SILAS LAPHAM GRIFFITH

The Santa Claus Bandit: Vermont's First Millionaire

ANN K. ROTHMAN

SILAS LAPHAM GRIFFITH

The Santa Claus Bandit: Vermont's First Millionaire

Copyright © 2022 by Ann K. Rothman and Danby-Mt. Tabor Historical Society

Ann Rothman completed the manuscript for this book in 2008. She died in 2010.

Edited by Susan Buckley
Cover and Interior Design by Debbi Wraga
About this book by Charles F. Tobin Jr.
About the Author by Donna Rothman

Thank you to our readers: Bradley Bender, Lauren Dever, Jane Johnson, Tricia Katz, Craig Moran, Herb Ogden, Terry Parker, and Charles F. Tobin Jr.

Photos courtesy of:
http://www.mtdhistoricalsociety.org
https://vermonthistory.org/digital-resources
http://cdi.uvm.edu
Scanned hard copies from the SL Griffith Memorial Library, Danby, VT

All rights reserved. Printed in the United States of America. No part of this book may be used or reproduced in any manner whatsoever without written permission except in the case of brief quotations embodied in critical articles or reviews.

For information contact:
Danby-Mt. Tabor Historical Society
http://www.mtdhistoricalsociety.org

ISBN: 978-1-60571-628-2 (hardcover)
ISBN: 978-1-60571-616-9 (paperback)
Library of Congress: 2022934936

ShiresPress
Manchester Center, Vermont

Printed in the United States of America

This book is dedicated
to
the residents of Danby and Mt. Tabor,
to Hugh Bromley,
and to Donald,
without whom it never would have been.

Contents

About This Book 3

Chapter 1. DEATH 5

Chapter 2. THE VIEWING 7

Chapter 3. THE FUNERAL 125

Chapter 4. THE CORTEGE 228

Chapter 5. THE BURIAL 245

Chapter 6. THE AFTERMATH 266

Noteworthy People Throughout the Book 344

Griffith Family Tree 346

Appendix 348

Acknowledgments 361

About the Author 365

ANN K. ROTHMAN

Throughout this book you will see different fonts used. Below is a font key.

Text from a Book

Text from a Diary

Text from a Church Record

| Text from a Newspaer |

> Text from a Legal Opinion

: SILAS LAPHAM GRIFFITH

About This Book

This book is the product of the financial and organizational efforts of Robert Tobin, Tim Cameron, and Danby-Mt. Tabor Now, Inc.

Bob and Tim met Ann Rothman on a skiing trip to Vermont in 2001. In 2002, after a year of negotiating, they bought property from Annie in Danby, and became full-time residents shortly thereafter. As their friendship with Annie grew, Bob and Tim began to learn more about her efforts to restore and revitalize the village and about her research into the life of Silas Griffith. They also quickly learned how important it was to Annie to share the unique history of Danby and its most famous citizen.

As the years passed and her health declined, Annie saw the necessity of finding ways to keep the revitalization work going and to pass the Griffith research on to someone who someday might bring it to fruition. Towards that end, in her will, Annie left the Silas manuscripts to the historical society and named Bob and Annie's daughter Donna as trustees of the Rothman properties in Danby. Through the efforts of Bob and Tim and many others, these properties are now as beautiful as they have ever been.

Getting *Silas Lapham Griffith* published was a proper extension of their earlier work with the properties. Annie's research and crisp writing style will now be available to all who want to learn about this remarkable man and town.

Bob and Tim thank the Mt. Tabor-Danby Historical Society and the many other citizens of the town for their generous contributions to the publication of this book.

In writing this work of narrative nonfiction, the author conducted extensive research using historical records, oral histories, diaries, and other sources. Ann Rothman based people's dialogue and thoughts on those sources.

ANN K. ROTHMAN

Return of Death Certificate
Courtesy of Mt. Tabor-Danby Historical Society

Chapter 1
Death

ON JULY 21st, 1903, a sixty-six-year-old man died in California. The stated cause of death: Pityriasis Rubra, a self-limited skin disease which disappears in six weeks without treatment. About as fatal as eczema, its most disturbing feature is that one of its accompanying symptoms may mimic secondary syphilis. Whatever the cause, the man died at his San Diego, California estate.

A member of the ancient, oft-times hell-raising Welsh family Griffith, who claim descent from Llewellyn the last king of Wales who was beheaded by the English in 1282, the deceased, Silas Lapham Griffith, a resident of Danby, Vermont, was also a king. He ruled a 50,000 acre mountain realm, whose seat of empire was situated in the township of Mount Tabor and its sister township, neighboring Danby. From their inception, the two townships had been bound together like Siamese twins.

Word of Griffith's death preceded his casket home for he was a prominent man. Newspapers categorized financial success, broad public spirit, benefactions to town and church, and his political service as a Republican state senator. But although he had been ailing, the suddenness of his death took many by surprise. In its July 23rd, 1903, issue, the *Rutland Herald* pronounced his death a shock, since he had been out shooting a fortnight before he died.

And the talk!

"Why, God, the bandit's dead!"
"Wonderful man, did so much good"
"You can't buy your way into Heaven."
"It says here he died of a skin disease."
"He died of syphilis. All those women..."
"Why, that's nothin' but town talk. I don't believe that."
"Well, you're about the only one in town who doesn't."
"The hell with all that! Are they goin' close down is what I want to know!"

The body didn't arrive in town until two weeks later. The funeral took place on August 3rd at the lovely, small Congregational Church that anchored the south end of the village center. Overseeing the village from a knoll on the east side of Main Street, the church was a simple white clapboard structure, yet infinitely elegant. Above the front door was a lofty, Gothic-arched tripartite window. Embellished with stained glass, the window was set in the bottom block of the building's rectangular steeple, which terminated in a lacy wrought iron gallery, reiterating around the topmost block, where its delicate tracery reached towards God.

The casket arrived at the church at eight o'clock in the morning and was readied for the funeral.

Chapter 2
The Viewing

IT WAS TEEMING RAIN and humid the day of the funeral. Judging from the temperature, it was going to be a scorcher.

The Family

The immediate family members straggled in before nine o'clock, having felt their presence obligatory for the public viewing, even though that meant enduring a five-hour wait until the funeral started at two o'clock that afternoon.

The first to arrive was Silas's older brother, Charles.[1] As he entered the church, he was reminded of the years this exquisite picture of serenity became the hub of all manner of aggravation, misery, contentiousness, and war, for which his dear, dead brother was largely responsible. *Ah, Silas,* he thought, remembering as he walked down the aisle to the flower-laden, open coffin. Relieved that his brother's face

---

[1] See page 344-345 for a list of Noteworthy People and pages 346-347 for a Griffith family tree.

looked remarkably natural, Charles stood there for some time, visibly moved. Finally, sniffling, he turned away and seated himself near the coffin as it lay in state in the church Silas had supported.

Their younger siblings, William and Mary, filed in shortly after. They were followed by Griffith's ill-composed daughter, Jennie Riddle, accompanied by her husband, William. William had managed his late father-in-law's numerous business ventures.

Last to arrive was the young widow, Katherine Mason Tiel Griffith also called Kate or K.T. Since her fine home was directly opposite the church, she had only to travel across Main Street. She came alone, leaving the company of her parents and sister who had come from Philadelphia to stay with her throughout this ordeal. Because of the rain, her father had driven her across the street in his buggy, dropping her off as close to the church door as possible. Regally aloof, she didn't have much to say to her husband's siblings and even less to her red-eyed, sniffling stepdaughter. Jennie was a scant ten years her junior, but the women had exchanged as few words as possible since Silas's remarriage in 1891.

Each of the family members prayed silently that the dreadful weather would deter the expected throngs of people. Their prayers were not to be answered.

The Public

At nine o'clock sharp, the doors were opened to the public. It had begun. Despite the rain, they all filed by—laborers, customers, fellow dignitaries from Montpelier, relatives, businessmen, local folk, multitudes of people come to take a last view, to pay their respects and to mutter appropriately to the family.

Composed, emotionless, coolly proper as always, the widow Griffith accepted the condolences of the endless procession that trooped past her late husband's coffin. It was a grand coffin; bronze, imposing, suitable. (The undertaker had done a remarkable job, everything considered.) K.T.'s expression was inscrutable; she seemed adrift in reverie.

And so she was.

The Widow Griffith Remembers

Thank you, Lord. Dear God, thank you for setting me free to live a life at last, she prayed silently.

Among the large number of people present from out of town were some of S.L.'s most prominent business associates as well as numerous former associates from the Vermont Senate of 1898, most all of whom K.T. knew and greeted cordially.

Now, the widow Griffith recalled the entertaining, the luncheons prepared by their excellent, long-time chef, Barnum, and served in the vast lodge—the "hotel" the locals called it—that Silas had built right after their marriage. He wanted to ensure the proper stage for the life he envisioned, luncheons that afforded the tycoon the opportunity to tour his guests around his realm, having met them at the railroad station with mountain wagons hitched with fine horses. The tour always started with his splendid private office, finished in rare, beautiful wood, included lunch at the Lake House, and terminated with a tour of his fish hatcheries before getting his guests to the station in time for the evening train. Beyond that, the tours varied, depending on his guests. When appropriate, his Works might be included or the greenhouse and, sometimes, frolics on Lake Griffith for which he provided boats and fishing gear. He let the gentlemen play at fishing in a lake so vastly overstocked with speckled trout from his hatcheries that the fish would frequently crowd each other out of the water and flop into the boat or get hooked somewhere in the body rather than the mouth.

Remembering Silas

"Starchy lady, that," one of Silas's former legislative associates said to his companion as they settled into one of the pews for the long wait until the service began.

"Yes, indeed," agreed the other gentleman, "but S.L. more than made up for it. Hospitable man, a pleasure to be with."

"As fine a host as you could hope to find. Why, that meal after that tour of his Works, that meal would've been a credit to the Waldorf Astoria."

"But fishing in the lake up there, that took the cake. I'll never forget it. Never saw anything like it. There were so many trout it was hard to catch them by a hook in the mouth. One fella struck one in the tail. I made a cast and hit one of them in the back, hooked it in the back, I did, and brought it in that way," the man recalled with a chuckle. "Thought I'd split from laughing."

Stop and start went their conversation.

"...A setup like that here, and property on the west coast and Lord knows where else... -Wouldn't be surprised if he's Vermont's first millionaire."

"No question. Why, shucks, he'll be a millionaire easy, without even counting all I'm sure he's got hidden away."

The friends considered that, at length.

"A real hustler, that one," one of them picked up. "Do you recall him pushing that bill? Griffith's Bill."

"Sure do. The Fish Bill, Senate bill No. 23," the other senator recalled with a grin. "His weekly gifts of flowers did lend unusual charm to the Senate chamber as he was pounding away to allow the sale of trout from private hatcheries during February, March and April when trout sell from $700 to $1200 a ton. If he raised ten tons which I seem to remember he expected to do, it would've given him quite a little bonus."

"You've got to admit, that was quite a hatchery he had. I remember being mighty impressed when he said it had a capacity for hatching

7 million trout eggs. Had 75,000 fry in the nursery ponds and 25,000 large trout."

"One Burlington paper described it as the largest trout hatchery in the world."

"Griffith poured a fortune in there, no question. When he found Otter Creek water too warm for fish culture, he had two artesian wells sunk about 160 feet to keep the water temperature at 48 degrees."

"$20,000 that venture cost him, read it in the paper."

"It's still operating, I suppose."

"Nope. Closed down years ago."

"Closed? How come?"

"What I heard is that somebody was sore and threw a case of Paris Green-arsenic-of-lead into the top dyke and it went all through the hatchery and killed all the trout and that was the end of the trout business."

"Pity." The senator shook his head and sighed and thought some more. "Still and all," he picked up, a few minutes later, "for a poor boy to have amassed such a fortune, he must have had some help somewhere."

"He may have been poor, but he was a Griffith," his companion grunted and continued conspiratorially, "and those Griffiths, they have hooks everywhere. Wherever those people's ancestors settled, they made it their business to ensure proper marriages for their children, important affiances for the family, you know. It's a tight family, real tight, and those people's kinship ties are legend. You want to know where Silas got help from, I'll bet you dollars to donuts, it came from relatives."

God knows, there were plenty of them marching down that church aisle. Probably no family in Danby in 1903 had more relatives than the Griffiths, all descended from the old ancestor's six children. Without even counting the women who had married locally and stayed, the town had as many Griffiths as there are mushrooms after a rain.

Thanks largely to his Great Uncle George, Silas had been overwhelmed with second cousins whose ancestors had the good sense to raise their families right in town.

Wondering at the Past

Brother Charles did what had to be done, thanked them for coming, said a few words. It became rote after a while, a blur. But when he heard Bill Riddle greeting an M.J. Scouton, who had come all the way from New Whatcom, Washington, and when General E.L. Bates, Secretary of Civil and Military Affairs came by with Governor J.G. McCullough, Charles marveled: *Whoever thought when we were kids there'd be a turn out like this for* one *of David Griffith, Jr.'s children... You fought Silas every bit of the way, Pa, and you didn't live long enough to find out he was right...*

And as the people kept coming down the aisle and the rain beat against the windows and the church started to smell and his brother lay dead in his coffin, Charles remembered back when they were real little, growing up on one of the 130 farms that dotted the township. He thought of how the chores had started as they were barely old enough to do them.

Silas had been put to work gathering eggs and feeding the chickens and weeding their mother's garden. But when the day came that he was enlisted to help his older brother fetch wood to fill the wood box, he commenced grumbling.

"I don't know why we gotta do this. Why doesn't Pa make one of the hands do it?" he piped in his little boy's voice.

"He'd have to hire another hand to do all this miserable stuff," grunted his seven-year-old brother.

"Well, why doesn't he do that?" Silas persisted, struggling to pick up a chunk of wood. "Because, dummy, that takes money," Charles retorted.

"Money? What's money?" the four-year-old asked.

"What we could use more of."

"Oh," Silas said, falling silent, frowning in thought.

With a subdued but wry chortle, Charles recalled that it hadn't taken very long for S.L. to figure that out.

The day came when David Griffith said to his sons, "I'll pay you young fellas a penny for every pile of stones you make." So the boys did that, but Charles made a few big piles and Silas made a lot of little ones with only a few stones in each.

"What's this, Silas?" their father questioned when he surveyed their work. "See these big piles your brother made, and yours so small?"

"Well, you know, Pa, a heap's a heap," Silas retorted and held out his hand.

David gave him a peculiar look as he paid him. "That's pretty sharp, young man," he said, "pretty sharp. Too sharp," he mumbled, as he walked away.

"I didn't know your head could earn you money," Silas remarked to his brother with an amazed smile, as he clutched his fortune in his hand.

That was the start of it, Charles reflected, that and those Sundays spent with Aunt Elizabeth and Uncle Jesse at the Lapham's fine home, Maple Terrace, the residence of the richest man in town.

The Griffiths and the Laphams

Jesse Lapham was one of ten children born between 1781 and 1804 of the union of Nathan Lapham and the former Elizabeth Arnold. Nathan was a poor young Quaker when he settled on the farm of one Joseph Button, also a member of the Society of Friends, with whom he had much in common. Active, energetic men of business talent, determined to make a mark for themselves, they became partners and engaged in the manufacture of potash from the trees they cut while clearing the place. Potash, used for cleaning linens and woolens, for processing fur and in making soap, fetched a goodly sum, and before long, Lapham & Button was flourishing, along with Nathan's burgeoning family. Over the years Nathan set aside his "laborer's hands" and, in 1790 the men opened a store on Button's farm. The store, which they kept for several years, was undoubtedly patronized by the Griffith ancestor, Lemuel, who lived nearby.

Lemuel Griffith arrived in Danby along with his wife Elizabeth and most, if not all, of their six offspring, who were born quite regularly at two-year intervals. David, the eldest, was twelve when the family migrated from Dartmouth, Massachusetts in time for Lemuel to be included among the 1778 roll of Danby's freemen.

It soon became obvious that the new settler was a man of means, for he had hardly settled on a farm parcel when he started buying land. And, before too many years passed, Lemuel became one of the town's largest landholders, at one time owning six or seven farms of several hundred acres each. His holdings encompassed part of what would become the Borough and continued some distance up into the hills.

Although elected Representative to the State Legislature in 1789, Lemuel didn't attend, devoting himself instead to the business of being family patriarch. As his six children matured and grew to marriageable age, he ensured proper unions with families he wanted to be allied with, unions that would benefit the family Griffith forever. To each married son who stayed in town, he parceled off a farm from his own vast holdings.

The time came when David, Lemuel Griffith's oldest son, married Lydia Coates and settled on a farm south of Lemuel's homestead. David industriously farmed away his days and devoted his nights to posterity, begetting nine children who were about the same ages as Nathan Lapham's brood of ten. And the passing years brought prosperity to Nathan Lapham, who eventually moved down from Button's farm to the Borough.

Success in Danby

Nestled between the looming Green Mountains and the Taconic Range, Danby's lands consist of rolling hills interspersed with stands of pine and rushing brooks and streams. There are meadows strewn with birch and maples, sugar maples that in the fall create a living palette of reds and yellows that blend with the evergreens to make it a place of great beauty and majesty and serenity, a place one feels privileged to call home.

Although the census of 1800 counted 1,487 citizens in the township, most lived either up in the hills, near the town's other village, Danby Four Corners, (for it was up there that the settlers had entered the township) or north of the Borough, near Otter Creek. The turn of the century found but two houses in the Borough and a hotel serving the needs of the travelers journeying on the highway which was one of the state's major north-south arteries.

Armed with courage and conviction, Nathan Lapham erected a home in the middle of the deep, deep woods where he commenced to invest heavily in land in the valley. Anticipating that it was only a matter of time before the Borough would be built up, he bought property. Eventually casting his eyes east to the Green Mountains, the canny old Quaker decided to partake in the building boom to come. He invested in the lumbering business by acquiring a sawmill in neighboring Brooklyn, as Mt. Tabor's village was called, all the while guiding his maturing progeny, introducing his sons to the intricacies of trade at an early age.

In 1803, Nathan's two oldest sons, Joseph and Jesse, opened a store on their father's property. With their father looking over their shoulders, training them, the boys proved ready students, especially Jesse. He was a handsome lad. A charmer. A born salesman.

The store on the highway was but the first of a series of stores and other ventures Jesse and Joseph would undertake over the years. They included their brother Elisha when he was old enough to join them,

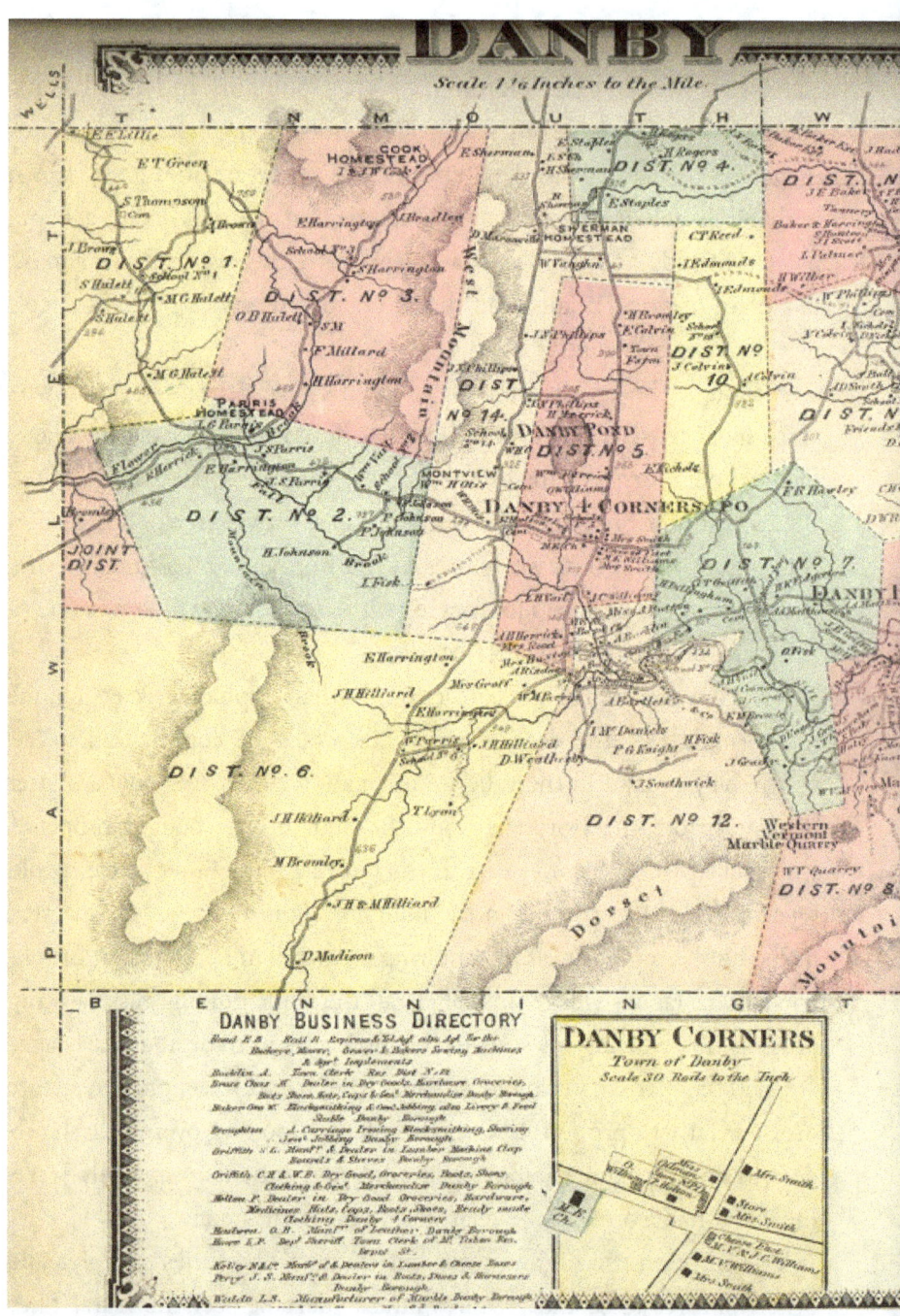

Beers Atlas, Danby and Mount Tabor, 1869, Courtesy of Mt. Tabor-Danby Historical Society

SILAS LAPHAM GRIFFITH

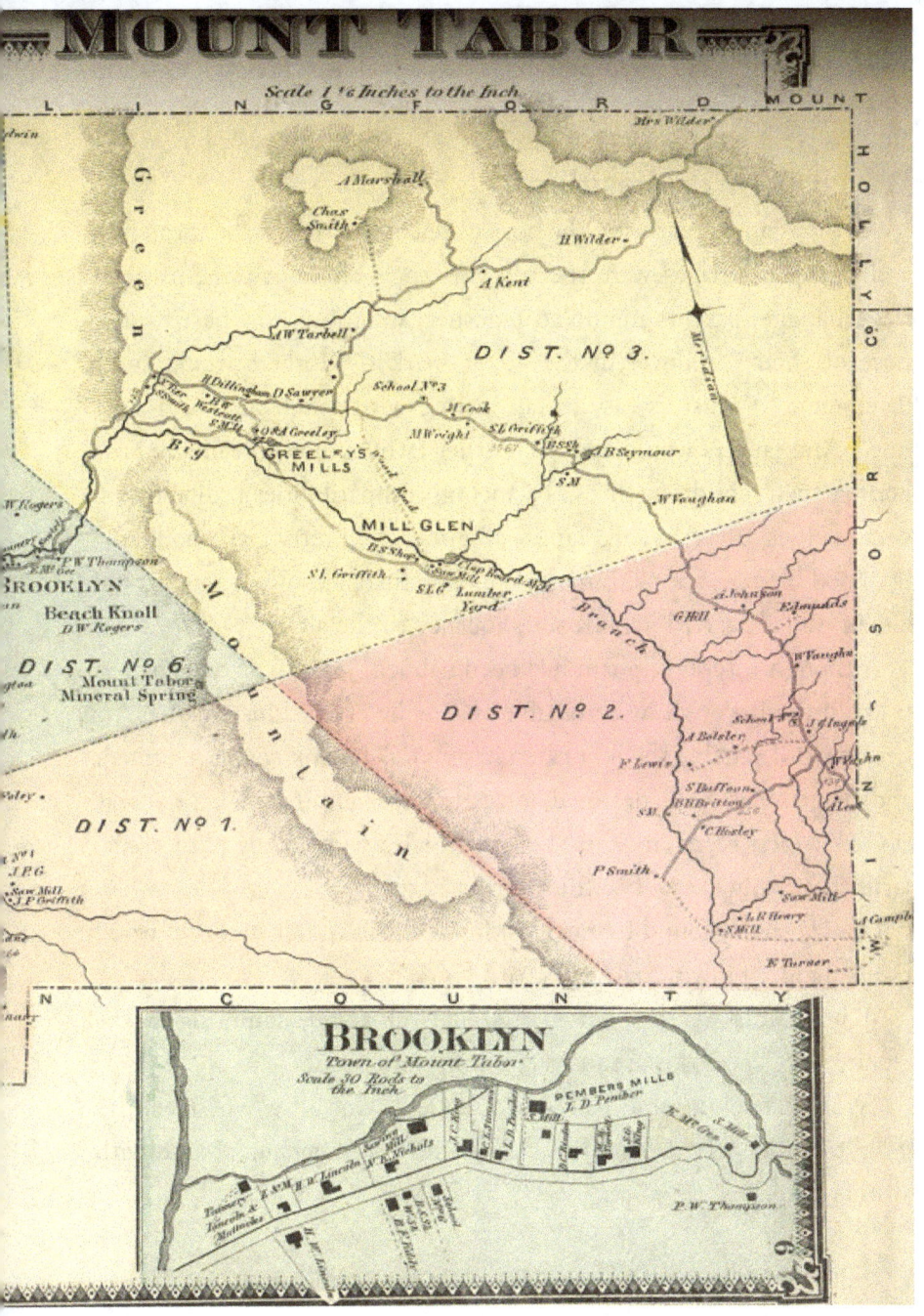

establishing a pattern of family partnerships and demonstrating the business acumen inherited from old Nathan, whose talent his sons and countless other descendants would perpetuate.

A Marriage Proposition

As they gained maturity, the boys were considered excellent catches, and young marriages were the rule. As their children came of marriageable age, parents mumbled together, weighing how best to dispose of their "product" in the going market. Mothers would tutor daughters, "It's just as easy to fall in love with a rich man as a poor one." And fathers would approach other fathers, not unfeelingly brokering their children's lives, balancing compatibilities, suitabilities, personalities, doweries, and family alignments. "Pretty girl, good family, good blood—and within easy courting distance. What more could a man want?" started many a son's journey to the altar.

Although Joseph Lapham had been nabbed, Jesse, who had entered trade in the Borough, was available and, as he entered his twenties, he became indisputably the best catch in town. A man of sound judgment and determined will, destined to lead, Jesse dominated his generation's business scene in Danby. All of which was noted by old Lemuel Griffith, pushing seventy, still sharp as a tack.

One April day found Lemuel visiting with his oldest son, the two of them standing idly near David's barn.

"I hope this weather holds," Lemuel remarked, squinting at the cloudy sky. The roads are just beginning to dry out."

"Wouldn't count on it, Pa," David replied. "Cows are lyin' down. It's goin' to rain." "Hope not. Oh, it's an awful chore getting around with all this mud."

"Yep."

"I did get down to the Borough awhile back, during that cold spell, you know. Bumped into Nathan Lapham. He happened to mention that Jesse doesn't like that store he's in now, says he's going to build a new one rather than add on to or patch up the one he's got."

"Yeah, seems to me I heard something to that effect," David allowed, watching the sky.

"Ambitious man."

"Yep."

"Eh, David," Lemuel ventured after a little, "have you given any thought to your daughter Elizabeth's future? You should. It's time. She's the flower of your flock, you know."

"She's surely startin' to bloom," David agreed, considering his fourth born. "Oh, yes," he said reflectively, considering the grins his farmhands were casting in Elizabeth's direction.

"A girl like that deserves someone very special," Lemuel observed, "not just another farmer, but a man of substance. Like young Jesse Lapham."

David shot his father a look, rolled the piece of grass he was chewing around in his mouth for a little and then replied thoughtfully, "I wonder... Do you suppose we could pull that off? We're not Quakers."

"No, but we're Griffiths, descended from kings. That should count for something."

"Now, I've been thinking," Lemuel went on, "that maybe if I helped you with the dowery, bolstered it up, you know, we got a good chance for that. They're two mighty good looking kids, healthy, couldn't find better. Seems to me that if we can get Nathan to go for it, it's a done deal..."

"Season's comin' up, road will be dry soon..." David nodded.

Not long after, the day came when Jesse's horse's hooves clattered up the dust in his pursuit of the farmer's daughter. Jesse and Elizabeth married shortly after and started raising a family.

Good Times and Bad

The years went on—some good, some bad. The year 1816 was a year of famine, long remembered. The rains lasted into May, followed by a drought into the autumn. There were frosts every month and crops failed. Many people were destitute in the winter and spring following, and many cattle died. It was a bad time for farmers like the Griffiths who made their livelihood off the soil, their fortunes bound as inextricably to the whims of Nature as the Lapham interests were bound to enterprise. But from 1810 to 1840, no town the same size rivalled Danby in business, and no one in Danby rode the wave better than Jesse Lapham.

In 1821, with his brothers, Jesse started up a tannery, establishing leather as a business several of them would pursue. In 1824, he erected an impressive marble store in the burgeoning Borough. It was a bare stone's throw from Maple Terrace, the fine residence he built for himself and his family in the 1830s. The house sat on a rise of the hill at the south end of Main Street, with an unobstructed view of the Green Mountains to the east.

The 1830s were good years for the Lapham family, for two of Jesse's children, Henry and Sophronia, married the children of John Vail, knotting the Lapham family ties once more with the Vails. This fine family was already related through the marriage of Jesse's brother, David. Following the tradition of family partnerships, in 1838 Jesse established the firm of Lapham, Vail & Co., a mercantile business, in South Wallingford, taking as partners his children's father-in-law, John Vail, his son-in-law, A.R. Vail, and one John H. Vail.

The Union Meeting House

1838 also found Maple Terrace's view to the east interrupted by the erection of the Danby East Village Union Meeting House, a place of worship to be shared by the Borough's Quakers, Baptists, and Methodists.

A great friend of religion, Jesse had headed a group formed to erect and maintain a much needed Meeting House for the mutual use of the three religious sects represented in the Borough. The funds were to be raised through the auction of pews, or slips, as they were called. Jesse's personal subscription of $250 to the Danby East Village Union Meeting House Society, the largest of any received, bought him seven of the twelve pews owned by Laphams. Twelve more of the fifty pew total were purchased by Griffiths. By April 1838, with a total of $1,549.90, an architect was called in. For the sum of $25 he drew the plans and supervised the building of the structure directly across the street from Maple Terrace.

Throughout this period, David Griffith occupied himself marrying off the rest of his brood. The 1830s left him with a balance of two sons, Lewis and David, Jr..

Silas Arrives

On November 7th, 1833, David Griffith, Jr. married Sophia Hadwen, of the Newport, Rhode Island Hadwens. The couple's first child, Charles Hadwen Griffith was born on July 28th, 1834, a trifle prematurely. About three months before their second child was due, a slew of parcels of land were exchanged between (but mostly from) Jesse Lapham to David Griffith. And on June 27th, 1837, Sophia bore another son, whom they named Silas Lapham Griffith.

Family Matters

Sixty-six years later, the downpour outside the funeral intensified briefly, accompanied by thunder and lightning and wind, a breath of which found its merciful way into the stifling church.

Charles mopped his brow and cast a glance at his sister-in-law, impassively performing her social obligations. A fine-figured woman, K.T. was garbed, as usual, in severely tailored attire, today in appropriate black, from her shoes to the straw boater sitting above her tightly pulled-back hair. If anything, she looked better today than usual, for the humidity had caused some strands of curl to loosen about her face and her widow's veiling added an unaccustomed softness to her appearance. But no amount of veiling could conceal the pouches under those cold, dead eyes and the pursed slash of a mouth. Charles sighed, and considered how fortunate he was, never to have married and been forced to look at a face like that over the supper table every evening.

You might not have loved him, but just for once you might show a little something, his mind fired at her. *God knows, you'll be well paid for the twelve years you put into the job!*

Disgusted, Charles turned his glance on his brother and sister, noting, without much surprise, that they appeared more bored than anything else. Of course, Mary was twelve years younger than Silas and the two of them hadn't had much in common. An independent lady, his sister Mary married Isaac Kelley in '66, divorced him in '85, and lived on the $2000 alimony she received, Charles summarized in his mind. *Mighty independent woman, Mary. Mighty independent, taking back her maiden name of Griffith after she divorced. Disgraceful.* Charles thought with disapproval, damning that Suffragette, Lucretia Mott, who had lectured at the Friends' Quarterly Meeting in Danby in August of '66 on the subject of 'Real, Radical, Practical Christianity,' rousing all manner of feminist stirrings in Mary and who knows how many others; Mott and those editorials of Horace Greeley in the *New York Weekly Tribune* that Mary subscribed to, all his chatter about women's rights and the equality of husband and wife in all ways in the marriage union. *How many marriages had ruptured because of all that humbug,* Charles wondered, recalling the time he visited one local couple on a Monday to find the husband helping with the wash.

Mary and Silas hadn't been very close. William Barney (Willie), nine years younger than Silas, might as well have been a century younger when it came to closeness. Amongst the immediate family, besides poor Jennie who genuinely mourned Silas's death, so did Charlie, his big brother and confidante throughout so many of those early years.

At Maple Terrace

Charles tried to recall when, exactly, Silas had said, "When I grow up, I want to be just like Uncle Jesse." It might have been after one of those Sunday dinners at the Laphams, at Maple Terrace, that they went to now and again.

What a deal that was! How their mother would go on before they left. If he closed his eyes, he could hear her voice haranguing them.

"Now, let me take a look at you," Sophia would say. "Charles, put a little more water to that cowlick, hear! And Silas, you've got a scuff on the toe of your right shoe. You buff that out, young man - and hurry, your father's waitin'. Fingernails...all right, all right. Willie, what did you stick your thumb into? Now, remember, no loud talk and no chasing around. And keep your fingers out of your nose and away from all those little things your aunt's got on her tables."

Lapham House, Maple Terrace

Sophia would scrub them, buff them to a shine, and she'd go on repeating and lecturing until they got to the door. Once inside Maple Terrace, though, the house took over. It was so perfect, so fine and elegant, so different from theirs, it demanded they act in keeping.

Charles found it thoroughly intimidating, and hated those visits with a passion, a sentiment the two youngest children heartily shared. His father was so uncomfortable he never really sat in a chair in that house; rather, he perched on the edge of the seat. For her part, Sophia loved visiting with Elizabeth, but her pleasure was always tempered by the vigilant eye she trained on her youngsters.

Probably none of the Griffiths found those visits as fascinating as Silas did. Sometimes, as they sat there, Silas's eyes would register the difference in the look of the hands of his aunt and those of his mother, worn and rough, that told the story of her life, a life Silas wanted no part of.

Even as a youngster, he was much taken with the beauty of the house and its possessions, and you could see his yearning for all that in his eyes as they returned to the farm and all that went with it.

Chores—at Home and School

As if it were yesterday, Charles remembered how hard he and Silas had worked. Day in, day out, winter, summer, every day the same. And to work in the cold of those long, snowy winters...During the winter, they'd sleep sandwiched between two feather ticks—feather mattresses—for warmth, rousing themselves before dawn, sometimes finding that the wind had drifted the snow in under the door and across the floor.

After the chores it was time for a breakfast, and then the two of them left for school, joining the other 502 students between the ages of four and eighteen years of age who attended one of the township's twelve district schools.

Though Caesar's triumphs were too remote to rouse Silas much, his eyes gleamed as he learned of Napoleon's accomplishments and narrowed as he considered Hannibal's strategies. "Smart," he said, "smart." He laughed with delight upon hearing of the Trojan Horse. "Sharp thinkin' did it," he said with admiration, "Their smarts won it for them," he answered in class when called on.

Throughout his school years, Silas labored over his penmanship. With time and practice, his signature came to please him as a reflection of himself. His work was remarkably free of the ink spots customarily found splattering the pages of young farm lads. In the procedures taught concerning the transaction of ordinary business, he proved exceptionally adept at figuring.

When it came to matters of deportment, Silas's easy smile and glib explanations to his teachers usually succeeded in keeping the ruler at bay. Often, his escapades involved classmates who were less swift than he, for rather than suffer fools graciously, he outsmarted them, time and again. Whatever the game or competition, Silas played to win. More than anything, he hated to lose, and he was quite forceful to ensure it didn't happen often. Roughhousing with the other boys during noon recess, the feisty featherweight didn't fare too well with his fists, but his quick kicks won him a measure of respect from his peers who often selected him captain when they played war.

When school was over, back home the children would trudge in all kinds of weather, and work out the rest of the day on the farm. Now, behind shuttered eyes, Charles could picture them tilling and weeding, clearing stones out of the vegetable garden, haying and plowing and fetching buckets of water for the women on wash day. The children cleaned out the gutters in the cow barn, thankful for the heifers because they were smaller and didn't fill the gutters quite so fast.

And clear as a bell in his ear, Charles heard Silas one day, occupied in the barn, saying, "My days here doin' this are numbered. You can count on it, big brother. I'm goin' to be a businessman."

Big Dreams

Before he even entered his teens, Silas started his diligent pursuit of a business education; his school was Maple Terrace, As he grew older, Charles remembered how his brother would sit quietly indoors and listen to the men while his siblings were scampering around outside.

Everything came down to money. There never seemed to be enough of it to pay for the endless repairs for the Meeting House, a topic that was much discussed. If it wasn't the roof, it was water in the cellar or windows that needed caulking, or a new hatchway cover. There was always something. Finally, in 1848, Jesse announced a solution to the financial woes. "Well," he said to his brother-in-law, "we've formed this committee to grant privileges to people to use the Meeting House for such purposes as they think best. Of course," Jesse added, "nobody will be allowed the use of the house for the purpose of making any kind of exhibition for which pay shall be demanded of those who attend. We didn't think that would be seemly."

"Humph," said David, thoughtfully. "Contributions aren't excluded, though, are they?"

"Certainly not," Jesse replied with a smile. "And it will be a real community service, for the Meeting House will be the focal point of mental stimulation, bringing in thoughts from the outside world."

"Sounds pretty good to me. But aren't you afraid you might get too many newfangled notions here?" David questioned. "Those Spiritualists, you know, they're growing by leaps and bounds."

"But they're Christians, David," Jesse reminded him. "Very liberal, of course, but Christians all the same."

"Or so they call themselves," David muttered. "Sundays they attend Meeting and worship Christ, during the week they attend those circles, those seances, and speak with the spirits. It doesn't seem right," he said, shaking his head.

Silas, Uncle Jesse, and the Danby Bank

When Jesse's son, Henry, was visiting from New York City, where he was a leather merchant, Jesse would expound on business practices and lecture on the economics of production. On other occasions, he would go on and on about the forever-coming Western Vermont Railroad, in which he was a large stockholder, seeing nothing but a sure thing for his investment. And always with the talk of the railroad, the subject of the Danby Bank would come up. Jesse always tied the two together, the railroad and the bank, the bank that he had been dreaming of for years, and for which he finally secured a charter in 1850.

About the time the bank started going up, the closeness between Silas and his older brother lessened. Charles had left school by then and was working full time on the farm and Silas's constant barrage of "Jesse Lapham told me" or "Uncle Jesse says" or "Uncle Jesse's this or that" was driving Charles wild, even more so because you didn't need to be a genius to know where that was going to end up.

By the time Silas was about fourteen, his ingratiating ways, quick mind, attentiveness, and obvious hero worship had impressed as well as flattered his uncle, who had become used to his nephew's company. So it was no surprise that Silas would spend every rare, available moment sharing Jesse's delight over the erection of the Danby Bank, the only brick building in the village.

Situated on a side street that would access the future railroad station, the structure was classic in design. Complete with four fluted Doric columns, it looked like a miniature temple transplanted from the Acropolis. As they watched it grow, Jesse's talk to Silas about vision, and planning ahead, and patience and success, was enlarged to include the mistakes one can make, despite any amount of planning.

"I didn't realize when I started construction," Jesse said one day, as he regarded the nearly finished bank, "that building straddles the town line between Mt. Tabor and Danby. I keep thinking to myself," he went on, musing into space, "that if that pile of stones that marks the boundary were over only a foot or two farther east, the Bank would be in Danby where it should be. I'd be much indebted," he continued, with a short laugh, "if the good Lord would see fit to work a miracle to that effect."

"Considering all you've done for the church and the town, Uncle Jesse," Silas commented after some long, thoughtful minutes, "...it appears to me that the good Lord owes you that."

Lapham was pleased when the Danby Bank opened its doors for business in 1851 with $50,000 in capital and Jesse as a member of its Board of Directors and the bank's first President. The timing was beautiful, for the first Western Vermont Railroad train finally chugged into town that same year, twenty years after the Rutland & Burlington acquired its charter.

"Wonder how they pulled that off?" some in town questioned.

Others scoffed, "You shouldn't need to wonder with Jesse's brother, Elisha, the State Senator from Rutland , and John H. Vail, his old business partner from back in the '30s, as the railroad's General Agent."

"I hear they're startin' to print their own money."

"Yep."

And, as if the good times weren't rolling in fast enough for Jesse Lapham, the day came when Silas said to Charlie, "What do you know! Turns out Uncle Jesse's Bank is in Danby after all."

"Really," Charles retorted, leaning on his pitchfork. "So tell me, Silas, what do you know about that?"

Silas didn't answer, having learned at an early age, to admit only to that which would enhance him. The fairy tales he would spin (included in ponderous, impressive volumes that no locals would likely see) are legend. No one was more facile than Silas Griffith when it came to ducking issues or spouting fantasies to upgrade or downgrade the facts.

Charles and Joel Baker Remember

No one in town knew this better than Charles Baker, Publisher and Editor of Danby's weekly newspaper, *The Southern Vermont Mirror*.

As he shuffled in that long procession down the church aisle, Charlie Baker didn't look well and felt even worse, having passed the evening before over-imbibing with his cousin Joel Baker, a judge and Silas's long-time attorney. A thoroughly raucous, hilarious time they had, discussing the endless lawsuits that had kept a steady flow of food on Joel's table and the massive advertising that had kept the *Mirror* alive.

"...and that biographical sketch on him that you published two months ago, oh, you buttered your bread thickly, your complimentary furbishes embellishing every fact Silas wanted known or believed true," the judge chortled.

"I put it down just as it came out of the horse's mouth," Charlie had agreed, drunkenly. "He dictated the whole thing, right before he left for California. You should've heard him, you should've heard him. What a performance!"

"But the lies, Charlie! You published lies that were public knowledge! Why, Gawd, I'm embarrassed to be related to a journalist who'd do that!"

Screaming with laughter, Joel grabbed a handy copy of the biography from a nearby table. "How could a Baker give forth some of this hokum?" he demanded, his eyes tearing with amusement. "Why, in years to come," the lawyer spouted on, theatrically brandishing the May 29th, 1903, *Mirror* issue, "these printed words of yours are going to be incorporated into the fabric of the town's history."

"Hogwash," Charlie commented mildly and belched.

"Maybe so, maybe not," Joel allowed, judiciously, reaching for the bottle. "But now that he's gone, those out-of-town papers, and who knows who else are going to be poking around in here for background stuff, and they're going to take your biography as Gospel." With great difficulty, the judge stifled his laughter, composed himself, and finally managed to say, as sanctimonious as the Pope, "For shame, Charles. How could you do such a thing?"

"Actually, I thought I did it damned well," was the haughty reply. "I did it with editing, and I did a magnificent job of it if I say so myself. It was an incredible job of reverse editing," he continued, basking in thoroughly sloshed self-satisfaction. "First time I ever did that. Instead of puttin' everything together, nice and organized, I spread everything so far apart that it was hard, even for me, to make sense of," the editor grinned.

"I gotta admit, I loved it," Joel muttered, perusing the piece with a chuckle. And the two of them had laughed the whole night long, drinking mightily to Silas's memory as they tore the dictated biography apart, paragraph by paragraph, until the early hours of the morning.

"…Sure, he lied. And ducked. And otherwise, eh, modified. You know it, and I know it, and the town knows it, and everybody knows why I did what I did. A man's gotta do what he's gotta do," Charlie summed up ponderously and let out a fart.

"Of course," he resumed, melancholy, "the bright side of it is that he didn't live long enough to feed me another story. I suppose I can safely assume that everything I wrote about him after that biography was accurate."

So much for last night. Now, having offered his sympathies to the family, Baker pulled out a pad and got to work noting down the incredible array of flowers, and who sent what to the man whose passion for them was well known.

Roses, lilies, and carnations were on and about the casket. Two set pieces, one representing Gates Ajar and the other Faith, Hope and Charity were sent by the employees of his Works. There was a large wreath from some Rutland bankers; lilies from E.E. Darling & Co. of Troy, New York, wholesale grocers; a crown and cross from Eugene McIntyre, his sometime partner and business associate; a harp from the employees of his six stores... The editor's list went on and on, noting wreaths, and baskets, and arrangements, to be incorporated in the *Mirror's* funeral edition. Despite his throbbing head and the overwhelming fragrance of the massive floral display which mostly overpowered that of the two-week-old remains in the summer heat, Baker made especially sure not to miss the family's offerings. Diligently, he noted the immortelles and asparagus fern from W.H. Griffith, S.L.'s cousin and office manager; and the pink and white carnations from the Tiels, Mrs. Griffith's parents and sister. Baker shook his head, reread the card, crossed out 'parents' and substituted 'mother'. Rolling his eyes and shrugging, he went on to list the roses and carnations from Bill and Jennie Riddle and the massive display of white roses from Charles, William, and Mary Griffith. And from the widow... The newspaper man checked and rechecked the cards on each and every one of the floral renderings but could find none from Silas's wife. *I guess she must've sent the ones on the casket,* Baker shrugged and took a seat in one of the pews.

Fact or Fiction?

Charlie Baker decided that he would pass the time trying to recall the list of the late Griffith's fakeries that Joel and he had picked up, and spun throughout his newspaper's dictated biographical sketch.

"...Mr. Griffith attended the district school in this village till about sixteen years of age..."

"...Please, Uncle Jesse, take me on..."

"I've got to admit, Silas, I can't see you with a barn for an office for the rest of your life. And I was already learning trade when I was younger than you are. But my father wanted it that way, and your father's dead set against it. And you'd sure be dumping on Charlie, and Willie's only seven... Silas, you know I'd like to oblige you, but I can't. Your father will have my hide right along with yours if I give in to you. I just can't do it."

"I'm old enough to decide what I want to do with my life, Uncle Jesse. Pa won't like it, but there's nothin' he can do to stop me. Please, Uncle Jesse, please. I'll work for nothin'..."

"If I let you work for me at all, young man, that's exactly what you'll get. Nothing." Jesse Lapham was a man of his word.

As reported in the *Mirror*,

> ...when he entered the employ of Lapham & Bruce as clerk in their general store in this village and continued in their employ for the larger part of two years.

"...I'm startin' right after school lets out," he told his brother Charlie. Uncle Jesse's agreed. I'm goin' to be gettin' $40 and board for the first year, $80 and board for the second..." (S.L. had omitted telling Baker he was getting board and substandard wages.)

"$40! A year's pay for a clerk is $750. or better! You know that! That's for an experienced clerk without board. I'm gettin' board."

"You're gettin' what I'm shovellin'. You're gettin' nothing but abused."

"He doesn't want me, don't you see?" Silas said. "He's doin' his best to discourage me, for what he'll get from Pa. But even for nothin', I'm goin' to do it and learn the business and get whatever money I can to pay for more schooling.

"Charlie, I'm sorry, I'm truly sorry for what the loss of my hands will mean. I don't know as I'll ever be able to make it up to Pa, but I'll make it up to you some day, to you and Willie. I swear it."

Silas Lapham, Merchant

In 1853, Silas commenced an apprenticeship as a clerk at Lapham

& Bruce, a general store housed in the stone store building Jesse had built some years earlier.

Jesse's choice of C.M. Bruce as business partner was astute, for Bruce, an experienced merchant and businessman, was as shrewd a Quaker as one could hope to meet. Silas couldn't have learned the meat and potatoes of store keeping from two finer merchants, and what he picked up from their thoughts was sheer nectar.

"That brother of mine, Elisha, he's nothing but a farmer," Jesse carped to Bruce one day, with infinite disgust. "That foolish farmer went and sold the sawmill he got from my father for $1,600. He'd have got a good deal more if he'd held on longer. With the railroad in and the down-country markets opened up, there's a fortune to be made in lumbering. All that money sitting there, waiting to be made... If I wasn't in my sixties, I'd get into it, but it's a young man's business..."

Lumbering?

> ...He then accepted a clerkship in the store of Mr. P.D. Ames at East Dorset, where he remained till about a year later, when he relinquished the position to enter upon a term of school in Kimball Union Academy at Meriden, N.H. Thus it was in the winter of 1855-56 that he and Mr. William Ames of East Dorset entered upon their term of schooling in that institution.
>
> By frugal economy during his employment in the stores above-mentioned Mr. Griffith managed to save enough money to pay a term's tuition in the academy but had little left to provide for his living expenses during the period of

> study away from home. Consequently, he and Mr. Ames decided to board themselves, and in this manner managed to complete the term and return home with empty purses but with a creditable addition to their stock of knowledge. Many hardships were experienced during the term, however...

William Ames Remembers

Having commiserated sufficiently with the family, a rotund, elderly gentleman, huffing and puffing and mopping his brow with his handkerchief, plopped himself into one of the front pews and fixed a baleful gaze on the coffin of the most impatient, impetuous, and impulsive man he had ever known, his late cousin, Silas.

You always had to have it when you wanted it, the way you wanted it, no matter, groused William Ames to himself. *For all your smarts, you never learned from experience. All that grievous shame you brought on your Church... And in the long run, no one suffered your actions more than you.*

Now, see you there in your box, Silas. Who did you push after me, Silas, into doing what they didn't want? Who did you push, after me? William Ames sat there, staring at that coffin for a long, long time, communing with Silas, cutting the years like butter.

Ames could hear Silas talking, long ago. "Oh, c'mon, Willie. It'll do you good to get out of here, live a little," coaxed Silas, a slight youth, all muscle, all energy, vibrant with anticipation of new horizons.

"I don't know...," from Ames, a chunky, easy going, placid lad, fond of all the comforts of home, with no desire whatsoever to rock the boat. "... for the winter term? I don't know... My mother's beggin' me to wait until spring, when the weather will be more clement."

"Of course, she is. So is mine. That's what mothers are for! Ah, Willie, c'mon. Be adventurous for once in your life. The more obstacles, the greater the challenge; the more challenge, the nobler the pursuit. C'mon, Willie. We'll have a dandy time..."

You always had to have it when you wanted it... Ames grumbled to himself.

Had they waited until spring, not only would they have avoided the forty below zero temperatures they encountered that dreadful winter, but they would have accumulated sufficient additional funds to put towards food...

"This is some dandy diet, here, you've got us on, Silas."

"Stop grousing, Willie. Think of it as applying some of our learned knowledge of physiology and hygiene."

"Buckwheat cakes and molasses are among the foods that possess more heat-giving properties than others"

"Exactly. They're also filling. And cheap."

"There was a time, centuries ago, when I was home, when I'd dream of girls; these days I dream of food - roast chicken and gravy and beef and my mother's pies and fruit instead of these *dang* buckwheat cakes and molasses three times a day, every day," Willie complained. "It ain't *healthy*. Why, my gums are startin' to bleed and I swear my teeth are loosenin' up and..."

Somehow, they survived the term, but their friendship didn't.

Had anyone looked at William Ames that day in Danby's Congregational Church, however, they would have seen his eyes welling with tears, for that dismal winter at Meriden, New Hampshire, was the only outstanding experience in his lifetime of complacent boredom.

A memorable biographical account of Silas's life appears in *The New England States, Their Constitutional, Judicial, Educational, Commercial, Professional and Industrial History,* Vol. 3, p. 1568. This worthy tome, published in the 1890s and not likely to have been read in Danby, contains all manner of fantasies that no one but Silas himself would have spewed forth, including the following portion that concerns itself with his time at Meriden:

> It was after two years of this work [at Lapham & Bruce] that Mr. Griffith began his academic life at Meriden and derived the technical part of his education. His attitude and ability to absorb information manifested itself at once, and in 1854 he was graduated with the highest honors, being the only member of a large class to gain the distinction of receiving the highest mark attainable. At the end of his student life Mr. Griffith accepted a position in Dorset as clerk of the store known as the Union Store; here he remained eighteen months....'

Hardly.

At the end of his student life, Silas arrived back in Danby hungry, broke and with no option but to return to his father's farm and the life that went with it, for Jesse Lapham's world had undergone great changes. 1856 found Uncle Jesse largely retired from trade and preoccupied with bank matters.

In 1855, an out-of-stater, a Chester Hitchcock from Buffalo, New York, had bought up about nine tenths of the bank and in 1856 a new Board was elected. Of the former Board, only Jesse remained to serve with a few others including two sons of Isaac Vail: Isaac J. Vail and John H. Vail. In January of 1857, Jesse Lapham's association with the Bank terminated, Isaac J. Vail was elected President and his brother, John H. became Cashier.

Finding His Path

In Charlie Baker's account:

```
    In the summer of 1857 Mr. Griffith had
an opportunity offered him to teach
school the following winter in a west-
ern town, and he forthwith set out for
that point,...
```

"A teaching job!" Joel Baker had hooted incredulously. "With his educational background! I don't believe it, not for a minute. And where out west? In what western town?"

Charlie Baker shrugged. "Oh, I asked him that. Just a western town he answered, bland as custard, and gave me the look and the smile of the Lord High Executioner. Lest I dare to inquire further."

"Well, Cousin, sometime before you got to him, some other fella interviewed him for a piece in the *New England States* and there's nothing in there about a schoolteacher's position. It simply says he got restless and decided to go west, as many young men did back then. His father presented him with $40 - probably glad to get rid of him - and off he went,

> ...stopping over at Buffalo, to visit relatives.

"Relatives... That would be A.R. Vail, Jesse's son-in-law. He'd left town by then and headed to Buffalo.

> ...While there the memorable panic of that period set in. He had no money to take him farther along toward his destination, and nothing except gold and Canadian bank bills would be accepted as currency. He was, however, equal to the emergency-as he has been to every subsequent one that has occurred during his business career ...

"Ooooh, Charlie, how could you?"

> ...and he engaged his services in the precarious occupation of rafting logs.

> While engaged in this work he received letters from home ...

There was a financial panic in 1857 and it hadn't been easy to find a job. But there weren't many takers for rafting logs up the Niagara River into Lake Erie for $1 a day (most of which Silas's landlord kept). Upon learning of the dangerous occupation Silas had embarked on, a barrage of letters arrived from home, specifically from his mother, Sophia, urging her son's return. An impossibility, Silas wrote back, not only for lack of funds but also for the reason he had left home in the first place: want of employment.

Determined to get Silas safely home where he belonged, Sophia applied herself to accomplishing this goal. She leaned, she cried, she begged, she assaulted her husband and every relative unmercifully, employing every woman's wile until, finally, she won out.

> ...urging him to return and open a general store in this village. But he had no money to pay his transportation expenses from Buffalo to Danby, to say nothing of the still greater sum needed to buy the stock of goods. It was finally arranged, however, that Benjamin Barnes should loan Mr. Griffith $1,000...

"Wait, now... Benjamin Barnes... Sure. He's the father-in-law of Edward Vail Lapham, Jesse's nephew David Lapham's son."

> ...$1,000, upon his note bearing his father's indorsement, and the cashier of the Danby Bank, which was then do-

> ing business in the building which now does service as a house of worship for the followers of the Catholic faith, would advance him the money needed to bring him back to Danby.

It is mighty generous of David Griffith, especially seeing as he hadn't advanced $10 when his son was all but starving in New Hampshire. Indeed, David Griffith and John H. Vail, the cashier of the Bank must have had extraordinary faith in Silas, especially considering the severity of the panic of '57.

> ...The offer appeared so tempting to him that he accepted it, and upon reaching his native town leased the lower floor of the building situated just across the stream from the MIRROR office and for many years past occupied by J.S. Perry and family - at that time being used as a shoe and harness shop.
> Mr. Griffith built counters and put in shelving and drawers at his new place of business, and in September 1858, with $1,000 in his pocket, started for New York City to purchase goods for a general country store.

It was at this point, Charlie Baker recalled, that he and Joel had dissolved in hysterics, for drunk as they were, they weren't sufficiently gone to miss the fact that Silas had, with the soundest of reasons, leap-frogged over the fall and winter months of 1857 to September

1858, a nimble omission for the balance of 1857 was best forgotten.

1857 was indeed a period of great economic panic that built up and seemingly increased in momentum. It was, in fact, a panic of great dimension during which failures of all sorts took place. Corporations went under, as did railroads and banks, including the Western Vermont Railroad and the Danby Bank which failed in September of that year. It is a matter of history that when the bank failed, C. Hitchcock and J.T. Hatch of Buffalo, owed it $80,000 which proved a total loss, and other bad debts made the loss exceed twice the amount of the capital stock.

Very likely, the Bank's $1,000 advance to Silas was one of the last it ever made; very likely, it was one of its last bad debts, too, for Silas omitted any disclaimer concerning repayment.

"Awful lot of coincidence there," Judge Baker ruminated. "What prompted that Buffalo man, Hitchcock, to buy up those bank shares in the first place? And then you've got Silas there in Buffalo with the Vails... Aaron R. and Sophronia had family, didn't they?"

"Yep. They had five children - Caroline, Elizabeth, Helen, George A. and Moses H."

"It's mighty possible they married Buffalo people. Could be, one of them married into the Hitchcock family or possibly that of J.T. Hatch..."

"You know, I'll bet you," said Joel, "that S.L. didn't hurry home so fast after he got that money. A lot of folks in town wouldn't have appreciated him waving his $1000 around when the Bank failed and they lost their shirts. I'd lay money on it, that he stayed out there with his kin until things settled down here at home. I'd bet about anything that Danby didn't see Silas Griffith again until spring of 1858..."

The Laphams, the Vails, and the Griffiths, Round and Round

Silas opened his first store in 1858 and went to market again in the spring of 1859 to replenish his stock, believing his credit good enough to pay for everything in thirty days. He was in for a rude awakening, for his suppliers had checked his financial standing and from the information they received, considered Griffith insolvent.

"Insolvent!" Silas told Charlie Baker with a chuckle, "Insolvent."

"Ridiculous!" Baker replied, suitably, and larded the biography accordingly.

In fact, however, chances are Griffith was insolvent or he would have had the money with him or, at least, would have given his distributors partial payment. Instead, he followed his established pattern and turned to his relatives for help.

> ...Mr. Griffith wrote to his cousin, Mr. H.G. Lapham, who was then doing business in New York City, telling him of the predicament he was in, and asking him to help him out of it...

Which Lapham did, personally guaranteeing payment, which

> ...act of his cousin gave him good credit, and...Mr. Lapham was never called upon to pay any of his bills...

The Laphams and the Vails and the Griffiths, round and round.

Who knows how S.L. Griffith would have fared without the Lapham connections that saved his hide so many times? The unstinting help that family gave their namesake, Silas Lapham Griffith, was invaluable in every area—for the first thirty-five years of Silas's life, through two generations of Laphams. And, in fairness, Silas returned these favors and, in turn, helped his relatives later in his life when he was able to do so. (On one occasion, in fact, he went out to Wisconsin and shut down an illegal patent infringement operation there to help a Lapham or a Vail who had the patent for cheesecloth.)

The failure of the Danby Bank and the losses he sustained from his Western Vermont Railroad stock when that company bottomed-up in 1857, took all the wind out of Jesse Lapham's sails and brought an end to his business enterprises. He sold the Stone Store to his partner, Bruce, and retired from Danby's commercial scene, remaining inactive until his death in 1863 at the age of seventy-five.

The Store

Despite Henry G. Lapham's demonstrated willingness to help his cousin when necessary, 1859 ended Silas's financial tribulations. From May 7th, 1860, to December 17th, 1861, Silas held the position of Postmaster, a plum every storekeeper lusted for. Helped substantially by the traffic the job generated, business in the Corner Store thrived to such a degree that Silas found he needed more space. Consequently, in 1861 he built the S.L. Griffith & Co. store.

The building was ideally situated right smack in the middle of the west side of the block-long main drag, at the terminus of the road that led to neighboring Brooklyn, Vermont. Not only did it dominate the Main Street scene, but it was conveniently neighbored by family. To the north, his widowed aunt, Lydia Hadwen Brancroft lived with her brother, Obediah, in a handsome Greek Revival residence, behind which Obediah maintained a tannery. The third house south of the store was the residence of Silas's parents, his father having sold the 133-acre farm in 1860 for $3,500.

Oh, it was a fine store, Griffith's store, the biggest in town, over 5,000 square feet, big and exuberant and soaring. Three stories high, with a flat roof, a boom-town front and a nifty paint job, Silas's grand emporium was the skyscraper of southern Vermont during Civil War years.

The Civil War Years

Besides building a skyscraper, how else did Silas occupy himself during Civil War years? Charles Baker of Danby's *Mirror* knew better than to ask, but the inquiry did arise when he was interviewed for *The New England States*. Having already supplied fantastic biographical data on his schooling at Kimball Union Academy at Meriden, New Hampshire, Silas just kept right on being creative about the Civil War.

"Oh," he answered, "I couldn't serve in the army on account of my aged mother," (who died in 1890 at the age of eighty-two). "But the fact that I didn't enter the army didn't prevent me from appearing in Union Camp whenever a battle loomed on the horizon," he expounded.

"Really!"

"Of course, I wasn't always successful in forecasting those events," he continued, "but I was with the Fourth Vermont Volunteers at the close of the Battle of Antietam, and I was on the Fredericksburg field directly after the engagement. I was also with the regiment on the three days' march from Hagerstown to the Potomac and spent many a night in camp."

"But how could you pass the lines, particularly after the Battle of Fredericksburg?" the interviewer asked.

"Yankee smarts," Silas said airily. "A few days acquaintance with the clerk of the War Department and a letter from Senator Solomon Foote. That's how I got the necessary papers."

A Grand Store

Between those fantasized Civil War engagements, Silas occupied himself in his grand store. The soul in Griffith's coffin twitched a smile, just remembering it.

CLOTHING HATS CAPS BOOTS & SHOES was emblazoned between the second and third floor windows. Another sign, mounted on the face of the front porch near the smaller entrance, read **FLOUR**

FEED MEAL CORN & OATS. Besides these items, the store had wares of all descriptions - furniture, carpets, rugs, luxuries, and necessities. Carpeting went for $2.20 a yard, a set of chairs for $2, a bedstead cost $1.85. A good many farmers brought their meat to the store for Silas to sell; a half a hog went for $4.50, and beef sold for $.50 a pound. Produce ranged from such staples as apples, onions, and winter squash to such fine fruits as bananas and oranges which were sold for a penny apiece. A bushel of ears of corn went for $5, six bushels of potatoes for $1.30, raisins for $1 a pound. $3.30 was the price for a pound of coffee. Tea was considerably more. Soap cost $1.50 a gallon, flour went for about $3.80 a half bushel, $5 was the price of a bushel of oats, and whey butter was $.80 a pound. In later years, on Saturday nights, the men who worked his Mt. Tabor jobs would write in the amount of lumber they had cut that week after their names tacked up on one of the main doors, and the fellow with the largest cut got to smoke a cigar with the boss. A congenial man, Silas was a born salesman, and adept at figures. When he was figuring an account, he'd go, "Ought from ought, two from two, all for me and none for you." And smile. Of course.

Oh, what a kick Silas got, outside his emporium, watching the world go by.

Main Street Danby

Main Street was a mighty busy thoroughfare, for it was part of the main north-south artery that served the western side of the state. In the winter, in snow and ice, sleighs and sleds mingled with the horse-drawn buggies and wagons and carts, riders on horseback, and, occasionally, bicycles, all of them having to skitter around for the pedestrians who constantly maneuvered their way through the traffic as they went back and forth, east to west, often sprinting from the sidewalks.

There was always noise, a mixed harmony of whinnies and clanks and clops and bells and shouts and hails and, often, muted cussing on the part of the foot traffic. Trying to cross was a process decidedly more trying for the women with their long dresses and shopping baskets, especially in mud season.

Even in the heat of summer, the village ladies wore high-collared, long-sleeved blouses or dresses, generally practical and tailored, made of unpretentious cotton dress goods, with some favoring apron-like garments with sashes drawn back to produce a bustle-like effect. Flat brimmed, high crowned hats prevailed as the women made their way in and out of the shops, especially the general merchandise stores, like Griffith's and the Stone Store. And occasionally they frequented an old place run by Bill Bond. It was a leisurely, sociable process. In fine weather, the women bumped into each other and stood around visiting and gossiping on the sidewalk as they made their rounds, marginally protected from the sun by the towering shade trees. In their three-piece suits, white shirts, bow ties and bowlers, the men took to lounging on the steps of Griffith's store as they shot the breeze.

The heart of the commercial district was anchored on the north end of the long block by stores on both corners. At the south end, the Union Church and Maple Terrace faced each other, elevated on their hill, elegant and apart from the mercantile scene. The stores and residences in the middle of the block were primarily on the west side of Main, for the village's vast hotel occupied the southeast corner opposite Griffith's store.

The hotel grew and grew over years of different owners. It was a large, window-shuttered, farmhouse-like structure, that sprawled east and south through a series of connecting front-porched structures. At least six chimneys rose from this almost block-long establishment that housed a restaurant and a livery and a large hall about forty feet wide by eighty feet long. There, balls and dances were held, as well as exhibitions and whatever other uses were required by the conventions that frequented the hostelry.

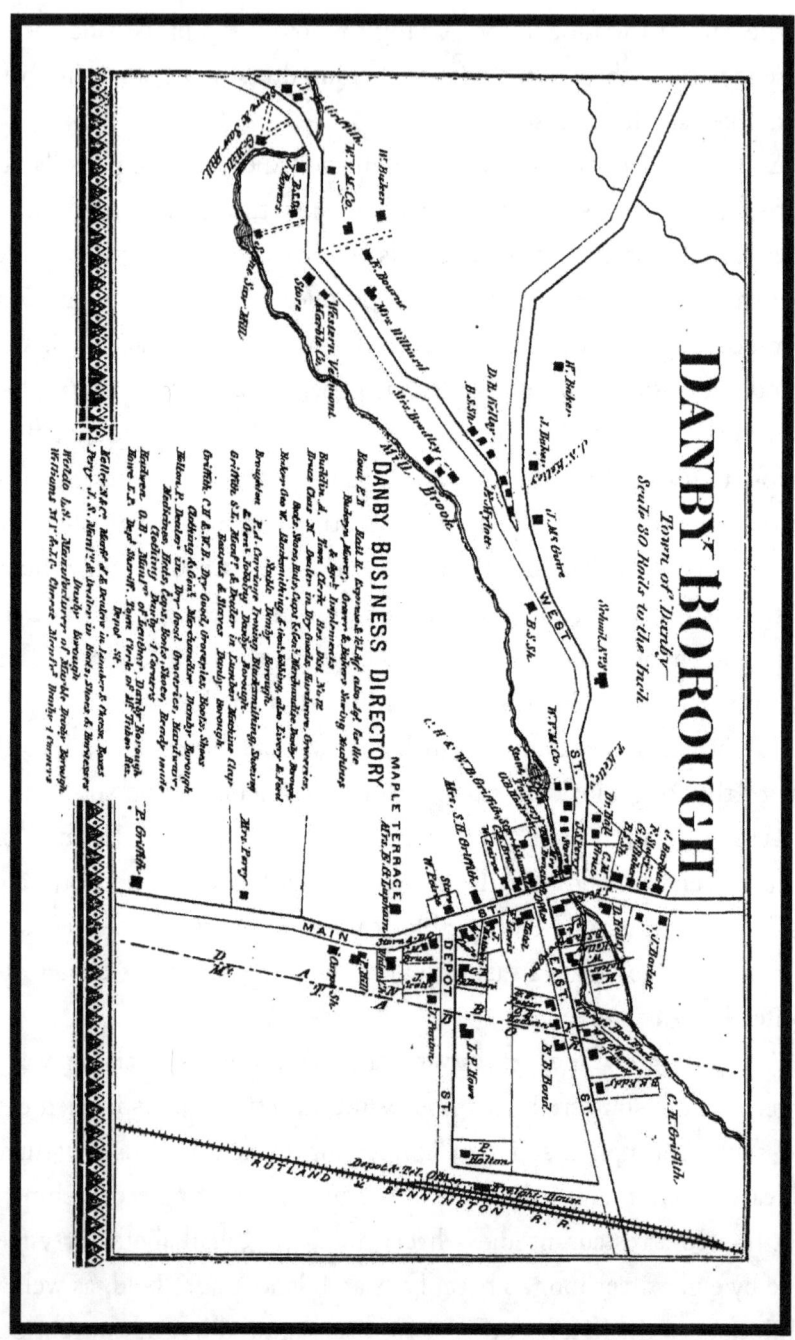

Danby Borough

There was Silas, at twenty-four years of age, an important part of the commercial scene just like his uncle, Jesse. Well established in business, with more than sufficient income to support a wife, Silas was a man to be reckoned with and one of the best catches in town.

Wedding Bells

Silas was ready to get married. Foresighted as always, he had his bride-designate all picked out. Elizabeth Mary Staples, known to the world as Libbie, was the object of Silas's affection. She was the daughter of Edwin Staples, one of Danby's leading farmers and a well-reputed man of taste and means. Edwin had married Louisa Vail, Ira Vail's daughter and their union was shortly blessed by a daughter, Libbie, who was born in December of 1844. Tragically, Louisa died in 1849, when she was twenty-five years old and five-year-old Libbie was brought up by Edwin's second wife, Margaret Vail Lapham, Jesse's niece. (She was the daughter of his brother David Lapham and his wife, Samantha Vail.)

The Laphams and the Vails and the Griffiths, round and round.

Libbie was a handful. A beautiful girl with a regal way about her, she was spirited, independent and proud, and Silas wanted her enough to endure the process of courtship. On Sunday afternoons in those days, virtually all male members of polite society sat, at one time or other, perched on the edge of an overstuffed chair or sofa in the front parlor of his lady's home, courting. The young men sat under the eyes of her collected family, Purity's remorseless guardians. So there sat Silas, trying to engage his lady, while Libbie's two younger half-brothers, George and Eddie, Margaret's sons, hovered and chased and giggled and applied every form of obnoxious behavior from the vast repertoire available to pre-teen boys. Where men hated the procedure, courtship, to the woman, was girlhood's last dance. Perhaps because her vow at the end was "obey," a man had to do some pretty good convincing her—even more so than usual, in Libbie's case.

"Well, well, Silas, what's this I'm hearing about you?" inquired his cousin, H.G. Lapham one day, smiling broadly at Silas across Griffith's expansive store counter, as his glance appraised the well-stocked shelves and the customers milling about. "Word has it you're courting Libbie Staples."

"For all the good it's doing me," S.L. replied grumpily, tossing his pencil down in disgust and looking up from his ledger. "Oh, I'm going through all the paces, all right. Every Sunday, in every kind of weather, I go up there and try to charm her into caring for me, with her brothers tee-heeing and the women knitting and watching. Not that I'd dream of taking a liberty, you understand..."

"Come, come, Silas," Henry murmured.

"...although I'll not deny the thought has been driving me wild. She's a beauty, you know. And proud and regal and smart, everything I could possibly want in a wife."

"It was bad enough going through all that hoopla at her father's farm up in the hills," Silas ranted on, "but then she took it in her mind to move over to Granville, so now I have to trot over to New York state, where she's staying with one of her aunts."

"Libbie, why did you move all the way over here?" I asked her. "Oh, I just had a little disagreement with my stepmother" she answered.

"I like Margaret, myself," Henry said. "A nice woman, but quite a bit younger than Edwin."

"She's somewhere in her early thirties," Silas supplied, "only six or seven years older than I am. We get along great. She's been married to Edwin ten, twelve, thirteen years, now. I don't know what's ruffling Libbie after all this time."

"What do you suppose they squabbled about?" Henry inquired innocently.

"I'll be blamed if I know. I surely wish that Libbie wasn't so riled up that she had to leave town. That's a miserable haul —two trips every Sunday, probably twenty-one miles between the Borough and Granville, two hours going, four hours returning home on a tired horse with most of the way uphill. And now it's coming up mud season."

"And how are things going, for all your trouble?"

"Even with the whole family pushing for me, Libbie's polite, is all."

"How old is she now, Silas?"

"Libbie's nineteen and I'm twenty-six. Old enough. I'm doing real well and I'm not all that bad looking. Libbie could do a lot worse for herself."

"Exactly. And if she hasn't got the sense to know it, then too bad for her. My best advice to you, cousin, would be to dump her and go elsewhere. There's any number of lovelies who would jump at the chance of being your wife."

"I don't want any of them! I don't want some farm girl, some simple, easy, compliant, simpering helpmate. It's Libbie I want. I love her with all my heart, and I'm determined to have her!"

"Oh, Silas, Silas," Henry sighed. "...Can't you see, this move to Granville... She's trying everything to put you off. Forget it!"

Silas answered his cousin with a set jaw, a sullen mouth and a stiff neck.

H.G. Lapham, in return, thoroughly roused, discarded his velvet gloves and bellowed, "Libbie's in love with another man, Silas, a Dr. Williams from Wallingford or Rutland or somewhere..."

"I don't care!" warbled Silas. "A lot of women get married to men they don't love and it works out fine. Families have been arranging marriages forever. I'll make her love me after we're married. She'll come to love me, I'm sure of it. I want her, Henry. And I'll have her. Getting Lib to marry me is the biggest challenge of my life, and I'm going to win it. If you want to help me, you'll apply a few screws of your own."

"Do you have any idea the pressure that girl is under now?" Lapham yelped forcibly. "My Uncle David is pressuring Margaret, who's sitting on Edwin, who's already getting it from his Uncle Abraham who married Catherine Griffith and from his sister, Lydia, who's 'applying the screws' to her husband, my cousin Joseph, who's getting it from his father, Elisha — all of which is making your Uncle Jesse, my poor father, miserable. Why, that poor man is on his deathbed, and he's the one who dictated I speak to you about this."

"Aside from driving each other crazy, every one of those people is pushing Libbie to marry you, every chance they get. It's a sign of the girl's fortitude that she's held out this long. And now, you're asking me to apply more pressure yet."

"Let me tell you something, Silas. I'm better than twenty years older than you and I'm a long-married man. I've learned a lot and I've heard a lot and, believe me, I'd be doing you no service were I able to persuade Libbie into this union."

"This is no docile cow of a farm girl you've picked for yourself. Libbie is a very independent, strong-willed young woman of great character, all the better to make your life with her a living hell, if she so chooses. If you think she's going to forget this other fella as soon as she crawls beneath the sheets with you, you've got another thing coming. And if she's successfully pressured into a match she has no heart for, you're going to pay for it, and dearly."

"I want her," Silas replied, stonily. "I'm determined to have her."

"You're making a mistake. This is a marriage that shouldn't take place."

But take place, it did.

And in the beginning, at least, to all outward appearances, Libbie was as happy in the union as Silas, for on the couple's first anniversary, on the 20th of May 1864, they repeated their vows and were married for the second time in Danby, an uncommon but not unheard of act of sentiment.

The soul in Griffith's coffin warmed with ecstasy, recalling one of the two sole periods of unadulterated joy he had experienced in his lifetime.

Joy and Sorrow

What Libbie's acquiescence to the second marriage ceremony meant, in terms of her feelings towards Silas, was yet augmented by her lusciously swelling belly that proclaimed his first child would soon be born.

In August of 1864, the Griffiths became the proud parents of a daughter, Lottie, a beautiful infant, whose arrival brought indescribable happiness to Silas and Libbie. But their joy was shattered beyond redemption on October 8th of the same year, when the infant took a fever and died at the age of one and a half months. Her poor little body was placed in one of Timothy Kelley's $1.25 wood coffins and buried in the Griffith lot in Scottsville cemetery.

At his own funeral that day in Danby, the soul in Griffith's coffin writhed at the recollection, and the rain teemed down harder and the stink of the flowers and the wet wool funeral suits and the perspiration from all those bodies in the hot, humid closeness of the Congregational Church affected all, but none so much as Jennie Riddle, who just then caught and acknowledged the transient eye of a heavily veiled lady of a certain age, who stood ramrod straight at the coffin and then, without a word to the family, turned and took a seat in one of the rear pews for the two hour wait for the service.

With a sigh—for the woman was Libbie—she remembered her surprise at the incredible happiness her marriage to Silas had brought her in the beginning. His kindness and generosity and adoration more than made her forget her beau in Wallingford and she was delighted and proud to be his wife. It was a period of joy, all too brief, that shattered after Lottie's death. Not because of the baby's death, she remembered, but because of Silas's insistence, immediately after the child's burial, that they "start making babies again."

"Silas, not now, not yet! To go through all that, only to bury the dear result...Give me time to get over Lottie."

"I know it was awful, Libbie, it was dreadful, I know—"

"How could you know?" she cried. "I had the baby. After twenty-four hours of labor, she came from me, she was part of me. I nursed her. While you ran to the store every day, I was with her, watching her fail and die. No, Silas, you don't know. No man can know."

"Libbie, please, Libbie dear. You know how many infants die, children die. We have to have another right away, to take Lottie's place."

"Not yet, we don't! I won't have it!"

"Libbie, I'm twenty-seven years old. I want a family and I don't want to wait!"

"I'm not ready to bear another child now. I will not!"

"It's your marital duty!" Silas demanded

"Duty be damned!" You want a child so badly, poke around elsewhere and get one! I'll bring it up for you."

Silas jerked his chin up at her words and clamped his mouth and gave her a look she never ever hoped to see again, a look of fury and pain and sorrow, and she thought she saw a suspicion of tears in his eyes, but he never said a word. He just turned on his heels and stormed out. The subject was not broached again, for a very long time. All these years later, in the heat of the Church, Libbie shivered at the recollection of that frigid year, of the please-pass-the-salt politeness, of the awful loneliness of a married couple sharing a house as strangers but going through all the motions as if everything were fine between them.

Silas Griffith, Lumberman

Silas, of course, went to the store every day and buried himself in business. As the newspaper described,

> ...his business continued to increase till 1864, during which year he sold $48,000 worth of goods. The following year he sold out the business to his brothers, C.H. and W.B Griffith, to devote his entire efforts to the lumber business, which at that time he was operating in only at North Dorset, on some timber land which he had been forced to take in order to liquidate an indebtedness.

"... he was operating only at North Dorset..." Joel Baker had parroted the night before, "Hogwash, hogwash! Why, you knew, Charlie, the whole town knew about that lawsuit where I represented him against Willard. It was Griffith vs. Willard, September Term, Rutland County Court, 1865. The Report of Referee that was incorporated within the decision of the Rutland County Superior Court in 1868 said it like it was:

> The plaintiff at the date of contract, dated November 28th, 1864 ...was a merchant at Danby Borough, and also largely engaged in lumber business, which lumber business was done in the town of Mt Tabor.

"Why do you suppose he lied that one away?"

"He lost it, that's why. In 1869, the Rutland County Court found for Willard. Silas was charged $46.27 plus interest from the time the Referee's report was filed, which amounted to $47.40 plus costs of $64.66 and $700 on top of that.

"The case didn't receive much coverage," Joel continued, "since I was on the staff of the *Rutland Herald* at that time and pushing for Editor, so I kept it out of the paper, but, oh, S.L. hated to lose and he very rarely lost after that; he settled rather than lose," his lawyer nodded and drank some more.

"What was that case about, anyway?"

"Oh, it was a convoluted contractual matter between him and Willard and old Risdon and Henry Howard, who had the Button Mill. Ohhh," Joel groaned, rubbing his brow, "I'm much too drunk to remember all those ins-and-outs, which don't much matter anyhow, seeing as it was one of them who-owes-who deals. But I do recall a couple of things. It was up to Silas to sell the lumber and receive the sales and keep true and accurate accounts and his books were to be open to inspection. But when the Referee of the Court examined the books," Joel chortled, "it was impossible for him to determine a thing that went on before the lawsuit began, since no copies of the accounts were furnished for his inspection until after the hearing and those that were lacked the dates of all charges. The bottom line on that was S.L.'s bookkeeping. You know, I wonder, if maybe that wasn't when he brought in Minnie Bushee to help him with that? Do you recall when Minnie started in with him?"

"Gawd, no," Charlie replied. "Seems like he had her for always. What I do remember, though," he added with a leer, "is that before she started in with him, the Head Office at that time was one large room. Minnie hadn't been there long, when Silas figured he needed a private office, so he put up a wall and added that fainting couch to his space."

"Something else I always wondered about," Joel mentioned after a little, "that profitable store business he was forced to sell to go into lumbering. That $48,000 he grossed in 1864 sounds tremendous. But I happened to speak to William Pierce in '67 after he had been running the Stone Store awhile. (He'd bought it from C.M. Bruce in November of '66.) And when I asked him how he was doing, Will said he couldn't complain. A good trading day would bring upwards of $120, a real high day would bring sales of more than $200. When you divide S.L.'s $48,000 into days, you get about $131.50 a day. Considering that Pierce's store couldn't be more than about 2,500 sq. ft. and Silas's big store is more than twice that in size, Pierce was doing much better in terms of sales per square foot. Everything considered, S.L. wasn't about to become a millionaire in storekeeping, where he'd already found out in his dealings with Willard that the cost of cutting, piling, drawing the logs to the mill, sawing them into lumber, and drawing the lumber to the station was $12 per thousand and the value of the lumber at the railroad station was $16 per thousand. Which might have had something to do with why he sold out to his brothers."

"You happen to check how much he sold it to them for?"

Joel laughed. "Sure I checked. He sold it to them in for $2000 — a ridiculous price, a gift, really. I guess he figured he owed them..."

Jennie Griffith Arrives

On September 19th, 1865, when Silas sat down to supper, he said to his wife, "I have a couple of things to tell you, Libbie."

"Oh?"

"Yes. First of all, I sold the store today to my brothers, sold it for a song, with the understanding I could use part of the land for a lumber office and if I wanted, I could buy back a part of the operation and use it later on.

Second, I wanted to tell you I took some advice you gave me, quite a while back," Silas informed her and started eating.

"Advice? What advice?"

"Well," S.L. said, chomping and swallowing before answering, "you remember you said if I wanted a child so badly, I should poke around elsewhere and get one. So I did that," Silas informed her, and went back to his chicken.

"You didn't," Libbie gasped, aghast.

"Oh, I did, indeed. You didn't want to bear it, Libbie, so you didn't, but you will rear it as your own. With luck, I'll be able to get the Town Clerk to list you as mother."

Silas was partially successful. In the more popularly consulted Index, at some later time, some obliging Town Clerk did what he could. Lacking a proper line, he squeezed the name Jennie Elizabeth Griffith between two lined signatures, thus legitimatizing the child in that volume anyway, although the Index does refer the listing back to page 29 of the Vital Records Book as reference. In response to 20th century genealogical inquiries, later clerks graciously and gratuitously legitimatized the birth by furnishing Libbie's name in answer to inquiries.

However, in the Vital Records Book, Volume 1, Page 29 of the Birth Records for 1865 notes that an unnamed (misspelled as "Know name") female child was born in the 8th District of Danby on September 23rd, that her father was a merchant and that both parents were born in Danby. Under the column, "Name of Parents", the September 23d entry is the only one. Obviously, no amount of persuasion could convince the Town Clerk to change the mother's name from "Lydia" to "Libbie" in the Vital Records Book.

Who *is* the birth mother, Lydia? Who knows?

In any case, Silas's daughter, Jennie Elizabeth Griffith, was born on September 23rd, 1865, eleven months after Lottie's death. Jennie was in all ways reared as Libbie's own child and was accepted as such by all. Not a hint of scandal was ever heard concerning the circumstances of her maternity.

Silas reveled in his daughter, indulged her, adored her, played with her, loved her to distraction, for he was a person who inordinately loved children and Jennie's presence in his home relieved the underlying chill of his relationship with Libbie. Still, he longed for a son.

SILAS LAPHAM GRIFFITH

Vital Records

Danby Registry of Births, 1866
Courtesy of Mt. Tabor-Danby Historical Society

The Lumber Business

S.L.'s entrance into the business of lumbering was not as immediately satisfying. For some time, he made a point of telling his customers and others that he had been forced into lumbering and that merchandising was his occupation of choice. Silas further admitted he didn't think lumbering was a good business, and that it was, in fact, a rather disreputable one, although after a time he came to the conclusion that it took about "as good a head" to conduct it successfully as it did the mercantile business. Griffith's conclusions proved more than accurate.

> At the time Mr. Griffith sold the stock of goods to his brothers, a man

> by the name of Howard owned what was then known as the "Button Property" in Mount Tabor and was engaged in the lumber business there. Mr. Griffith had assisted Mr. Howard in money and goods to the extent of several thousand dollars and had taken a mortgage on the property as security. In order to get what was due him Mr. Griffith was forced to take the property.

Howard had paid over $9,000 to acquire the better than nine-hundred-acre parcel with the sawmill which reverted to Griffith in the summer of 1866, when Griffith foreclosed.

A search of the Land Book indicated a dollar amount on the transaction of $2,500.

> ...This was the nucleus from which he built up his present extensive Works, commencing in 1869.

("Wrong, Charlie!! 1866 is the year!" Joel Baker interjected.)

Like it or not, Silas was stuck with the mill and stuck with the business and, if truth be told, starting out into lumbering took a lot more "head" than merchandising ever did. For Griffith, it was a new business, a new game, a new and thoroughly absorbing challenge that tested every facet of his varied abilities.

In actuality, the lumbering business was a good deal worse than "disreputable."

Most of the big operators and a lot of the small ones, too, when they owned three-quarters of an area, they started cutting. And after they cut the three-quarters they owned, they went on to cut a good part of the quarter they didn't and if the owner came in to protest, they would put their logging crews and cutters on him and run the poor guy right out of the woods and only pay him stumpage if it got to Court. Which it generally didn't.

In the courts of the day, a *Plea of Trespass* was the legal classification of timber banditry. And judging by the number of cases of this type on record, it was an all too common practice. Operators large and small were accused of trespassing with force and arms, breaking and entering and removing logs and/or cutting down trees and causing damage and loss to another man's timber holdings. And Griffith was indeed a party to a number of these actions, sometimes as plaintiff, but most frequently as the defendant.

It would seem Griffith quite successfully outgrew his initial aversion to the disreputable aspects of the industry. Many people would call Griffith many things, but the most common of all was "Pirate."

There are some pretty good stories about Griffith in later years. They used to tell about the time Griffith was cutting over an area adjoining Hadwen's and old man Hadwen called out to him, "Stay away from my line, Griffith! If you or your men cut one log from my side, I'll kill the lot of you!" And Hadwen sat on his porch with his gun and his telescope and watched them.

In later years, a lot of people would stand around and talk about Silas. Some said he was a decent man. Some told what an old crook he was. "Well, he wasn't a crook," in one man's opinion, "but you could say he practiced mighty sharp practices."

With the preface that the constable, deputies, and sheriffs were in S.L.'s employ, there were stories told that if some old timer didn't want to sell his timber, Silas would invite the old guy up, get him drunk, have him arrested for intoxication, have the fine set high, pay the fine, and take the timber.

But that was later.

ANN K. ROTHMAN

Choppers and Teamsters

In the beginning, Silas manufactured clapboards and staves in his mill on the Button property and sold the product behind his brothers' big store building. It was a limited operation, confined to the borders of the property he had acquired from Howard, but the operational process was quite standard.

The chopping went on in all seasons, but winter was when the bulk of the work got done. The choppers worked under woods bosses who told them what areas to go into. And when the wood was cut, the softwood required for the clapboards and staves was skidded out with oxen and put on skidways to wait until winter when the roads were frozen and ready. Then it was hauled to the mill, cut and loaded onto sleds—double sleds—to bring it down the mountain when there was snow.

For brakes, heavy chains called *rugglers* went around the nose of the rear sled and were hooked around the back runner or runners of that sled right before it headed down. The hardest part for the horses, big western horses, was to pull the sleds back up the mountain, but it was a mighty dangerous job for the teamsters that drove.

The teamsters would put a horse blanket over a 2" hardwood sapling called a *log binder,* that was pulled over the logs to put tension on the chain that held the load down. And while it wasn't the most comfortable seat in the world, it worked fine, most of the time. Unless the sapling broke, which they did, now and then, catapulting the men off and down, God knows how far down. Some of the cliffs alongside the roads were sheer drops of hundreds of feet.

Handling the rugglers going down was tricky business. Since the horses couldn't pull the sleds on flat ground with the rugglers on, at the bottom of a hill the teamster would unhook the chain and let it slide alongside the runner until they got to the next steep place. The rugglers would handle the breaking job very well so long as the teamster knew what he was doing and kept his mind on it. But if he forgot the pitch of the road ahead or daydreamed or started to fill his pipe or something, or, if for any reason, he'd got down a little too far before thinking to hook on his ruggler, by then it was too late. Too steep. No stopping. And he would end up over a bank somewhere and the horses and the two sleds, loaded with four or five tons of wood, would end up someplace else. Or maybe they'd all come charging down the mountain, out of control, on down-bound ice.

That was the operation.

Fortunately, when there were accidents, the doctors in town would go out after them, anywhere, at any time. They would think nothing of driving their horse up the mountain in any kind of weather, a snowstorm, if necessary, to get to a man who needed them.

God Sent Harry Ralph

Lumbering was a rough job, from start to finish, with a good many considerations, but for Silas, starting out, one problem loomed above all the others.

There was Silas, up high on the Green Mountain, surrounded by timber with a mill to cut it, swamped with inherent profit and no way to realize it without getting the lumber off the mountain and down to the freight cars of the Rutland & Burlington Railroad Company, the successor firm of the bankrupted Western Vermont line.

What he needed first of all was a road builder. And God heard him and sent him Harry Ralph.

Years later at the funeral, Harry had tears in his eyes when he spoke to Jennie Riddle. "Oh, this is a sad day," he said to Jennie. "You know," he said, "I was one of the first men he hired and I worked for him over thirty years and only once in all that time did we have words, and that wasn't Mr. Griffith's fault, the blame for that rests right on the shoulders of Eddie Staples. As far as I'm concerned, he was a good boss, Mr. Griffith, and I enjoyed serving him while he was alive much more than I'll enjoy my final act here on his behalf, that of pallbearer of his coffin."

And Harry, a very fit man around sixty years old, lean and straight as a sapling, took a seat in one of the front pews and remembered and pondered and recalled how he had watched Griffith grow his empire from the very beginning. Shortly after Griffith's acquisition of the timber tract and sawmill, a lanky twenty-three-year-old drink of water, a Canadian just down from Montreal, he came knocking for a job at Griffith's lumber office behind the store.

"I'm Harry Ralph," he said. "I need work."

"What do you do?"

"I'm a woodsman," he answered, "a good one. Heard you have a tract of land you want to lumber off, thought you could use me."

I might be able to." Griffith looked him over, his hands, his eyes, his spare frame, his controlled intensity and he liked what he saw. "I don't suppose you've had any experience building roads?"

"Sure. Some."

"Well, I might try you out. I don't pay much."

"I ain't ever got much." Harry answered with a laugh.

"I expect a full day's work, dawn to dark."

"You'll get it."

Harry Ralph. His qualifications: woodman. His genius: engineering. His worth: incalculable.

Six months to a year before the logging crews were scheduled to move into an area, Harry would go into the timber and walk back and forth, back and forth in new areas of virgin forest. He had an uncanny sense of direction; he never used a compass and never got lost. When he was cruising the timber, he had a very deliberate gait. The first hour or so, it was pretty easy to get ahead of him and a lot of men that went with him thought that Harry was pretty slow in the morning; after lunch, they were quite certain he'd speeded up some;

and by five o'clock, when they were pretty well beat, they would have sworn Harry was practically trotting. But of course, he wasn't. He just kept his same deliberate pace all the time, and kept going, on and on... thinking all the while.

He had plenty to think about. For one thing, he plotted his roads, making certain to leave most of the merchantable timber above - Silas would have been more than a little displeased having any problems stand in the way of gravity-oriented, time-saving removal procedures.

Ralph mapped the road out as he went along, not on paper but in the terrain itself; he laid it out, marking trees. With his eyes as the only surveying instrument he ever used, Harry plotted his grades over ways sometimes so steep and rough as to be almost impossible for a man to ascend on foot, and he never displayed the pressure he must have felt knowing that the safe transport of life as well as load depended on how well he performed.

With the road laid out, on a strict schedule, he started the second part of his job - supervising the road's building by his road crew over whom he had complete charge and for whose performance he was entirely answerable.

From start to finish, practically every wood road on the Green Mountain was Harry Ralph's creation, and almost without exception they were built with whatever materials were naturally available at the site. If they went across a very steep place, a granite ledge or something, they cribbed that up with logs and covered it over with dirt and whatever else was handy and, when necessary, they blasted. The end results were roads with some of the most beautiful grades imaginable along the mountains. Beautiful but as steep and hard going as could be imagined.

Sitting in the church that summer day, Harry figured that one of the reasons he and the boss had gotten along so well, was because they were both perfectionists.

He remembered one particular Sunday when he was making fence posts and he didn't notice that Griffith had chanced by and was standing there, watching. Harry was a great axeman, and he'd cut through a log and every blow just the same on each side. His posts looked as though they had been put through an over-sized pencil sharpener, they were so even and their points were so sharp. That's the way he wanted them, so he could more easily drive them into the ground with his hammer, the eight-pound maul, he used.

After a little he looked up and saw Griffith standing there, beaming. "That's why your roads are so good, Harry, because they have to be perfect to please you."

Now, looking at Silas in his coffin, Ralph blinked back his tears and already missed the respect Silas had always shown him, respect for a job well done.

Change of Plans

Then, remembering way back, Harry recalled a brief period, about two years after he had started working for Griffith, when he found himself temporarily unemployed.

It came down to this: in the short time Silas had been lumbering, he had an awful lot of aggravation and not much to show for it. His lawsuit with Willard had dampened his initial enthusiasm for the business and endless problems with the railroad proved an ongoing worry.

In January 1867 there had been no trains or mails with any regularity and, for a week, no freights at all, which thoroughly disrupted business. Griffith attended most of the many meetings that were held all over to see what could be done to get a railroad connection with some road south. As the year progressed, the meetings were invariably accompanied by a lot of warm discussion over subscribing to a bond issue to pay for the extension. (In the long run, Danby was too selfish to contribute.) Then, in August, a man at his mill broke his arm and leg, one bone of each. It felt like just one more thing, on top of the basic fact that Griffith truly didn't care for the lumbering business.

It's no wonder that when an opportunity came along to rid himself of it, he did just that. In December of 1868, Silas sold the Button Mill to some men from Boston, hoping to be done with it; and, with some time on his hands he turned more of his attention to the boiling pot of goings-on in the village.

Village Goings On

There was plenty of it for everyone and always had been. The Velocipede School at George Baker's Hotel was lots of fun for the boys. The Sewing Circle was popular with the ladies, as was Dancing School. Most everyone enjoyed the picnics, and there were lots of them. One great Union picnic up at Danby Corners was attended by about a thousand people! And quite a number of men found it unfailingly agreeable and pleasant to watch the Company Militia's training exercises and the Baseball Club's matches, especially when the Danby boys won. Griffith didn't have much interest in any of that, though.

About the last thing in the world Silas was interested in doing was attending any exhibitions like the slight of hand performance at the Hotel one evening with some Spiritual manifestations through one of the Eddy mediums. The onlookers saw several externalized hands, different from the medium's. No, that was definitely not Silas's cup of tea. Nor were the frequent lectures like the time when Mrs. Kingbury spoke one evening on the condition of the Freedman. That kind of thing—that and the circles, the seances they attended all the time—was all fine and good for the liberals, the radicals, Silas thought. If the Spiritualists who prevailed around town (Methodists, most of them) took pleasure getting rappings from the dead and speaking to Thomas Jefferson and such, fine for them, but that wasn't for Silas. Philosophically, Silas was a conservative, a Congregationalist, quite rigid and orthodox in belief, one who took the Bible as true and authoritative, compared to those who saw the Bible as a source book of man's seeking and had a considerably more "mental" approach.

Despite the different religious factions in the community, people lived and let live without any difficulty whatsoever for a good many years with the Meeting House, the Union Church, a focal point for all. Beyond purposes of worship, the house was a place of mental stimulation, a conduit, where all manner of thought of the times was presented for the community's consideration by those who lectured there in return for contributing to the building's insatiable upkeep.

Understandably, then, when once more concerns about the building's maintenance and increasing state of disrepair arose, meetings were held and major repairs on the house were commenced in 1866 with the support of the entire community. A good many citizens became involved in the project, which took better than a year to complete.

William Pierce

Various happenings in addition to the church repairs fueled the town talk, including deaths (lots of deaths, like the dysentery epidemic of August,'66 that killed more than four children and adults). Some goings-on were watched with particular interest. Among these was the saga of one William Pierce, who had moved down to the Borough some years earlier, after selling his farm. Philosophically, Pierce was a liberal, a radical of the first order, who discarded or ridiculed the old Biblical beliefs. A man of inquisitive mind, he was a great reader of a philosophic bent. A leading Spiritualist in the community, he passed countless absorbing evenings with his good friend Austin Baker, (Charlie Baker's father) who was a medium of the first order. It was through Baker that any number of Spirit Friends, from Tom Paine to various deceased members of the community, made themselves heard.

Pierce was a good citizen. He duly paid his taxes ($27.15 to the town plus $2.47 for the school tax), put in his time on jury duty, went to the Corners to town caucus meetings that were managed ...

as corrupt as H...," He wrote in his diary. And he attended state elections there where Town Representatives were elected "...with the aid of Rum, Rowdyism, and Howling..." He attended too many Town Meetings that were "... very noisy and a Disgrace to Half Civilized Man" thoroughly fulfilled his obligations as a voter, attended Freeman's Meetings and held town office.

Once moved to the Borough, Pierce took advantage of an astonishing number of the lectures, exhibitions, dances, and other activities the village had to offer, and, of course, he patronized its stores for his needs, methodically putting down his expenditures in his little account books.

Expenses of Interest:

Barrel of flour	$5.87
½ tt of tea	.30
Tribune for one year	$1.00
3 yards of calico	.36
1 dozen buttons	.12
1 pair of shoes	.62
100 sap buckets	$14.00
Paid Spencer Green for writing lease	.50
Three yards of carpeting	.66
Paid E.O. Whipple for doctoring	$1.25
Paid O.B. Hadwin for one half pt. of Brandy	.35
Moses Shippy worked for 4 days @ .25	$1.00
April 1st Lydia Buxton commenced work her for one dollar per week as long as she stays with us	$1.00
For one fish	.10

For the first volume of JSC Abbots History of the Rebellion	$3.50
Paid C.M. Bruce for his hat	$1.60
Sold two cows for	$25.00
Paid for one cow	$30.00
For school tax	.58
For 1 lb. of coffee	.33
Paid for ½ of a washing machine	$6.50
Paid C.M. Bruce for one pair of pantaloons	$5.00

For a number of years after he sold his farm and moved to the village, Pierce dabbled, casting around for a livelihood that suited him. For a while he dealt in furniture; then he tried money lending. But his life changed over the years. His first wife died and he remarried the former Katie Kelly, a lively widow with a child, little Georgia, whereupon Pierce felt he had to get back into a steady, dependable field of endeavor. He decided to go back to farming and applied himself to searching out a new farm.

Hither, tither and yon, for a full five months, Pierce traveled in rain, in shine, through mud, on boats, any number of trips all over the state. One trip alone, he spent three weeks footing it, looking over farms. Some land, good; some land, poor; some very good land, but always with a lot he didn't like about it. He finally headed for Michigan, got as far as Buffalo, then got to Adrian where he saw some good farms, but the price very high, from $60 to $100 an acre. Four miles from the center of the city he found a 120-acre farm for $55 an acre, considered cheap.

Finally Pierce gave up. He got back to town in October and on November 12th, 1866, with some qualms about his snap decision born out of frustration at having tramped those interminable soggy acres, but buoyed up by the prospect of never, ever again having to endure the rigors of farm hunting, William Pierce paid $9,000 for C.M. Bruce's Stone Store and the house and lot that immediately neighbored the David Griffiths' residence.

"Ye have nothing to worry about, Pierce," the old Quaker, Bruce, reassured him, as he clutched his money in his hand. "Ye've made a wise choice. Ye are a smart man, good at figuring, with a little background behind ye already, for trade. Why, ye'll do fine," said the Borough's oldest, most successful surviving merchant of his day, as he handed Pierce the keys of his late empire. "What could possibly go wrong?"

And it was quite true that the Borough's stores, even those that didn't house the post office, had done quite well. The township's population numbered just below 1,400 with most having shifted down to the village area (also known as the Borough) since the coming of the railroad. Although there were several other stores in the township, in the Borough proper (also called the Village) there were only three at that time that dealt in general merchandise: Griffith's, an old store occupied by William Bond (that took fire and burned down in March of '68) and Bruce's. (J. S. Perry's store up-street dealt in harnesses, boots, and shoes exclusively.) Money had become the most plentiful article in the community and with the Griffith boys running S.L.'s former establishment, Pierce figured all in all he had made a wise choice.

On November 26th, Bruce accompanied Pierce on a buying trip. They left for Troy in the morning, bought goods and started for New York City at night by boat. They finished trading on the 30th, settled up, ran to the boat and started for home.

ANN K. ROTHMAN

Expenses of Wm. Pierce Going to New York:

Fare to Troy	$2.35
Fare to N.Y. by boat	$3.00
For Supper	$1.00
Breakfast at Lovjoys	.50
Supper Tuesday	.85
Breakfast & Supper Wednesday	$1.00
Breakfast & Dinner Thursday	$1.00
Breakfast & Dinner Friday	$1.00
Room Lovjoys	$3.00
Fare to Troy	$3.00
TOTAL	**$16.70**

On December 5th, 1866, Pierce brought his goods to his store. There he and his clerk, James Fish, and C.M. Bruce marked the merchandise. Thus Pierce began a successful career as a merchant, as life in town puttered along—the bad and the good, round and round, and sometimes, both at once.

The village was alive with music, virtually any occasion provoked it. The Cornet Band, for example, played at the funeral of Benjamin Griffith, a Band member, who died in May 1867 of congestion of the brains after an illness of twenty-six hours—a funeral that, of course, Silas attended.

Silas loved music, and there was plenty of it in those days. There were pianos in many homes, and there were "sings," lots of sings. Sometimes the choir would come over to people's houses and sing away the evening, and sometimes the band would likewise visit and blast away. And then there were dances and balls, which were held either at the hotel or in the hall in C.W. Bruce's new store, a happening of interest to everyone, but most especially to William Pierce.

Five months of inactivity was enough for old Bruce. May of 1867 found him scuttling around for real estate and in June, he bought a house and lot for $500, "...rumor says to build a store on it...Considerable excitement over Bruce's moves." All in all, William Pierce was a good person indeed, but his nature was somewhat marred by his nose, which was unfailingly stuck in the affairs of the Borough and its citizens, all of which Danby's Pepys diligently noted in his daily diary entries. Needless to say, his attention was riveted on C.M. Bruce:

Mrs Jesse Lapham called on us and sympathized with us in regard to Bruce's movements against us.

With malevolent fascination, Pierce watched his competitor's work-in-progress: Not that he could have missed this expensive job as it went on just opposite his store windows.

Bruce store basement nearly finished.
Bruce is raising his new store today. When part up, it fell. No one hurt.

Repairing the Church

Without question, in the way of small-town shunning, Pierce looked right through C.M. Bruce, the Society's Secretary, the following day, on the occasion of the Union Church's rededication.

Virtually every family in the Borough had participated in the building's repair. Some had contributed their time; many others had furnished labor and materials. The largest bill of all was from C.M. Bruce, who charged the Society $197.50 for the carpet he supplied, demonstrating his continuation of trade even before his new elegant emporium was finished, which it was, shortly thereafter. The other local merchants were also owed monies for expenditures. C.H. and W.B. Griffith and William Pierce were jointly owed $138.51 by the Society.

S.L. Griffith and J.B. Nichols had both supplied about $20 worth of lumber. Austin Baker, the Spiritualist Treasurer of the Society, presented a bill for $17.86 for labor and materials — the list went on and on, and when September 15th, 1867 finally came, they were all there, the town was all there, to celebrate the completion of their handiwork.

An amazing assortment of neighbors—friends and enemies—were present for the occasion, as was the Reverend Z.C. Picket, who had commenced serving the Methodists. After the ceremony, there was a fight in the street, Pierce recorded, and though the men were parted, their faces were "pretty black" the following day, and they were very much ashamed. Theirs was the first documented battle revolving around the Union Church and was an unfortunate omen of the future.

A Heavenly Scene

Years later, after Pierce's death and some years prior to Griffith's, one could imagine this scene: old Pierce's consuming interest in other people's business found him cooling his heels outside the Pearly Gates, hovering with his coterie of Spirit Friends, waiting to be summoned at a time when Spiritualism had waned.

Later, the Lumber Baron's funeral found Pierce floating above them all in the Congregational Church, taking it all in and refreshing his abundant memories of his life in the cauldron. Passing over the bier, he winked down at the benefactor, with whom he had gotten along without acrimony, despite their diametrically opposed philosophical viewpoints. Pierce couldn't forget the evening he and his second wife had spent visiting Griffith's home during Silas's interregnum between wives. But he could and did forgive just about everything else, always excepting C.M. Bruce's actions and his store, with the post office installed in it. That was a cancerous growth in his craw that no amount of time would heal.

As he wafted above, Pierce relived his life through his entries, penciled in his little booklets in his less than Spenserian scrawl.

George Eggleston is and has been sick for two weeks, from drinking ice water.

Just being in the building brought back all manner of recollections of the years when the church battles rocked the community and venom replaced the good will among its people. How did the church wars start? When did they start?

Ah, yes. I remember, Pierce thought...

Us and Them

It began after the leaves began to put on the appearance of old age; in the fall of '67, after we went up to S.L. Griffith's mill in Mt. Tabor to view the foliage, after that, Pierce recalled. When all the leaves were down and the cold, grey days had started; in mid-November, when David Staples, commenced tearing down the old Quaker meeting house. That's when "We" became "Us" and "Them."

The Hicksites were a small group of Quakers taught by Elias Hicks, who had preached in Danby around 1830. They maintained their old church for occasional monthly and quarterly meetings, but it was primarily used for funeral purposes, there being an old Quaker burial ground connected with it. When the building was over sixty years old, it had been sold to David Staples, who demolished it amidst cries of *Sacrilege!* from those in the community who had friends and family buried in the connecting cemetery, and those who wished the decrepit structure retained, if only for future funeral purposes. It was the tearing down of that old church that abruptly shattered the good will and unity that had existed among the different factions in the community.

"Desecration!" the traditionalists screamed.

The ensuing hue and cry completely disregarded the condition the building had been in, most conveniently forgetting that the first Quaker church had been sold in 1805 and had since been used for a barn without creating any havoc whatsoever. And who knows, whoever knows about these things? Perhaps the matter would have blown over, had it not been fanned a mere week later by Dr. Holden's liberal retort to the community at large which had gathered to pay their last respects to the newly-late Mr. Wolcott, husband of Mrs. Wolcott, the prominent Spiritualist. Pierce noted in his diary:

> December 5th, 1867 – Mr. Wolcott's funeral. Dr. Holden spoke ably as usual and very demolishing to the Old Theology. . . .The Funeral sermon stirred the Orthodox to the bottom."

Sadly, Pierce considered the entry proof in itself of how stirring Dr. Holden was. His own consciousness was roused, all right. "Old Theology. Orthodox." Those were the first of many instances of that ilk to be found in his diaries. Indeed, Dr. Holden's speaking ably fired the community up to full boil.

Had Mr. Wolcott departed this life a month before or after the fact, all that followed might have been averted. As it was, his funeral was the first barrage of happenings that thrust the formerly unobtrusive Spiritualist contingent most prominently before the public at large.

Above it all, Pierce's soul radiated pleasure as he recalled those thrilling days for the believers in the new, spiritual philosophy! Finally, they were out in the open, proudly taking their rightful, prominent place in society. And their spirit friends rejoiced with them. The following evening, not surprisingly, within so hospitable an environment, they celebrated by calling on their own accord at a meeting of the Sewing Society which occasionally met at Pierce's house.

December 11th, 1867 – The sewing circle had an attendance larger than usual, a good time and a good supper and after the close, we had some spirit manifestations, very good ones.

Oh, the look on those women's faces! Pierce's spirit trembled with remembered hilarity.

Talk about salt in open wounds! Spiritualism had become as obvious a part of the town's existence as a runaway cart or a man's being knocked down for insolence.

Closing his eyes, with a shimmer, Pierce thrust himself back to that earlier day, recalling, recalling...

Pierce Remembers the Competition on the Dance Floor

That's when the competitions started, the dancing competitions between C.M. Bruce and his traditional following and George Baker and our liberal crowd. Oh, that was lots of fun, Pierce remembered.

Bruce's actions were behind all of it, of course.

Hardly any time at all after he'd gotten his new store up and operating, C.M. Bruce acted against my good friend George Baker as he had acted against me, Pierce recalled. He entered into competition with George Baker for the Borough's extensive dancing business. (None of this took place on Saturday nights of course, as that would have infringed on the Sabbath.)

George Baker, the then-proprietor of the hotel, had commenced holding dances in December of '67, one a week before Christmas, one on Christmas day itself. He had a whole series planned, including a New Year's Ball. Then we learned that C.M. Bruce was holding a dance in his new hall on December 31st as well.

"He's enterprising once more, entirely too freely!" Pierce observed at circles and around. And acting to benefit one of our own, we mobilized our forces for the forthcoming engagement. What better way to start a new year than with a good hot contest!

Thrust, parry.

"Come on," I coaxed the ladies as I rang up their holiday sales, "Come on! We're going to have a ball at Bakers!"

"He's homing in again," I agitated to the men gathered around the wood stove in the store, on evenings. "Here, have some more cheese, take another pickle—and be sure to show up at the hotel on the 31st!"

I can't remember that I've ever had a happier New Year.

January 1st, 1868 – Ball at George Baker's in the evening. Well Attended. Musick grand. One at Bruce's a fizzle and broke up early.

So, on the 5th, after a Spiritualist circle, Austin, having spoken under influence, was a little weary. I, being his close associate in all matters, picked up the conversation and after we'd finished rehashing a lawsuit up at the Corners between Frank Bromley and his father-in-law, the talk turned to speculation about Bruce's up-coming dance and what, if anything, we were going to do about the one Baker was holding two days later.

"We mustn't let Bruce beat Baker! The gall of him! I think we should teach him a lesson..."

Recalling his own active part in all that transpired, Pierce was filled with a certain wonderment, for he had always been a peaceable man. It hardly made sense that a man whose entire orientation was geared to thoughtful rationality and whose political leanings were constantly grounded in the Reformists who unanimously advocated peace, would do anything in the world to promote a war. Pierce was just having a little fun, is all, getting his uppers and helping out George Baker, his friend. And evening-up with C.M. Bruce, of course. A troublemaker? Pierce? Never!

January 8th, 1868 — There was a dance at C.M.Bruce's Hall this evening. Small company.

January 10th, 1868 — George Baker had a dance, a good one, about 40 couples besides spectators.

With great glee, Pierce remembered, we energetically mustered our troops to parade once more before the bandstand. Which show of strength, carefully gauged by the opposition, added considerably to their bile, for try as they might, they simply couldn't match us. As the competition continued back and forth, back and forth, between Us and Them, with invariably good turnouts at Baker's and small affairs at Bruce's, their frustration and fury as our victories mounted, energized us all the more.

Thrust!

January 16th, 1868 — Another festival at George Baker's to get an organ for the church a good one. Bruce and company opposed it enough to make it a success. The Festival cleared about $180.

Oh, sweet joy of galling!

Danby's Liturgical War

From the perspective of years, William Pierce realized this incident could, retrospectively, be considered the first real skirmish of Danby's Liturgical War, although no one realized it at the time, least of all Pierce himself.

Remembering it all, Pierce looked down at Silas, looking so composed, so serene in his coffin. So unlike himself.

Of course, Silas had been included in the "company." He was thick with C.M. Bruce and conservative to his very marrow. Besides, he was a feisty man who loved competitions and was always prepared to leap into the hottest issues. Still and all, the organ situation must have wrenched him something fierce, Pierce reflected, especially seeing as how, in later years, Silas contributed his own fine hand-pump Estey organ to the church. Indeed, no one liked good music more than Silas Griffith, who, on occasion, fostered it, paying for organ lessons for Will Risdon and singing lessons for Minnie Bushee, two of the community's most outstanding talents.

As time would demonstrate, Silas Griffith undoubtedly wished his crowd were on the other side of the issue, because he detested poor music and the organ serving the church at that time was very poor. But side with his own, he did, always, although the dance competitions were all but over.

"I don't know," one of the farmers said at our next Spiritualist circle, "I don't know but that maybe we ought to stop this whole business. It appears to me," he commented, "that this is getting out of hand. They're getting mighty angry at all of us, flaunting our numbers. I've got nothing against them," he said, directing his remark to George Baker and myself. "Bruce is your problem. My problem is one you two gentlemen don't have: having to get up at five in the morning to milk cows! I'm all for helping friends out, but I'm getting very tired of all these mid-week dances. Fun's fun, but enough is enough."

"He's not had enough yet," Baker protested, blowing hard.

After a little gassing, George Baker agreed to curtail his dances in February and the others agreed to participate through the end of January. On the 22nd, Bruce had another dance, another small one, followed short-on by Baker's glorious double finale—a good large dance on the 24th and a quite large dancing school on the 27th. Bruce's small affair on the 29th followed by Baker's large dancing school on the 7th of February put an end to them.

What were they, anyway, those competitions? The philosophical old soul considered this retrospectively as he floated above the rapidly filling church. They were fun, of course, in their way, but they were divisive manifestations of the Age of Enlightenment and beneath the patter of all those gay, dancing feet was the staccato drum beat of a nation at the end of war.

On the surface, at least, the hostilities ceased.

Seances and Dances

With a sigh, Pierce went back to his diaries. He read that there was an exhibition at Bruce's Hall on the 18th, a slim affair. Bruce and Cook were very sore over the failure of their show, over which there was a little tittering, but that was the end of it.

On the 20th, there was an Old Folks Concert at George Baker's, a rich thing, attendance large.

Pierce remembered that in January, the Rev. Z.C. Picket commenced his second year of service as the Borough's only regular attendant preacher, his Donation having come off a success, at which the sum of $236 was raised. By then, 1868, the Baptist Society had died out and the Quaker church was failing. Of our township's former, predominating denominations, the Methodists had survived best. Their donation festivals had been held every year since 1830 to supplement their minister's yearly salary of about $500. These had become popular events that promoted community good will and effected understanding between the people and the ever-changing progression of pastors who supplied them, almost without exception, for only one year before moving on. (Two years of service by the same preacher was usual.) But many of us, myself included, Pierce remembered, liked Picket. He recalled that he took to attending more and more of Reverend Picket's Methodist meetings.

It was a quiet, peaceful time, Pierce remembered.

...A large ball at Baker's in March, musick fine, I came home

about 2:00 o'clock. ...William Bond's old store burned. ...Circles in the evening at Austin's with our Spirit Friends. The usual.

...Trade was slow, even more so for Bruce. ... I watched his new goods arrive at his store ...I heard about his help problems - his clerk was drunk, complained of, fined and was discharged.

Pierce, floating high, swallowed a guffaw.

May found my family all sick and under doctor's care, he remembered. Katie recovered slowly but little Georgia grew gradually worse. I thought it doubtful that she would recover but her disease finally reached its crisis and she survived for another year.

And so things continued, humdrum and easy, too easy, too peaceful, the lull before the storm..

William Pierce kept thumbing through his 1868 booklet.

August 18th, 1868 – (Tues)...Mrs Calvin Bruce found dead, as it was supposed Saturday morning but is not buried yet.

August 19th, 1868 – Mrs Bruce's friends met to bury her last Monday but came to the conclusion that she probably was not dead.

And then, in early September, the Spiritual Convention took place in the hotel, with N.B. Slocum, President and Peleg Griffith, as Secretary. Peleg was Silas's second cousin and there was a touch of mysticism running through that branch of the family, Pierce remembered.

In any case, none could deny the numbers that attended the four-day Spiritual convention held that September, for it was a large gathering. The meetings, ably addressed by Mrs. Wiley, Fanny Davis Smith, and Dr. Holden, were jammed with more people than the house could hold. All attendees agreed it was the best ever held in the state.

Increasingly, Pierce recalled with pleasure, believers in the new philosophy came to head up various community doings which drew like-minded participants. Right on the heels of the convention, Mr. Eddy of that spiritually gifted family (once, at the Chittenden Eddys, Pierce had seen 12 or 15 externalized spirits, several of them several times) well, Mr. Eddy, he started up a singing school in October. And shortly after that, Fanny Davis Smith gave a number of able lectures to good audiences.

It became more indisputable than ever that the liberals had become the predominating faction in the formerly exceedingly conservative community. And it rankled. And these events combined were the factors that sparked, ignited, and rekindled the smoldering bed of embers on which the Union Meeting House rested.

The Choir Wars

Two days after General Grant was elected President by a large majority, a great furor about the singing schools started off the fall campaign and the chain of events out of which was born the Congregational Church of Danby and S.L. Griffith's part in its birth and being. Actually, Pierce sometimes wondered if there even would have been a Congregational Church in Danby if We hadn't been so blatant and They so reactionary to Us.

November 22th, 1868 – The War in the Choir came to a crisis. The belligerent party staid home in disgust because they could not rule the church.

Did the 'belligerent party' include Silas Griffith? What do you think?

The acrimony grew.

November 26th, 1868_ – A dance at the Hotel and a great row because the young folks preferred to dance at the Hotel instead of Bruce's Hall. Which row ended in a few bloody noses and considerable excitement.

Two weeks later there was another skirmish.

December 13th, 1868 — A tremendous row at the church concerning the project of abolishing the choir and have.

Pierce squinted, trying to decipher his ancient scrawl.

...of abolishing the choir and have Congregational singing.

Although there wasn't a Congregational Church in town at the time, it was coming... And S.L. Griffith was involved up to his neck in all of its growing pains.

Of course, Silas was relatively idle at that point, having completed the sale of his mill about two weeks earlier, on December 11th to be exact. He had free time, probably too much of it, and, as the old saying goes, "Idle hours are the Devil's powers."

"Oh, what a scrapper you were, Silas," Pierce beamed down and then returned to the affairs of yesteryear.

Being one who took matters concerning his Church and Meeting House business very seriously indeed, Silas had already started accumulating slips, as had I, the Spiritualist recalled. Slips, pews, shares—same thing, really—entitled one to some say in what was transpiring. But "say," wasn't enough for S.L. Griffith, always one to prefer action to words.

In any case, the row at the church on the 13th of December created great excitement and was still running high a week later, terminating in the crowning incident of the Rows of '68, when...abruptly, the ancient soul stopped strumming his diaries and coughed out a laugh, shook his head, and, containing his amusement with effort, recalled a foiled act of banditry that had occurred at the Union Meeting House on the 29th of December.

SILAS LAPHAM GRIFFITH

December 29th, 1868 — Still warmer this morning & cloudy. It snowed a little in the forenoon and turned to rain toward night but stopt before dark. S.L Griffith tried to get the organ out of the church but Austin would not let him.—

For a moment, the old soul closed his eyes and tried to imagine the unimaginable. Of course, A.S. Baker had told Pierce, told the world, how he arrived, just in the nick of time, as S.L. and his troop—well, a couple of good men, anyway—were endeavoring to maneuver the organ through the door. Silas was determined to have his way, determined to have it out and he had more sense than to try to remove it by himself, after all. So he and his like-minded crew were wrestling it out when Austin came upon them.

Now, Austin wasn't a very large man, but aside from his personal views on the matter, he was an officer of the Society. He had a responsibility, and his determination lent him strength. He hopped right on the keyboard, and, clutching the pipes, supported himself as he thrust his weight against their efforts, caterwauling away until, finally, the group desisted and left.

What possessed Silas to do such a thing? Who knows? Possibly he felt his deed might kill two birds with the same stone, for the organ was poor in quality and then, obviously, without an organ, it would make singing very difficult.

It was an outrageous act by a notorious hot head, known for his high-handed ways. That is what many objected to, but, although in the minority, the orthodox were the majority shareholders in the church, which they largely ruled.

January 5th, 1869 — The church association had their annual meeting and elected new trustees. All on the Rebel side voted by stock and so were whipt.

C.M. Bruce was a good part of that, too. As Jesse Lapham's executor, he controlled Lapham's shares. Consequently, S.L. Griffith, the organ bandit, was elected Vice President, and C.M. Bruce, Secretary.

There was great anticipation among the citizens as they awaited the major upcoming event, the Rev. Z.C. Picket's history-making third donation. The speculation... How much would it bring in, without their support? Although lacking the Aristocracy, the preacher had many sympathizers among the people and they, along with those others who deplored the state of the community's affairs, registered their feelings by casting their support to our Rev. Picket, by putting their money on their man.

January 7th, 1869 – Mr. Picket's Donation came off this evening, a great success. $225 cash and $350 subscribed towards his preaching here another year.

January 8th, 1869 – Griffith and company very glum over the Donation and its results.

What to do? They put their heads together and got themselves another preacher. And before long, we were chortling again.

January 18th, 1869 – Considerable sport over Mr. Walker's sermon. His employers got hoisted with their own petard...for he preached right at them.

Finally, the community at large was reacting to the troublemakers and Bruce was feeling it. Not even his post office could drag them into his store.

February 6th, 1869 – To all appearance, Bruce's and Griffith's trade has fell off a great deal since they started this row in the church.

SILAS LAPHAM GRIFFITH

How could Griffith's trade have fallen off? There was a deal that went with that $2000 sale to his brothers, no question. Pierce certainly knew the value of stores. His took fire (or fire was set) around midnight in March of 1872 and it and the adjoining building both burned, along with nearly all the contents of his safe. They saved but little. By compromise, his insurance company agreed to give him $7,000, after which he insured his store, fixtures and goods for $9,500, their true worth.

In any case, Griffith's trade fell off, along with Bruce's. Why, the entire Borough was up in arms over their effrontery. Their aristocratic airs. Their share-waving. How people felt was made abundantly clear on the evening of February 18th when there was a dance at the hotel the same night Bruce had a concert.

On the evening of Thursday, the 18th — The festival at the hotel came off, 3 or 400 people present and a very fine time They danced until 4 o'clock in the morning. That was 300-400 because we knocked the concert to pieces with our festival at the hotel… The concert folks very mad because we flopt them.

As Swift once said, "War! that mad game the world so loves to play." Their parry came on the 28th, at the Congo [Congregational] meeting with the Choir vs. Whipple matter, when, forbidden to join the choir, Mrs. Whipple, that poor, indomitable woman stood her step, and faced the entire congregation off that Sunday.

February 28th, 1869 — A row in the Congo meeting. Some of the Aristocracy would not let Mrs. Whipple sing in the choir and she sang on the steps of the orchestra.

The excitement through the community! The acrimony! The entire village was up in arms. The exhilaration was dreadful, as we ripped our community apart. *Yes, it was dreadful*, Pierce recalled, shaking his head, his fingers trembling a tattoo on the diary in his hand.

The ill will mushroomed and spread like a disease, infecting every area of community life, eventually reaching Marble Lodge No. 76, where Freemasonry is based on the practice of brotherly love.

March 5th, 1869 – A Temperance Lecture at the church by Mr. Atwood for the Good Templars. A Terrible Row about the singing so they had no singing at all.
March 7th, 1869 – A great row at the Congo Meeting to keep Mrs. Whipple out of the choir.

The excitement over the church row reached fever pitch, culminating with the choir business the following Sunday, Pierce recalled, as his fingers relayed the message of his jotting, when *Mrs. Whipple went to the Congo meeting and got in the orchestra and the choir refused to come in and sung in front of the pulpit.*

March 15th, 1869 – that was the day our little Georgia died, Pierce remembered sadly. *Our little girl had fallen ill, very ill, some days previous. Her illness dragged on for three days when she was taken worse and died about nine o'clock in the evening, without a struggle. The rheumatism struck to her heart. She was six years and eight months old.*

The old spirit sniffed and shook his head and dabbed at his eyes.

So we lost her, Pierce remembered, as the Colvins and the Otises and the Jessemiah Nichols and the Scotts and the Hills and the Silas Griffiths and so many other parents had lost their children. But Georgia, little Georgia did come back once. One Sunday night in July 1869, our little girl communicated by rappings at T. Maynard's.... Pierce's spirit quivered for a moment, his gaunt face etched with remembered grief. He didn't need his diaries to recall that he and Katie had Mr. Picket officiate at her funeral. Although they could've gotten Dr. Holden or Mr. Bent or any of the others, they were pleased with their choice. The funeral came off on the afternoon of March 17th, 1869. It was largely attended. The church was full. *Mr. Picket preached the best I ever heard him,* Pierce recalled. Professor Rogers played the organ, and the choir sang well.

We were all weary of the Congo rows by that time, the Congregationalist rows, myself weariest of all, Pierce remembered, but though things abated some, the acrimony continued its destructive course, raising its head in the Good Templer's Lodge in May, a terrible time, a strike for power between the two factions.

Things were bad enough for H.G. Lapham to come to town in June and try and quiet the row here. Henry was a commission merchant and dealer in hides and leather at the time - Buckley & Lapham was his firm, on Buckley Street in New York City. A much-respected man, H.G. Lapham, a friend and confidante of mine as well as of Silas's and Bruce's, a worthy mediator. It's possible his efforts helped some, but there were still incidents. H.G. Lapham had barely been gone a week when there was a town caucus to appoint delegates to the County Convention. The Congos were defeated, did not get a delegate. And then, in July, three days after our Little Georgia communicated with us, the Good Templers met at my hall and part of them seceded and went to Bruce's Hall and those that were left organized and went on with business. We had a great deal of fun over that.

Now, throughout all these hostilities, Mr. Picket, a man of great forbearance, had kept his peace, a level-headed course that earned him my deepest respect, for the coming of the Congregational Church was not easy for the good Reverend. Finally, in August 1869, Mr. Picket broke his silence with his memorable Hail Columbia sermon, his ultimate sermon, his courageous, determined stand against his Orthodox enemies.

ANN K. ROTHMAN

August 8th, 1869 — ...he preached the best sermon I ever heard him preach. He gave his Enemies Hail Columbia. Congo meeting small as usual

Regrettably, C.M. Bruce was not in church that Sunday. He was ill at the time, suffering from dropsy on the heart with congestion of the lungs, which affliction he had had since June. After two months of lingering, he died on August 26 about two o'clock in the morning, age 54 years. I attended his funeral, a Quaker funeral, very large, more than the house could hold. The preaching was *Intolerably Poor*; not worthy to be called preaching.

Not only did C.M. Bruce's departure from his physical body put an end to the upheaval in the Borough for awhile, Pierce recalled, but my business was helped substantially by his demise.

From April past, I had made every effort to wrest the post office from Bruce's store. A.S. Baker had gone to Rutland on that subject and my former clerk, James Fish, now our elected Representative, had agitated on my behalf but nothing had been decided. Three days after Bruce's funeral found the post office removed to my store and Bruce's store shut up, his goods having been purchased by me from the executors of his estate.

Those Congos..., those Congos..., Pierce thought, becoming rather frantic as he flipped his diary pages. *I'm certain they organized their Church around now, why haven't I anything in here on that?* Somewhere overhead, the frustrated soul blinked, screwed up his eyes, trembled, prayed, held out his hand, and miraculously scanned the pages of a grey booklet from the future entitled, *One Hundred Years, The Congregational Church, Danby, Vermont.*

With cocked eyebrow, he read, *"The only record remaining between 1838 and 1869 is the subscription list for the securing of a bell...."* Oh! Those Congos! *Tut, tut, tut!* For he knew full well that Union House Records existed

SILAS LAPHAM GRIFFITH

between 1838 and 1869 which included the inflammatory decision of '48 to make the Meeting House available for exhibitions and such, as well as a legal action brought against the Society by the (late) firm of Lapham, Vail & Co. of Wallingford.

And, further on, *"On November 4th, 1869, The Danby East Village Union Meeting House was reorganized as The First Congregational Church of Danby."*

"*No, No, NO!* the old Spiritualist countered between gales of laughter. *Trust those Congos to hide the truth under the rug of history!*" he gasped with glee.

On November 4th, 1869, the First Congregational Church of Danby was organized, he corrected. The new body, numbering twelve persons, included Silas's mother, Sophia Griffith, transferred from the Methodists. The building itself wasn't sold or the Society terminated until the 1880s, long after the founding of the Congregational Church.

"*I'm glad I'm not alive to catch the flak over that discrepancy,*" Pierce thought.

And on the 24th of December, the Congregationalists had a Christmas Tree at the Church, (a great splurge) with Silas undoubtedly at the bottom of it, having accumulated thirteen of the forty-eight slips by 1871. As majority slip-holder, he had lots of say, and Pierce remembered how thoroughly S.L. Griffith used—and abused—that power. Finally, weary from reliving those tumultuous days of yesteryear, William Pierce faded out of the church with a wave to Silas.

"*I'll see you in Scottsville,*" he called out.

And old Will was gone from the confines of the Congregational Church and its universally fidgeting, desperately uncomfortable occupants, each and every one of them trying to escape the heat and humidity and the increasing stench, for the sheeting rain against the windows forbade their being open more than the barest crack. What to do before the services started?

ANN K. ROTHMAN

Remembering Silas

Nothing to do but think, remember. For the widow Griffith, it was about her marriage to Silas.

The last thing in the world K.T. Tiel had wanted was to be the second wife of a man eighteen years her senior, for whom she had no attraction whatsoever, and to be uprooted from a happy life in Philadelphia, where she had family and friends, to live as a rich woman in a small, rural Vermont town. What good would all the money in the world do her in Danby, Vermont?

But her dear cousin Charlie had pushed for it, as had his wife. And K.T.'s parents, being all for the union, had forced the issue. So, she and Silas were married on August 1st, 1891. Now, here she was, on August 4th, 1903, having survived twelve years of him, plus that dreadful, month-long honeymoon at Yellowstone Park, Seattle, San Francisco, Salt Lake City, and Montreal in addition to a few other stops she couldn't even remember.

How strange. On my wedding day, I felt as if I was attending my own funeral, and now, at his funeral, I'm finally looking forward to the future, she thought.

For Minnie Bushee, S.L.'s long-time employee, her thoughts were of her equally long affair with Silas, the love of her life, whom she remembered through her tears. To others, Griffith wasn't a particularly attractive man. He was slight, and his always calculating expression made some feel he had a rather "weaselish" look to him. But that wasn't at all the way Minnie saw him. In her mind's eye, her glance swept across his trimly bearded, mustached, fine-featured face, the picture of contentment as he puffed away on his cigar. Behind his inconspicuous spectacles were the most incredible eyes she'd ever seen, brown, unusually dark, flecked with black, their color changing with his mood and his thoughts, sometimes so dark as to seem impenetrable black voids. But usually, they were alive with humor and zest, intelligence and thought, all kinds of thought. She considered his mouth and the operation of its neighboring muscles: straight, down, tight, quirky grin and all the nuances of variation that joined his eyes to force command upon his face. He didn't need pretension. He was what he was. A man of amazing vitality and energy who bore the sexuality of power.

What a time we had, my dear! Minnie thought, remembering how she was his comfort, his only comfort, through the deaths of his children. How he had broken her heart, when he wouldn't marry her after his divorce.

How we hurt each other! she also remembered. And Minnie thought of all the talk about S.L., the philanderer. And who could blame him, really, for he was a man and had needs that weren't being satisfied at home. And she thought about all the stories about the Italian women, how their men would lock their women in when they saw Silas riding into the Job, or how Silas would send the men out to work while he took their woman, stories she mostly scoffed at, stories that some attributed to Eddie Staples. Of course, after Louie and then, after his divorce...

But he would never force himself on a woman, Minnie knew. And knowing him as an always discriminating man of fastidious personal cleanliness, she knew any woman he consorted with had to be immaculately clean and bathed and sweet smelling. She doubted too many of those women fit that description, considering the nature of the work so many of them performed. As she considered the talk that he had syphilis, she just shook her head.

Married or not, we loved each other, through better and worse, 'til death did us part. Minnie thought.

Jennie's husband Bill Riddle's thoughts concerned themselves with his father-in-law's surprising, unexpected death. He remembered when he had been out to the west coast in May, looking at some timber land S.L. owned in the state of Washington and then visiting Silas at The Palms, his newly purchased fruit farm. K.T. had been even more quiet than usual and ate sparingly, but Silas had been in excellent spirits, serving and helping Bill demolish, with great appetite and enjoyment, a huge dinner fit only for a man in excellent general health. As Riddle remembered it, the meal consisted of roast beef, new potatoes, asparagus, green peas, cauliflower, turnips, strawberry shortcake, strawberries and cream, angel food, bananas, oranges, olives, apples, guavas, tangerines, kumquats, raisins, dates, English walnuts, tea, coffee, Bradley carbonated water, and port and Riesling wines to wash down this astonishing quantity! Nor could he forget the equally memorable table decorations, consisting of a cactus centerpiece of purple-pink, shading toward the center to lavender; orange and lemon blossoms, a calla lily with a five foot stem and blossom eight inches long and five inches wide, wild larkspur and lantana. Between the blatant celebratory floral display and the amount of food consumed it was inconceivable to Riddle that his father-in-law, whom he had left in the best of spirits and lacking even a stomachache, should have so failed and died a scant two months later.

What killed him, exactly?

A Lumbering Empire

As for Harry Ralph, Harry was trying to remember a date... *When was that? When was that anyway, when those fellas from Boston bottomed-up on the Button property and Silas got it back and we started lumbering in earnest?...It was about a year before he started in charcoaling, and that was in 1872. 1871, that's when it was, that's when I got my job back.*

1871, Harry remembered, was the year his boss started building his empire, block by block, until it grew to what it became. When Fate forced him back into the tall, tall timber, by obliging him to take the Button property back, Griffith undertook it as a personal challenge to make it a success where others had failed, as a proving ground for his capabilities. The first thing he did was to move his operation from Main Street east, to Mt. Tabor, near the Depot. Harry could barely remember Headquarters back then. There was a modest office building, a lumber yard, a small barn, maybe, but it grew in no time and changed completely over the next ten years or so, as did the Works on the Mountain. By the 1880s, Button's approximately 900-acre tract with the sawmill had grown to 13,000 acres.

Like the Green Mountain it was part of, the Button acreage consisted of a dense growth of hemlock, spruce, beech, pine, poplar, birch, and other evergreen and deciduous trees, the evergreens predominating, giving title to both the range and the mountain.

Over the years, the area around the old sawmill was increasingly cleared to an area of about fifteen acres, enclosed by wilderness. As time went on, houses and boarding houses and all manner of various buildings required for the Works went up until there were forty or fifty different structures up there that combined to make a village. It was way up high, near the peak of the Green Mountain, a community with the postal address, Griffith, Vermont. where Harry Ralph and his wife were living. In fact, Harry had left there early that morning, to come down to his boss's funeral. The winters were hard up there, cold and windy and the snow frequently eight to twelve feet deep on the mountain, but aside from that, it wasn't a bad place to live in. There was music and laughter. The inhabitants had nearly all the facilities they would have had in like-sized villages in the valley.

The housing for all the employees was provided free at a time when you could rent a five-room cottage in Mt. Tabor with half an acre of ground and a nice barn for $1 a month.

The single men were housed in two large, spacious boarding houses that were situated opposite the kilns. The boarding houses were run by people specifically employed by Griffith for that purpose, who saw to it that the workers were served plain but very attractive food. Since everything was done by day labor, Griffith believed it economical to feed his men well, that a well-fed man will do more work than one who is not satisfied with the quantity or quality of what he's eating. In later years, he employed a man who did nothing but buy cattle and swine and butcher them. And he had another man who distributed the meat among the boarding houses at his various villages. At that point in time, those nine mill villages were cutting an annual output of 25 million feet of lumber (24 million of spruce, 1 million of hardwood) plus about 1,000 cords of wood cut yearly for charcoal.

The married employees, about thirty couples or so, lived in cottages with gardens. One of these was occupied by Harry, who took pride in his cow horn potatoes: very mealy, very good, grown in all kinds of sawdust and horse manure, with no phosphate. Some of his neighbors played tennis. They'd set up a net and played with small Wright & Ditson racquets.

Griffith workers in front of the duplex on Depot Street extension

Near the cottages there was a school for the kids and a big general store, the S.L. Griffith Company Store that housed the post office and an office with an adjoining residence for the chief clerk or manager. In the village, Harry usually passed a number of women, most with bags in hand, traveling to and from the store or standing outside, visiting together. Griffith made a point of saying that the supplies were furnished as close to cost as possible and were stocked with almost all the household necessities and a good many of the luxuries, too, which nobody disputed. Although Griffith insisted his employees could buy their goods where they wished, a number of his employees insisted they were made to trade at the Griffith store. Ralph had heard a few stories, such as when the wife of one of his employees purchased a bonnet in Rutland and Griffith also stocked bonnets, she was charged for the item as if she had bought it from him ("It was there; you could've had it.").

The old Button Mill was long gone, replaced by a steam mill built in 1880 that was forty by eighty feet in size, and had a cutting capacity of 20,000 feet of lumber a day or 2-3 million feet a year. Birch was the hardwood. Spruce was the softwood, used for the manufacture of shingles, clapboard, and lathe. The largest logs of both were sawed into lumber, the smaller ones were burned for coal. But birch was required for the hard coal that was used for the manufacture of barbed wire. Of the twenty sawmills the boss was operating in Vermont at that time, this steam mill was his favorite. Oh, Griffith was proud of that sawmill, Harry recalled whenever he passed it.

Besides the mill, there was a big lumber yard up there and four of the thirty or so charcoal kilns situated on the mountain. And there were stables and sheds for the equipment and horse barns and ox barns and a harness and blacksmith shop with four forges that served the needs of the animals. Everything in the settlement was neat, orderly, and extremely well-maintained, for Griffith was real fussy about that.

Oh, but it was mighty quiet that day of the funeral, with the Works stopped and the pounding rain that kept just about everyone indoors. The unaccustomed deadness gave Harry the willies, for he was used to animals and people and wagons and noise and something going on.

Usually, Ralph picked his way through shifting troops of chattering, shrieking little black-haired, black-eyed ragamuffins, congregated around the cottages and running riot around the big barn and stables and shops and sheds near it. Most of the kids up there were Italian, the children of the immigrants, some of whom Griffith fetched himself from the New York docks. From the boat to his wagon to Mt. Tabor it was a trip that for many comprised their only sight-seeing tour of their new country.

Of the one hundred choppers Griffith employed year-round, some were Canadian, a few were French or Irish, and there were even a couple of Native Americans, but most of them were Italians. They had their own way of doing things and the woods bosses over them had to be prepared for anything.

For one thing, there was the Friday Taboo to be reckoned with. One of the woods bosses' jobs was to travel the woods with the choppers and tell them what section to move into. This one time, the men had just finished up one area on a Thursday and had to start another the next morning and oh, they were upset about it.

"We can't start a new job today, Boss" they said on Friday morning. "It'd be a lot of trouble and no finishing."

"That's all right, boys," the boss assured them, stopping a strike before it started. "Nothing to worry about. I realized that, so I sent two men up there and they started the job yesterday, so it'll be all right."

But the bosses' primary job was tallying up the cut and sending the tally down to the Head Office in the valley. The choppers got 75 cents for each cord they cut, and Griffith's cords weren't standard. A standard cord-was 8' x 4' x 4' whereas a Griffith cord-was 46" high, which, of course, they knew when they took the job. On the 30th of each month, they went down to the Head Office to collect their pay and they got mighty upset if they felt they'd been short-changed. Those immigrants were hot-tempered men. Excitable. And since most of them didn't speak much English, if any, they tended to negotiate their differences with their fists. Their bosses took the brunt of that.

"I counted this cord already."

"You didn't, either!"

And things warmed up. The extent some of those choppers went to cheat on their cut was mind-boggling. One of them actually piled his wood over a tree stump! And they played all manner of games to get their cords counted twice. To outsmart them, one of the woods bosses, Ellis Millard, came up with the idea of taking one of the bigger sticks off the top of a cut cord and laying it crosswise, which meant that pile had been measured. But he soon found out he couldn't do that with the Italians because the next time he came around, there wouldn't be any stick crosswise there at all and the choppers would insist that he measure the pile again. So after that, Ellis got to carrying around a paint pail and he would paint the ends of a few sticks on each pile. But the Italians soon got onto that, and as soon as Ellis left, they'd take a hammer and another stick and drive those painted ones out a bit and saw the painted end off and bury it. Of course, Ellis realized what was going on and finally he confronted one of the big, northern Italians who was standing there with two of his boys. "I measured this pile, "Ellis said. They had quite an argument over it, when finally, in a fit of rage, the chopper grabbed his axe and made a rush at Ellis. Now, Ellis was kind of a stocky guy who did everything slow and deliberate and acted as if he had all the time in the world, but he could move if he had to, and moving kept him alive that day. Ellis grabbed a 4' x 6" stick off the top of the pile and subdued the man right there, quick and easy. "You killa-ma-fa, you son-o-ma-bitch, you killa-ma-fa!" screamed the man's sons, the big fellas in their late teens that had been working with their father. "You killa-ma-fa!" they yelled, coming towards Ellis all the while.

"You come a little closer, you bastards, and I'll kill you, too," Ellis replied with some force. The boys backed off and Ellis went about his business. Turned out he hadn't killed the father at all, he'd just stunned him a little and smartened him up some.

Those jobs, there was quite a lot that went with them. Lumbering was a rough operation from start to finish, Harry remembered. And the men who worked the woods earned every cent of the pay they got.

In October the choppers were sent into the timber where they remained until April 1st, spending their nights either at the boardinghouse or in shanties in the woods. Griffith insisted the choppers looked forward to the winter season, despite the cold and snow. "They lead a life of excitement and, to them, one of pleasure," Ralph heard the boss explaining to tourists one day. "They go to work as early as it is light enough for them to see," Griffith went on, "and chop until dark. Then, they repair to their shanties and spend their evenings

Italian worker's home

and many days together, too, for that matter, when it is too stormy to work-in singing dancing, card playing, and thrumming musical instruments of some kind."

Sometimes the men, sometimes a whole family of Italians would build themselves a little shanty on the mountain and start cutting the area over. Some of these improvised houses were of logs, sometimes covered with boards, many constructed with runners that were moved with the progress of the chopping. Those that housed single men had a cook. Supplies were drawn to them on sleds. Those who wished to live in that manner, did. The other Italians lived in the settlement proper. but the fact that virtually none of them spoke English made things difficult.

As he traveled through the surprisingly harmonious community, Ralph was constantly amazed at how few incidents there had been, considering that the village was a world unto itself, where Vermonters, Protestants like himself, lived tooth and jowl with "Papist foreigners," mostly hot-tempered Italians.

As he maneuvered the wet road and the mud heading down the mountain to town, Harry figured that it was no wonder that differences were negotiated by force rather than by mouth, since, aside from so many not understanding or speaking English, there was no law up there—no constables or anything. Everything considered, it was a very peaceful community indeed. But occasionally, once in a long while, some particularly grisly incident would allegedly occur, like the time when a Native American settled up with an Italian laborer who had done him some wrong. Supposedly, the Native American got the man drunk, put him in one of coal kilns, and covered him over with a cord of wood. By the time they started looking for the Italian in earnest, the pile had been fired.

But back in the church, no matter how much he wool-gathered, Harry Ralph couldn't escape the reality of this day.

Normally, even in the rain, the cadence of uproar assaulted Harry as reached the bottom of the mountain and made his way through Headquarters, near the depot. The sound's fabric was textured with the sometimes mournful, sometimes protesting bawls of cattle descanted by the clanking of chains and the noise of the wagons they drew and the shouts of the men that drove them. But today, there had been that eerie quiet, with the Works shut down because of the funeral.

Making his way over to Danby, Harry had passed the impeccable gingerbread creation that housed Griffith's $6,000 Head Office. The large building, draped this day in mourning, was situated just across the track from the railroad station, and it was landscaped with beds and urns of plants and flowers, tended constantly during the season by Griffith's private gardener. The structure was a large-windowed, two-story clapboard concoction with shingled trim and a lacy iron gallery encircling its relatively flat roof, anchored by a frothy lightning rod at each corner. It was a romantic building that could easily have been mistaken for a grand residence were it not for its location in the midst of the Works and the sign OFFICE that was discretely mounted over the front door. Lighted with acetylene gas and heated with hot water, the office was equipped with a large fireproof vault and housed Griffith's private telephone line. (That line, said to be the first in Vermont, required sixty-five miles of wire and thirteen instruments that connected him directly to his various mills.) Inside, also, was Griffith's elegant private office, a room beautifully paneled with rare woods and furnished with the best of everything (including a fainting couch).

It was after Lottie died that Griffith first came to realize the therapy of occupation. Even on the worst of days, the bustle of the industry he created warmed him, increasingly so as the years went on and the complex that was his headquarters grew. Since he worked six days a week when he was in town, Griffith made his private office a home away from home and so it was, an inner sanctum to which only he and Minnie Bushee had the key.

Nearby was a complex of clapboard structures consisting of a stable and mills and shops and sheds for storage. There was a shop for making and repairing sleds and wagons and another for the making and repairing of harnesses. From twelve to fifteen men, skilled blacksmiths, wheelwrights, and harness makers, were employed in these two shops alone. And then there was a blacksmith shop, where there would always be a bunch of kids standing, feeling all sorry for themselves because the smithy had thrown them out.

Two of the clapboarded structures were mills. One of them converted unmarketable lumber. The unmarketable spruce was converted into shooks, packing cases for piano factories and knitting mills. The edges sawed from the boards went to make charcoal. The unmarketable hardwood went into making chair stock. The sawdust was utilized or sold for bedding horses and cattle and filling icehouses. Nothing was wasted. Everything interlocked. Insofar as possible, the needs of the operation were fulfilled within the operation.

Silas Griffith's office

Adjoining this mill, in a building the same size, was a large steam mill for grinding feed for the teams. The horses and oxen used in the business consumed about 20,000 bushels of corn and 10,000 bushels of oats and 600 tons of hay a year, about a third of which was cut from Griffith's lands, much from the Ten Kilns Meadows on the Mountain, said to have been the largest farm in the state!

By a siding near the depot, there was a large lumber yard where all the lumber and charcoal ended up for shipping. Off to the side were four charcoal kilns, around which there was always activity except during the cooling period. A little beyond the group of kilns was the freight shed equipped with a derrick and a loading platform that was built high enough so that the top of a freight car was about level with the platform. That made for convenient top loading when the freight car's hinged top covers were open. Griffith owned about fifty railroad cars, each with the capacity of about 1,150 to 1,300 bushels of coal. Even with delays caused by having to wait for the cars' return, Griffith shipped an average of 100,000 bushels of charcoal a month, quite a bit of it to New York City hotels. Even after natural gas came through as fuel, the hotels had to take the charcoal anyway, because they were locked in, bound by contract.

The Barn Raising

And then there was the big barn that housed twenty oxen and forty horses, a fraction of the eighty oxen and 213 horses in Griffith's total operation.

The barn, 69 feet wide and 100 feet long with an L and 16-foot posts, had been built by Barney Decker, a master joiner. Decker was the best there was. And he had built it the way he did all his barns: he built it on the ground, on each side of the foundation. He'd laid out his 8x8s and morticed and pinned them and put them together, a job that took months for the hand hewing and drilling involved. And when it was all ready and the rafters cut and on the ground, it was raised on the 22nd of July in 1882.

This was in the midst of Griffith's time of greatest joy, Libbie having borne him a son, in 1878, Harry, a small lad who carried with him Silas's dreams of dynasty.

Harry Ralph remembered the barn raising as if it were yesterday. The whole town turned out that glorious Sunday. People came with their kids and families and picnicked and the men had some cider or home brew. After they'd taken their liquid refreshment, they put their backs to it and first erected the sides and ends. Lifting them with plenty of manpower, they put them in place. And finally they fitted and tied the four corners together and drove in the wooden pins that held them. Next came the rafters and after they were up and the ridge-row on, one or two daredevils in the crowd who had quite a little cider in them, danced a jig from one end of the ridge-row to the other. And shortly thereafter, the barn was put into service.

Griffith big barn

Griffith's yard boss, Odolphus Nichols, was the overseer of the barn as well as being in charge of loading the lumber and charcoal on the cars and ensuring the orders were right. It was a responsible job that entailed a good deal of work, for there was a two-lane track and trains went through every hour or so.

When he was a young man, 'Dolph had gone out west for a spell and he had liked it, but he returned to Danby to marry the daughter of one of Griffith's masons, Jessie Johnson, who taught school at the Old Job. So 'Dolph started in with Griffith and worked his way up. After they were married, the couple moved into one of the houses Griffith kept for his employees.

In his capacity as overseer of the barn, Odolphus Nichols became Squealer Nichols, for he would hide in the hay mow and spy on the men, the teamsters, especially, to see how they cared for their horses when they brought them in after work. He checked to see if they unhitched them and cleaned them up, for Griffith was known to take excellent care of his horses. If a man was too tired to curry his team and water them and put them in their stalls, 'Dolph would report the guy to Eddie Staples, Griffith's Superintendent (and brother-in-law). There were an unfortunate number of these reports, since the guys were pooped at the end of the day and wanted nothing but to fall into bed.

The average workday was from dawn to dusk, twelve-hour days. But those of the men who lived on the mountain had only had a few hours' sleep, seeing as how they had to rouse themselves around 4:30 in the morning to get down on time, and wouldn't make it back up until 11:00, 12:00 o'clock at night. And then there were some other men who had to walk to the job from way far off in the township, miles and miles away and back in all kinds of weather.

Regardless, Odolphus spied on them, and the day came when the men caught Nichols peeking around the barn door. He had his head right in it and was snooping away when the guys on the other side slammed it on him, shut his head right into it. *And good enough for him,* thought Harry, as he had made his way over to the church, through the teeming rain. All that he had passed en route was only a fraction Griffith's empire, Harry thought. *What's going to become of it all now?* he mused. *What's going to become of me?*

Church Wars—Again

Of course, Harry and every other employee had felt the same way in 1872 when bankruptcy was all but a certain end to Griffith's career in business. Had Griffith gone bust, multitudes of his fellow townsmen would likely have felt it was Little Caesar's God-sent punishment for his shocking behavior that kicked off the year 1872.

On January 1st, 1872, the Union Meeting House Society held its annual meeting. After disposing of general business, the agenda arrived at Article 5: *To determine what Societies shall occupy said-Meeting House and the proportion of time that each may occupy same for ensuing year.*

The first three votes of the meeting were concerned with dividing up the use and occupancy of the church between the Methodist Episcopalians and the Congregationalists. Seeing as how the latter had contributed liberally towards keeping the church in repair, the Congregationalists were permitted to occupy the church from 1:00 P.M. until 4:30 P.M. every Sabbath and on Thursdays and Saturdays, both daytime and evening for religious purposes and on alternate Sabbath evenings. The Methodist Episcopalians could occupy the church only in the forenoon of each Sabbath, but it was agreed that they could also occupy it on Mondays, Wednesdays, and Fridays, both daytime and evening, and also on alternate Sabbath evenings, "always provided the Grantee of Jesse Lapham's heirs assent thereto." (i.e. A.R. Vail)

Then the meeting voted that the Congregational Church and Society be permitted to occupy the Meeting House of the Society one half the time for public worship and other religious purposes according to the usages of that denomination. The members of said Church and Society owning a majority of the stock of this Society and the Grantee and representative Jesse Lapham deceased who conveyed the site of said House to this Union Society having assembled hereto.

Finally they voted to appoint a committee of three to confer with the Methodist Society of Danby Borough or such committee as they may authorize to act on their behalf to apportion the debt of this Society and to devise a way of raising same.

S.L. Griffith was one of the committee of three appointed to apportion the debt - the traditional war cry. But one would have thought even the most irrational of them would have considered what he was doing before he erupted.

Congregational Church Records

January 2nd, 1872 – The Church had their annual meeting, a great row. The Methodists had an Injunction in Chancery served on them for interfering with their meeting.

January 3rd, 1872 – The Congoes are making a great rowe because they were enjoined by the Court. The ill will between the denominations was horrendous.

January 4th, 1872 – This church, having been informed that the so-called Methodists have procured an injunction, by which we are, at least for a short time, excluded from the right to occupy the Union Meeting House, of the stock of which is owned by personas favoring our organization therefore voted, that we will hold our Services next Sabbath and until further notice at Bruce Hall, and not as heretofore in the afternoon but at 1/4 before 11 o'clock in the forenoon, and at 6 1/2 o'clock in the evening and that the Sabbath School be held immediately after the close of the A.M. Service.

January 6th, 1872 – The Congoes are very Long Faced about the Injunction.

April 5th, 1872 – Still unjustly kept out of the Meeting House and holding our meetings in the Bruce Hall.

SILAS LAPHAM GRIFFITH

May 30th, 1872 – Hopes are entertained that the Society may succeed in obtaining another Minister. Otherwise, what will become of this little Church? May the Lord help his people here, and send the right man to go in and before them and break unto the bread of Life and under his ministrations may this little Church live and prosper and many be added to her membership of such as shall be saved.

In January of 1874, William Pierce sent a note to J.C. Baker that he would not pay any of the cost in the court Chancery suit, then pending.

It was divisive and bitter, infinitely ugly.

Certainly, Griffith's part in the church rows earned him a good deal of ill will. It may well have been at least a contributory reason that S.L. Griffith's name is so notably missing in volumes of Vermont's great men. In the definitive *History of Rutland County* of that period, John B. Griffith, one of George Griffith's sons is listed as is Silas's brother, Charles H. Griffith, but there's not a mention of S.L.. In the community, the cost of the ill will on Griffith's life and hopes, was enormous.

From beginning to end, Griffith was a staunch activist in Congregational matters. Indeed, it is highly doubtful that the Church would have survived without his funds, but how much he was in a position to contribute during 1872 is questionable, for it was a year of massive expansion.

With roads in and his basic structures in place at Headquarters and on the mountain, Griffith started accumulating more land.

In August of '72, he purchased 2,700 acres on Dorset/Danby Mountain from various Laphams and Vails for $430, which translates into $6.28 an acre. That was the going price and that's what he paid.

Charcoaling

In addition to land acquisitions, Griffith branched into the charcoaling business. Before oil, coke, and gas came to be used as fuels in foundries, charcoal was much in demand for industrial purposes as well as being used as a source of fuel for residential heating.

There was a good deal of money to be made in charcoal. Hearsay puts the cost of a cord of wood at less than $3. A cord of wood would generate forty to fifty bushels of charcoal which fetched Griffith a good price when loaded on the cars at Danby Station.

Griffith manufactured his charcoal in kilns. These were huge, beehive-shaped structures, ranging in size from twenty-five to thirty feet in diameter, nineteen feet high overall, built on a floor of hard brick with walls a foot thick.

Charcoaling was a tricky business. There was a special way to pile the wood: sixteen-foot piles of logs on each side, with kindling in the center and four feet more on top of the pile, for the fire had to begin at the top and burn downwards.

The burning process was especially complicated. The vents had to be opened and closed throughout the burning process for proper draft. If too much air got in, the fire got away and the wood ended up as ashes; if there wasn't enough air, the fire went out. Either was catastrophe. The fault for catastrophes rested entirely with the colliers.

Griffith employed old men for that job, fellows who needed the money and couldn't work anymore. For all his faults, Griffith was always concerned about the welfare of the old. He didn't want his old workers to starve when they were laid off. As long as a man could hobble, Griffith kept him on, tending kilns, which had to be watched constantly during the ten to twelve days minimum burning process.

The secret of good coal was to take time, and Griffith preferred to give twelve days to char unless he was behind in his orders. All told, it required fourteen days at least to burn a kiln. After the charring operation was complete, the vents were stopped, the body of the kiln was whitewashed, and the crown was covered with tar to make everything airtight. After two days of cooling, the coal could be taken out immediately.

Tourists Arrive

SILAS LAPHAM GRIFFITH

One fine July day in 1882, Griffith looked out of the window of his Head Office and said to Eugene McIntyre who was sitting there, "Uh, oh. Tourists."

Travelers from afar had been coming to the Green Mountains since the coming of the railroad. *The Afternoon Flyer* was the crack train from New York. It zoomed up in about five hours or so out of Grand Central station. Tourists would come for two weeks or a month or two months or sometimes for the whole summer.

Of course, the wealthy tourists stayed at the big old Equinox Hotel in Factory Point. They were picked up at the station by the hotel's fine carriages and liveries that met every train that came in. They brought the guests back to the elegant hostelry where a lot of them spent most of their time sitting in the rocking chairs on the big, long front porch.

Over time, the Orvis family acquired the big hotel in the 1840s and there was some feeling about "the foreigners" having taken over the town.

One time, as McIntyre had heard the story, a foursome of some very English hotel guests was playing on the hotel golf course. In the course of their game, they played up to a green where an old hotel

Griffith's charcoal kilns, Danby Depot

employee who was pushing his hand mower back and forth. The four men waited a reasonable time but the old fella just kept puffing on his pipe and mowing, back and forth. Finally, one of the men stepped up to him and tapped him on the shoulder.

"My good man," he said, "could you stand aside while I stroke the ball?"

But the old timer turned right around with his mower and paid no attention to him. When the old man came back across the green the next time, though, he had to stop because the guest was standing square in front of him, repeating himself, this time a bit more forcibly.

"My good man, stand aside while I stroke the ball!"

The old Vermonter braced himself right up in front of the Englishman and said to the tourist:

"Born under the eaves of the Green Mountains! A distant relative of Ethan Allen's! Move for you red-coated sons-of-bitches? Never!" Later that afternoon, when the guests got back to the hotel, they complained to Orvis who summoned the old timer. The old man took a deep breath and related the entire incident, expecting to be fired. But it pleased Orvis so much, he gave the old guy a cigar and sent him home.

The three gentlemen approaching the Head Office that day in 1882, however, were low-keyed people, come to enjoy the beauty Nature had lavished here.

"The state of Vermont has justly been called 'the artist's paradise,'" one of the travelers held forth. "I know of no state in the Union, and no portion of any state, that presents such a diversity of charming scenery as this favored portion of the earth's surface. This area is replete with pictures that would honor the easel of any painter."

"I wonder," said the third man of the threesome, "that these rich artistic places have not been discovered and utilized long ago by artists of New York, Boston, and nearer cities. They seem, however, to have been overlooked in the furor for the more fashionable White Mountains, coast of Maine, Yellowstone or the Rockies. Here lies a region whose every acre is a mine of artistic wealth and every mill is filled with artistic rapture."

"Count your blessings. When others have made the discovery of this charming Switzerland and shall have found how cheaply they can live and travel in it, they will come in crowds; the fashionable world will follow, and then adieu to the charming simplicity of its people, its reasonable rates and unadulterated honesty. Let us enjoy it while we may."

"I know these three. I promised to tour them around." Griffith remarked to McIntyre, and rose to greet the men.

"Mr. G.! Mr. G.! We're here to have that tour of the Works you promised us." one of them called, enthusiastically, waving to Griffith with one arm while trying to hold his easel firmly under the other. "This is the third year we've spent a two-month vacation here. This is where we come," he declared, "to knit up the raveled sleeve of care by climbing these mountains, threading these valleys, following up the streams and filling our portfolios with sketches."

"This year, however, we encountered grim Death at the depot," one of the travelers reported. Griffith gave him a startled look, but the tourist went on to say that they had learned from one of the men handling the coffin, that the deceased was a sawyer, killed by some logs rolling onto him.

"Was he killed instantly?"

"Yes, as far as I know," the chap replied, "he must ha' been. He sent all his men off somewhere else, and, as he wanted a log for some purpose, he went out to the pile and must have started it while standing in front of it. When his wife went out to look for him, she found him with a log some sixteen feet long and two feet through lying across his chest, and he stone dead. It must ha' crushed the life right out of him."

"Yes, it was a sorry accident," Griffith told them, as he guided them around.

ANN K. ROTHMAN

The Charcoal Business

It soon became evident the tourists were most fascinated by every aspect of the coal burning process. The tourists described it in an article of their trip that was published years later:

> ...the whole interior was filled with a fine charcoal dust, in which it seemed impossible to breathe. Three or four men, who looked more like imps than human beings, were breathing it, however, for they were engaged with long iron rakes in tearing down the …. ranks of charred logs, which, as they fell, crumbled and sent up showers of dust, through which the sunlight, entering at the opening above, sent athwart the picture of a ray that produced a very weird and startling effect.

As they watched, a tall, gaunt apparition of a man stalked out of the entrance of this kiln. Carrying a large, shell-like basket of coal, he mounted a plank to gain access to the top of an enormous coal wagon. "That wagon will take 250 bushels of charcoal," Griffith explained. "Sometimes we extend that capacity by adding 8" high sideboards," he continued, as the workman emptied the basket into the wagon and made his way back to the kiln for another load.

Often as not, while their men worked the woods, the Italian women cleaned out the kilns, exactly as the men were doing. Many spent their days emptying out the 1600 bushels of charcoal, one two-bushel basket a trip, carried on their heads. The charcoal fell all over their hair and onto their faces and over the rest of them, as they walked back and forth, back and forth with their loads all day.

By evening they would be an awful sight. And a lot of people didn't wash much in Griffith's day. One night, up in the store, the workmen and the teamsters and the choppers got to discussing taking baths. Most of them agreed that men that sweat a lot didn't have to bathe as often as men that didn't, because the sweat worked the dirt right out.

"What amazes me," remarked one of the visitors, as one of the large double coal wagons approached the freight platform, "is that loads like that can be safely transported on roads so steep that nothing short of a goat could climb them."

"The horses here are trained to take the most precipitous hill at a gallop and to keep their gait when going downhill," their host replied as the wagon pulled up to the loading platform.

By the time the three gents visited Danby, history reports Griffith's annual charcoal production was about 1 million bushels, for which, it stated, 20,000 cords of wood were burned yearly. Griffith represented his coal operation as one of the largest in the country. From the beginning, charcoal was his biggest money maker.

As Griffith dictated it to the *Mirror,* in 1872, when just commencing the manufacture of charcoal, he was awarded a contract with Barnum, Richardson & Co. of Lime Rock, Connecticut, which called for 1 million bushels of charcoal at $.1350 per bushel on board the cars at Danby station. That contract was subsequently increased to 1.25 million bushels with the sale of the Lime Rock Iron Company to Senator Barnum.

Aside from his luck, consider the connections that led the small-town man to the likes of Barnum. And once having made that gentleman's acquaintance, consider the salesman's personal charm and persuasiveness, to secure such an order to launch a new enterprise. What self-confidence to assume such a challenging obligation! What mettle! What audacity! All or nothing. Boom or bust. Get rich quick.

Likely, anger was the energy of Griffith's ambition in 1872, anger over his castigation by the community over his actions with the Methodists and frustration concomitant with belonging to a minority Church too poor to even afford a Pastor's salary.

For his own purposes and satisfaction, Silas wanted to be a very rich man and Barnum's subsequent contracts for 2.25 million bushels of coal at $.13250 each amounted to $298,125. Deducting $3 cost for each of the approximately 56,250 cords required to fulfill the order, left him a profit of $129,375 - a good start towards wealth. Griffith extended and over-extended himself to fulfill the contract stipulations.

After receiving about half a million bushels, however, both of the Connecticut concerns refused to receive any more charcoal, giving as a reason that the quality of Griffith's charcoal was not up to contract. Griffith of course disputed this, giving as the real reason the fact that charcoal pig iron had dropped in price from $65 to $40 per ton, and the companies could not afford to pay the contract price.

At the time of the contracts' default, Griffith commenced an inventory. He had $25,000 invested in kilns for burning the charcoal and a like amount in wood that was cut and decaying. When he got to the point where his liabilities exceeded $75,000, he closed the book and paid Senator Barnum a visit at his office in Lime Rock, Connecticut.

"See here, Mr. Barnum, the quality of the charcoal I've shipped you is fine. If you can't afford to pay for it, that's your problem, not mine. Either you'll immediately begin receiving the ccharoal as contracted or pay damages." "I'll do neither," Senator Barnum replied with some heat. "If you commence a lawsuit against me and my companies, Griffith, I'll make it longer than the distance from Lime Rock to Montreal."

"That's a long way," S.L. replied. "The sooner I commence my journey, the quicker I'll reach the end of it. Good-bye, sir," he said, and boarded a train, and without even stopping at Danby, took it through to Rutland where he engaged counsel to bring a suit for damages.

Having been advised by Rutland attorneys Wheelock Veasey and Joel C. Baker that the suit would have to be brought in Connecticut, Griffith and Baker went to Hartford and retained a Connecticut lawyer. Less than three days after their Lime Rock encounter, a $100,000 suit had been brought against William H. Barnum, as President of the two contracting companies.

Although lore has it that the suit dragged on for years, throughout which time Griffith stockpiled the charcoal, Griffith's dictated account to Charlie Baker has it that in less than two days after bringing suit against Barnum, a telegram arrived from that gentleman, requesting a meeting between them. Before another week had passed, they arrived at a perfectly acceptable settlement and Griffith returned to Danby "much relieved."

While it is true that 1873 terminated the economy's long upward trend and was marked by a panic of great magnitude during which charcoal pig iron dropped in price like everything else, it is more than likely that the charcoal, in fact, hadn't been up to snuff, for Barnum had his own man, Eugene McIntyre, come to Danby to supervise the job and ensure that the terms of the contract were strictly complied with.

Until the day of Barnum's death, he and S.L. were the best of friends. From then on, Griffith sold him charcoal every year on verbal agreements and attended his funeral when he died. Senator Barnum and Phillip M. Moen of the Washburn & Moen Wire Company were his two best customers and his two best friends in business throughout their lifetimes.

And thanks to Senator Barnum, Danby acquired the McIntyres, a number of whom were twitching in their seats, when the organ finally began to play, signaling the start of the funeral of the community's reprobate benefactor.

Silas Griffith at Lake Griffith

K.T. (Katherine or Kate Tiel) Griffith

Main Street, Danby, Vermont, late 1800s

The Danby Congregational Church, early 1900s

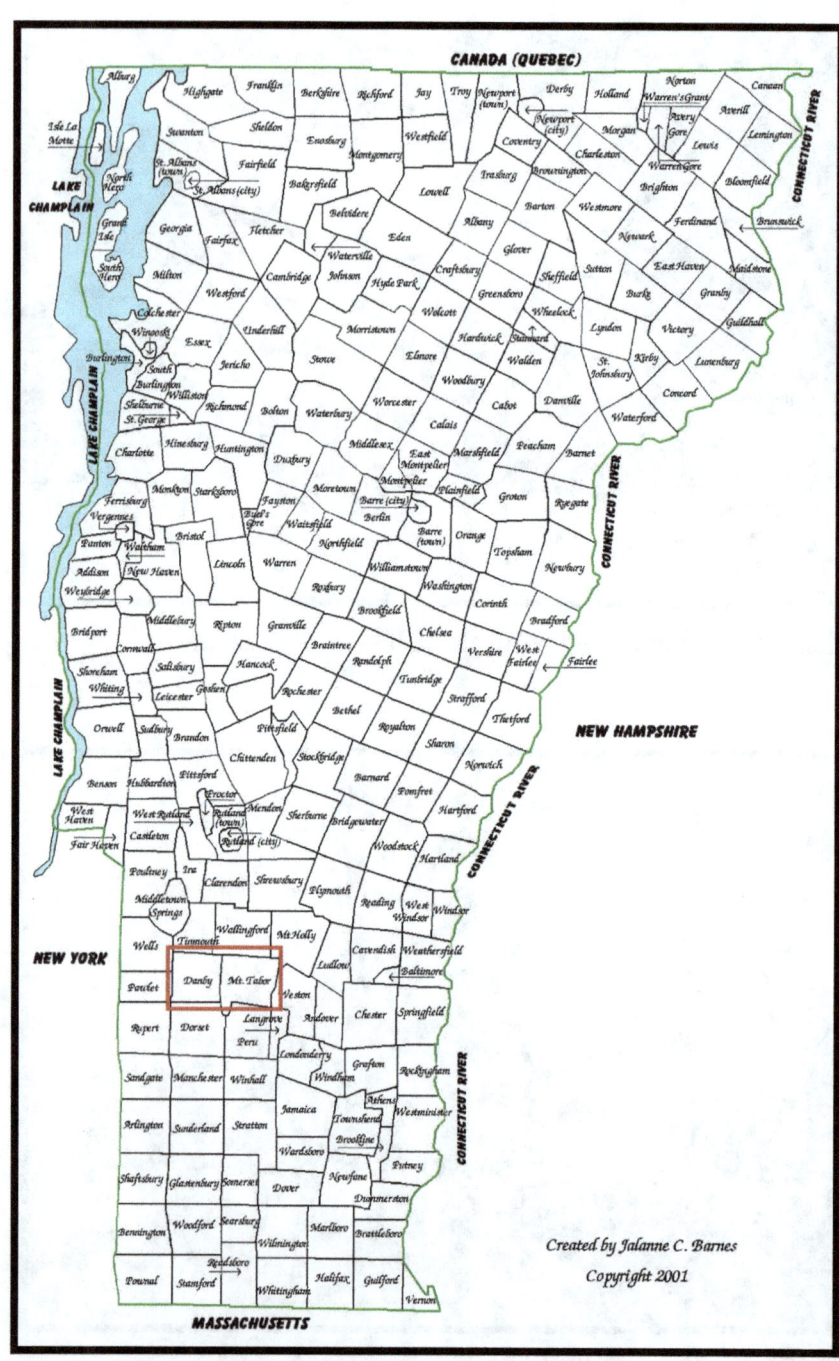

Map of Vermont Townships

Suffragist Lucretia Mott

Suffragists march for the right to vote

ANN K. ROTHMAN

Classroom in a country school

A séance

The Dummerston Railroad Bridge

The Danby Bank

ANN K. ROTHMAN

Kimball Union Academy

Buckwheat Pancake Mix

SILAS LAPHAM GRIFFITH

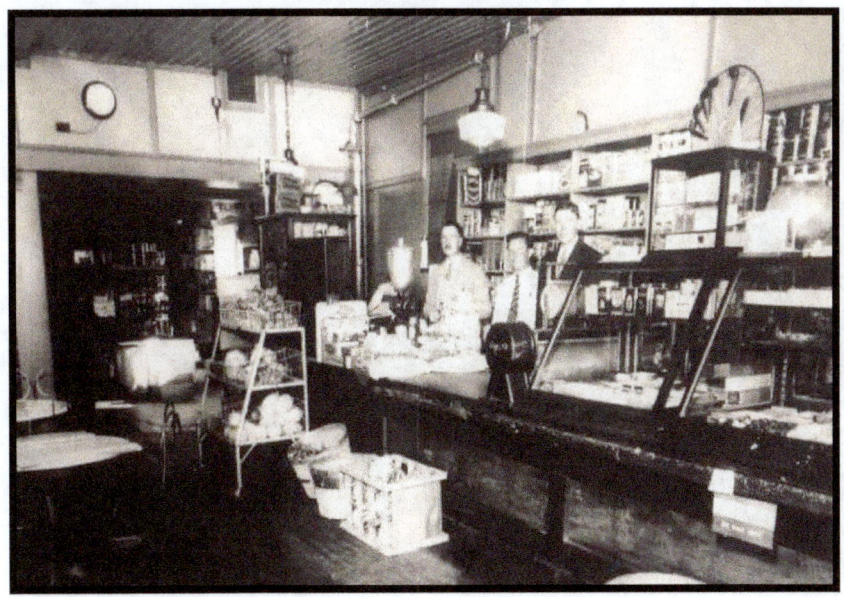

Interior, Dorset-Union Store

Log raft construction

ANN K. ROTHMAN

View of Danby downtown, 1940s

A party in the early 1900s

SILAS LAPHAM GRIFFITH

Chapter 3
The Funeral

THANK GOD! It was the beginning of the end, at last. A sigh of relief waltzed through the wilting congregation. All hopes for a short service were immediately dashed, however, by the sight of three officiating clergymen. Notably absent from the proceedings was the gifted organist Will Risdon, whom S.L. had had schooled. The end of Risdon's organ playing came the day that Silas had walked into the church to find him playing a dance tune, the "Downtown Strutters Ball" or some such, and had fired him. Therefore, it was a Mr. J. Harry Engels of Rutland who rendered, in sweetly solemn tones upon the church organ, Wagner's "The Pilgrim Chorus" to the accompaniment of the pounding rain. Everyone settled into their heads once more for what promised to be at least another hour of absolute, odiferous discomfort.

K.T., her invariably proper, emotionless self, bore the wait in joyous anticipation. How she had hated to leave Philadelphia, she remembered. But her parents kept pushing her, pushing her to marry, certain that somewhere there was a man who would appreciate their thirty-six year old daughter's mind and figure and forgive her facial shortcomings. The fact that unbeknownst to them she had a lover who treasured her but would have been unsuitable in their eyes, had made her marriage to Silas all the more repugnant to her. But now Silas was gone and she would have whom she wanted...

Eugene McIntyre Remembers

Eugene McIntyre, Griffith's notoriously close sometime partner and associate, was satisfied that his great floral splurge on the cross and crown arrangement was prominently placed. As he sat in the church, he let his mind drift from this to that.

A great many of the thirty-odd years since he had first stepped foot in Danby had been spent in close association with Silas. They didn't always agree, and they weren't close, but the years had bound them in many ways. They had been through a lot together.

Gene was the son of a charcoal manufacturer. Although his father had produced his charcoal in pits, Gene had become acquainted with the kiln burning process. In 1872 McIntyre was employed by Senator Barnum, who forwarded him to Danby where he was jointly employed by both Barnum and Griffith. He gave faithful service to Barnum by seeing that the quality of the commercial charcoal contracted for was fulfilled and that the terms of Barnum's contract were strictly complied with; he just as faithfully served Griffith by supervising the manufacture of the charcoal, to the end that there was no possibility of carelessness on the part of the workmen having charge of the many kilns. After a year of joint employment, McIntyre became solely Griffith's employee for three years. It was a good thing, too, that he was there. God only knows how Griffith managed before he came, for Eugene McIntyre was allegedly the first man in the area who really knew how to burn charcoal.

SILAS LAPHAM GRIFFITH

Gene remembered the summer night when the old guy watching one of the kilns down by the depot dozed off, made drowsy by the warmth of the kiln that soothed his arthritic limbs. He didn't notice when the heat went from warm to hot, but when it got very hot, the collier roused himself with a start and with horror saw the huge structure before him glowing red from its raging interior fire, transmuting its surrounding darkness, proclaiming imminent explosion that would endanger many lives. He didn't know how to correct it, but he knew enough to run.

"Help! HELP! FIRE!" he shouted. "RUN! Get away from here!" he warned the other nearby colliers, "Run or this thing will blow us to smithereens!"

"I'll fetch Gene!" one of them yelled and took off down the street for the home of the charcoal expert who lived nearby.

"We can't wait for McIntyre! Get the hoses!"

In a panic, the men at the site ran for the fire hoses and hooked them up and were just about to turn them on, which would have ruined both the charcoal and the kiln, when McIntyre came running down the road in his pajamas.

"Don't put water on that! You'll smother it! Block your drafts! BLOCK THOSE DRAFTS!" he yelled, stopping them just in time.

Once Barnum's money started coming in, there was no stopping Griffith. With proper supervision of the tricky coaling operation, Griffith was free to put his time into expansion, and so he did, buying land, starting up more and more of his sites on the Green Mountain: Three Shanties, Shippey Shanties, The Ten Kiln Meadows, The South End. Gene watched them emerge, and he watched Griffith tuning up his operations, improving every aspect of them when possible.

Griffith Works was responsible for introducing specially constructed saws. These were crosscut saws, two-man saws that replaced the old chopping method for cutting down trees, a method that was soon adopted by all the lumbering concerns in this part of the country and beyond.

Any improvement that could add to the efficiency of the operation was introduced at once. One time a fellow came down the mountain with a one-beam sled that worked better than the three-beam sleds they were using. Griffith stopped the job right there and had his men convert every sled he had from three beams to one.

Since the products of the forest were mostly transported by horse-drawn sleds in winter, Griffith soon replaced the little Morgan horses for which this area is famous. Instead he introduced big, western horses from Iowa and elsewhere. The Morgans only weighed about 800 pounds each, whereas the western horses weighed 1,500 pounds each horse. A team of those, weighing 3,000 pounds pulled better than three times their own weight most every load they drew. He also introduced efficiencies, so that all waste product was utilized.

Married to His Work

McIntyre was amazed at how much time and energy and thought and money Griffith poured into his business until, eventually, it became the largest individual enterprise within the borders of the state of Vermont and further. And, over time, as Gene observed and watched all this, he came to realize that Griffith, a man with many interests had no outstanding hobby nor any social affiliation, like the Masons of which he himself became a member in later years. McIntyre finally understood that, simply put, Silas was married to his business.

As to his marriage to Libbie, Griffith never mentioned it and Gene never asked, although he had heard stories. Indeed, McIntyre recollected how amazed the community had been when Libbie became pregnant in 1873 and finally gave birth to a little girl, Agatha, on February 24th, 1874. And he remembered the talk, the old women, the shrews with their glinting eyes and knowing nods, "An Anniversary Baby," they said. "They were married in May, remember? An Anniversary Baby, for sure. On their anniversary, in May, that's when Lib permits him his yearly pickings…"

Over the year little Agatha lived, Griffith was in notably better spirits, sometimes even leaving the Works a little earlier, sometimes even staying home on Saturdays. But then in early April 1875, the child died of congestion of the lungs and Griffith pulled even deeper inside himself, unfailingly putting in extra-long hours, holing himself into his office six days a week.

Earl vs. Griffith

Gene was right there when the matter of Earl vs. Griffith was brought before the Rutland County Court the March Term of 1876. It was a landmark case—in Griffith's career, his first cutting-over action.

In a Plea of Trespass, Roswell Earl of Wallingford accused Griffith of entering, cutting and carrying away timber from Lot No. 16 of the Steele Cliff grant in Mt. Tabor. The lower court found the defendant guilty and ruled that the plaintiff recover of the defendant $610 plus $110 in damages, a ruling Griffith took exception to.

"Why did you take exception to it?" McIntyre asked him, one day in Griffith's office.

"Wouldn't it have been easier to pay Earl off and be done with it? It was certainly affordable for you and it would have saved you the hassle of a Supreme Court case."

"Not the point at all," Griffith had answered in an uncommonly expansive mood. "Of course, I took exception to it," he said, after pulling forth a cigar and starting it up with great gusto.

"After all," he went on, "a man can't be blamed for his blood.

"It's been a source of some private amusement to me, that the acquisition of land - and women - has been a dominant strain in my family's line from its very beginning."

"Oh?" replied McIntyre.

"Certainly, I took exception. How can a man feel guilty, after all, for showing forth strains that have dominated his line from its very origins? Hell-raising is in my blood from way back," Silas assured McIntyre. "Would you like to hear about it?"

"I would, indeed," McIntyre replied.

"All right. Here's what it comes down to."

A Family History

"The origins of my family's history commence with one Rhys ap Gruffydd (AD 1132-1197), 'The Lord Rhys,' who was the last effective native ruler of the South Wales kingdom. He and one of his sons, Rhys the Hoarse, were commemorated by the Talbot family - the later earls of Shrewsbury, who, in the 14th century, set up effigies of the two at the Cathedral Church of St. David's in Permbrokshire," their genealogically knowledgeable descendant continued, after puffing up a storm of cigar smoke and tipping his ashes.

"Of course," S.L. picked up with a twinkle in his eye, "there was some little humor involved with those effigies of severe, dedicated figures with their crumbled hands raised in prayer. In actual fact, the Lord Rhys died excommunicate, having not long before incited some of his sons to chase the Bishop of St. David's from bed, to deliver a reproof.

"Whether Rhys the Hoarse was one of those involved in making the Bishop prance about in his woolen shirt and drawers, I wouldn't know. But when the Talbots installed those effigies a long while after, in the long-late Bishop's own territory, they may well have been evening-up for the scourging of the sons implicated in the incident..."

"There's another interesting throw-back," Gene thought, and asked his voluble employer, "How do the Talbots fit in there?"

With great relish and glinting eye, Griffith explained that the Talbot family traces its descent through a high-powered *ketch-colt* line of Rhys the Hoarse. *"Ketch-colt?"*

SILAS LAPHAM GRIFFITH

"Yes, ketch-colt. You know, bastard. Oh, they were an energetic bunch, my ancestors," Griffith related with great amusement.

"The apparent historical truth of the matter is that my ancestors pegged out their claim to the overlordship of South Wales by planting bastards instead of stakes to delineate their lines.

"Land and women, land and women," Silas mused, puffing on his cigar. "Like his father before him," Griffith picked up after a little, "Rhys the Hoarse left behind some dozen sons born in wedlock by several wives and twenty more sons begot by extramarital unions. When you consider that's not counting any of the old swordsman's daughters, that amounts to a lot of energetic philandering. Maybe that's why my conscience never took that kind of sinning too seriously," Griffith pondered. "I wonder if over the centuries it didn't build up an immunity...

"All those bastards," he wondered to himself out loud. "Imagine living back when illegitimacy caused no dismay. How much fairer for the kids..." he observed, thoughtfully. "You know," he informed McIntyre, "in the 12th century, bastard lines were recorded in pedigrees as basis for land tenure and payment of bloodshed fines.[1]

"Well," he said, getting up, "anyway, that's why I accepted in the Earl case. It's all in the blood," he shrugged, "Scrappers. Landowners. Kings. And womanizers," he nodded to McIntyre. "...It's all in the blood," he said, and left the office.

Earl vs. Griffith passed to the state Supreme Court, which also found against Silas and increased his damages to $422.

A Changed Man

McIntyre left town in '77 to go into trade for himself for two years, but he kept thinking of how much he had enjoyed his time in Danby,

---

[1] All information concerning Griffith's origins has been freely extracted from *Infants of the Spring*, Vol.1 of *To Keep the Ball Rolling*, by Anthony Powell (William Heinemann, Ltd., London, 1976)

especially during deer hunting season when he hied himself up the mountain and got about a quarter of the deer brought in to the legendary Buckhorn Camp. And he liked the village and the life and the work and the people. So, a few years later he returned to town with his wife and sons, Edward and Cecil. He settled them in a handsome house, set back a distance from the road to Mt. Tabor, on a generous lot surrounded by a fine wrought iron fence and commenced to build a life for himself as a permanent resident of the community.

One of the first things he did upon his return was to set up a meeting with Griffith to explore various business arrangements. The remarkably productive session gave birth to the first of a number of partnerships between the men, who jointly in 1880 purchased the Black Branch property on the Green Mountain. This was a 1300-acre parcel where, under the firm name Griffith & McIntyre, they installed a mill village with its compliment of kilns.

While they were discussing partnering a mercantile business in one of the village stores, McIntyre said to Silas, "You know, something's happened to you in the couple of years I've been away. You're a changed man."

"Changed? How so?"

"You're easier, somehow. Not as driven as you were. You keep shorter hours. You're more anxious to go home. You're happier, is what it is. How come?"

Griffith chuckled. "You're a smart guy, McIntyre. I am indeed happier. I became a father again when you were away."

"You did! Why, that's great news. What did you have?"

"A son," Griffith beamed. "Harry. 'Little Harry,' we call him, 'cause he's a slight lad. But cute as a button, a handsome boy, and sharp, you can tell how sharp he is. He's just starting to talk."

"When was he born?"

"On February 4th, 1878." *Ah ha! Another Anniversary Baby,* thought Gene.

"You have two boys," Silas continued, "Tell me something. You think when he's four I'll be able to take him trout fishing?"

"Why don't you wait," McIntyre replied, amused, "and see how he's doing when he gets there?"

"Jesus," Griffith said, soberly, "I'm almost afraid to hope he will get there."

In addition to his partnership with Griffith, and subsequent ones, over the years, on the mountain and also in Peru and Arlington, McIntyre maintained his own, separate holdings, as did Silas. Upon his return to town, McIntyre began accumulating land for his own enterprises. In no time at all, he settled in just fine.

Life in Danby

McIntyre's personal life was bringing him substantial satisfaction, as well. He was soon joined in Danby by his brother, Warren, and a cousin, M.O. Schutt. And over the years, the family McIntyre wove their own texture into the fabric of the town and its legends.

In short order, Gene was accepted as a member of the Masonic Marble Lodge No. 76, and he shortly became a fixture there, spending practically every night of the year excepting Sundays and deer season in the Masonic Hall. He would go after supper for a game of cards—King Peed, he played, a counter game. Night after night, that's where he was, and he became well known as an overly careful bidder who played with a deck of cards so old and used they were about as soggy as soda crackers and so sticky they'd have to unglue them to see what they had in their hands. The guys who played against Gene watched him pretty close and some of them would occasionally reach over and turn over his discards, into which he'd try to slip a counter card if he had bid too high. You had to watch him when he played croquet, too!

Not surprisingly, elements of McIntyre's character turned up in his conduct of business.

"You're a mean old sonofabitch," one of Gene's old, retired teamsters told Gene to his face one day, when he no longer needed his job. "By Jesus, you never half fed your horses. Men that worked for you had to work with horses that didn't have enough to eat and had old, broken-down harnesses and equipment." But Gene knew better than to try to get away with any of that on Griffith & McIntyre ventures.

Back at the funeral, McIntyre closed his eyes and stifled a groan, as the organ started in again. Having completed "The Pilgrim's Chorus," Harry Engels commenced Voigt's "Night Shades."

Flit! went McIntyre's mind, settling capriciously on Sam Vaughn, a fellow who owned a piece of land on the mountain between Griffith's and McIntyre's separate holdings. Both Vaughn and Griffith were cutting him off. With a wry grin of remembrance, Gene recalled how one day Vaughn had approached him, disgusted and fed up, and had sold him the parcel. And Gene recalled how, a couple of days later, he found out that Vaughn had also sold the parcel to Griffith. After he'd sold his property twice, Vaughn wisely took the next train going out west and never showed his face in Danby again.

Oh, yes, he and Griffith had been through a lot together, McIntyre mused.

Shortly after Harry's third birthday, Silas marched into the office beaming from ear to ear. For $4000 he had purchased Maple Terrace and its thirty acres from A.R. Vail, the executor of the estate of Jesse and the newly-late Elizabeth Lapham. By April 24th, he was already repairing its exterior. As the year progressed, McIntyre wondered if Griffith wasn't losing his senses.

On the afternoon of May 14th, the platform around his charcoal kilns near the depot took fire and burned with about five cords of wood. Did it bother Griffith? Not at all.

"Build it again," he ordered, bothered only by the appearance of the wall in front of the church grounds that presented an unsightly view out the front windows of his new home. He promptly rectified the situation by buying old stone and repairing it, to great improvement.

In June, he accepted eight horses and was in the process of building another house at the depot. In July, while everyone else in town and in the nation was talking of nothing but Guiteau's July 2nd attempt to assassinate President Garfield and the subsequent daily reports of the progress of his recovery, Silas packed up his family and took them all on an unheard of two-week vacation to Massachusetts. They stayed awhile at the seashore, returning home just in time to receive a verdict of $143,000 and costs from a lawsuit with one Ben Roberts. Was he pleased? Well, yes. "Better win than lose," he shrugged to McIntyre, but what really occupied him was trying to find water.

As August dragged into September and Garfield lay at the point of death, finally dying on the 20th, Griffith kept searching for a water source. To this end he hired Ben Hadwen to tear up the road in front of Pierce's Stone Store so he could drive in a pipe at the foot of the hill.

Sitting there, listening to the organist finally finish up, Gene remembered 1881 as the second year since his return to Danby, that Silas had divorced his business and married his family and his community. Sure, he met with Greeley, who'd come from Iowa to sell him a lot of timber land. And he bought thirty-one barrels of apples for their store, but his fire for work had diminished. His concerns focused on his home.

On February 17th, 1882, about a week after Little Harry's fourth birthday, the child became very sick. McIntyre remembered how haggard and upset S.L. had been, until the child's recovery. In March, the doctor was summoned again, this time for Libbie. Her illness was sufficiently severe to necessitate seventeen-year-old Jennie's having to leave Auburndale, where she had been staying, to move her things home on account of her mother's sickness, which lingered through June.

Gene couldn't recall if Silas had taken Harry fishing that year, but he did remember the huge firework display Griffith had down beyond the depot on July 3rd. Little Harry watched with delight from his perch on his father's shoulders, where he spent a good deal of time. It was the same on the 22nd, when Griffith raised his large barn at the depot.

Money Matters

Certainly, Griffith was disturbed when one of his men had some wood thrown on his head while filling a kiln on the mountain. He died two days later from the murderous incident, but for all of it, Griffith's primary occupation that year was spending money.

1882 was the year tight-fisted McIntyre became convinced Griffith had lost his senses. As soon as he became truly prosperous, Silas seemed to get as much pleasure out of spending money as he did making it. Not only was he spending it, he was giving it away!

Finally having found his water source, the Grady Spring, to fill his own needs, Silas was putting his water works through the village for everyone's use. In fact, thanks to S.L. Griffith, it was hard to maneuver the streets of the village without tripping over a man in the building trades. And what he was spending didn't seem to bother Silas at all.

McIntyre just couldn't figure it. At best, his teamsters could barely live on the $1 day he paid them, although Griffith was pretty good about jumping their bills at the store - forgiving them - if he knew a man was hard working and had a big family and just couldn't keep up. But still, $1 a day was low, awfully low. Some of the teamsters used to steal chains once in a while, he knew, to make a little extra. McIntyre had heard about one Vermonter, a Calvin Sampson, who started up a shoe factory in North Adams, Massachusetts in 1858 and paid his men $1.70 for a ten-hour day - a fortune compared to what Silas was paying, especially after he cut the wages even lower.

They used to tell how one old guy bought his horse "Cub, "cookies every day, but after his pay was sliced the old fella said, "No more cookies for poor old Cub at 75 cents a day, man and horse." And still, his men, most of them, considered Silas a good boss, strict but good to work for, an employer who kept work for his older workers and tried to keep winter work for all of them. And, of course, jumping their store bills helped considerably.

Griffith's lowest paid worker was his water boy, who got 25 cents a week.

Twice, Griffith endured strikes. The first was in consequence of a demand for more pay, which, Griffith said, his contracts wouldn't permit him to grant. Consequently, he paid off his old help the day after they stopped working and on the second day, started up again, with new help throughout. The second strike was instituted by the Knights of Labor. Griffith quickly reconstructed his work force and thereafter refused to employ anyone who belonged to that union. At one point, when the unions were trying to unionize the masons, Griffith got worried. The kilns burned themselves out regularly; they'd only last about a year before they had to be torn down and rebuilt, so he had a lot of masonry work and he didn't want any trouble. So he sent one of his bosses around with a piece of paper for his masons to sign, agreeing that they wouldn't join a union. One his masons, old Jim Johnson, a tobacco chewer, read it over and he spit tobacco juice on it. "That's my signature," he said to the boss, and Griffith fired him. Johnson went to Manchester and got $1.50 a day, a hell of a big raise.

No way was Griffith a big spender, no more than he was, Gene reflected, yet here he was, spending fortunes putting in a water system for the village.

It was quite beyond McIntyre's understanding.

One day in the fall, Griffith said to McIntyre. "You know, my life would be much simpler if I had a real good superintendent bossing the jobs on the Green Mountain. I'm going to take a little trip out west and speak to a guy about that. He might be just the person..."

ANN K. ROTHMAN

A Lonely Man

In early October, Griffith returned home from a visit to Illinois and Iowa to find a minor epidemic of dysentery in the village. One of the afflicted was Little Harry, who was very sick with the dangerous disease. Every day, McIntyre got a report. "Very sick." "No better." "Some better this forenoon but not quite as well this afternoon." "Very sick yet." "A little better this morning." "Worse yesterday afternoon." And so it went. Twelve days later, the boy was sufficiently better for Silas to go to the White Mountains for a short trip, despite Libbie's begging him to stay home. Three days later he returned to find his son not as well as he had been. By October 28th, Harry was considerably worse, and his condition was considered hopeless.

Griffith didn't get much work done that month. He went to the office and stared out the window, hollow-eyed, drawn, weary.

"You know," he said to McIntyre one day, "I envy you. I envy you your evenings spent at the Masonic Hall. There's no place at all for me to go, no place to talk to anyone, no place to socialize with men."

Gene didn't say much. He didn't know what to say. Everyone in town knew how desperately Silas wanted to be a member of the Masons. And everyone knew they wouldn't let him in.

It was no secret that practically every President of the United States since the founding of the Brotherhood, had been a Mason. For those smart enough to use its wide-spread connections properly, there was no limit to the help it could do them.

Aside from the connections he could've made and the enormous benefit it would have been to his business, Griffith, a remarkably congenial man, desperately needed the companionship the Lodge offered, especially since his marriage left much to be desired. But every time he was proposed for membership, the same black balls in the voting box kept him out.

In the beginning, he was pretty well convinced that religious difference had more than a little to do with it. The Lodge had been founded three years before the Congregational Church, with no overlap of membership. How many Spiritualists there were among the charter members of the Lodge, he didn't know, but it appeared to be packed with them, without a religiously orthodox member in the lot. Later, he was certain his actions against the Methodists perpetuated the Brotherhood's rejection. He tried everything to overcome it. Early-on, he contributed wall-to-wall carpeting to the Lodge, a rare, Masonic carpet of unique pattern, hoping they would accept him along with his gesture. But while they thanked him kindly for the carpet, they hadn't let him in. And how he courted Bill Bond, a charter member of the Lodge who held the post of the Society's Master, on and off, for eleven years. Actually, Bond was related to Silas through Bond's marriage to Alice Griffith, the daughter of Hiram, who was a Spiritualist. Bond was a big man in town. Besides his significance in the Masons, he had become the proprietor of the hotel in the 1870s. The original hotel and tavern had been situated on half an acre, but had been enlarged, over the years, to a two-acre complex, largely under Bond's proprietorship. Besides the hotel, Bond manufactured tin and sheet iron ware. And he had a store, too, built after his old one burned, where he dealt in hardware, agricultural implements, home furnishings, and fish.

Even though the voting process at the Lodge was supposed to be kept absolutely secret, after a while word got out that Bond was one of Griffith's constant blackballers, along with a shiftless, dishonest drifter who had once worked for Griffith. And then, Dr. E.O. Whipple might have retaliated for Silas's former efforts to keep Mrs. Whipple out of the church choir. Nobody knows exactly which Lodge members dropped those black balls into the voting box, but, in any case, no matter how many times his name was proposed for membership, two black balls always kept him out.

So, since McIntyre was there, it was McIntyre to whom S.L. spewed out the daily report on Little Harry's battle to survive dysentery. "Hopeless," Griffith had sighed on October 28th, 1882, "Hopeless."

But by some miracle, the boy slowly got better, and, though still weak, enjoyed a wealth of presents under the Christmas tree on the 25th of December. As Harry opened his gifts, Silas and Libbie exchanged a look of thanks on that best of all Christmases, so grateful to God were they, for having spared their son. And a few days later, Silas and Libbie welcomed the New Year, with Libbie's sister-in-law and half-brother, Eddie Staples who had arrived in town on the 28th, from out west, to commence Eddie's new job as Silas's Superintendent.

In 1883, Eddie Staples took over the mountain and, over time, became its unquestioned and universally unpopular ruler. He laid down the rules, straight off.

Harry E. Griffith

Eddie was the thermometer man. No thermometers were allowed on the mountain: Nobody was sick unless Eddie's thermometer said so.

No watches were allowed on the mountain. The work went on from dawn to dark, so they didn't need timepieces, except for Eddie's.

And there were other things, over time, lots of other things, but in the early months of 1883, Silas's concerns revolved around his son.

Little Harry was still weak from his bout with dysentery when he became very sick again, the third week in March and this time, he didn't get better. Except maybe for a day or two here and there, he got worse and worse while he lingered. By the 2nd of April, he was gradually failing, and by the 4th, he was just alive. He was no better by the 6th, and was reported breathing with great difficulty. On April 8th, 1883, Little Harry Griffith died at 5:30 A.M. of "Brain Difficulty." He was five years, two months and five days old. The large funeral was held at Maple Terrace, and. Mr. Mears, the Congregational minister, was the preacher.

A week later, McIntyre stopped in at the office late in the day, to pick up some papers he needed and was surprised to see Silas sitting in his office long after everyone else had left.

"What are you doing down here so late, Silas?" he asked him, quite disturbed at the appearance of the man. Unusually unkempt, his eyes deep in his head with black smudges even his glasses couldn't hide, S.L. just sat there, vacant, with his suit hanging loose on his gaunt body, at least ten pounds lighter than he had been. "Silas, man, are you all right?" Gene asked, concerned.

Griffith just looked through him as he sat there, surrounded by the paper of his wealth.

"For God's sake, Silas, say something!"

Finally Griffith swallowed and with dead eyes sweeping his files and records, he started talking.

"You know," he said, "in the beginning all this was a means to achieve my own ends, as well as to provide the creature comforts for Libbie and my surviving daughter, Jennie. After Agatha, there was nothing left but my work. I buried myself in it, drowned myself in it, escaped to it, and my industry became a substitute for my emotional wants. While my marriage to my business surely never brought me the warmth of love, it never caused me pain, either, and I reaped a good deal of satisfaction in perfecting my creation, that reflected me.

"And then, when the good Lord saw fit to bless our union with Harry, having suffered the loss of two children, I tried - oh, how I tried to save myself the pain, the possible agony of likewise losing my heir. So I steeled myself," he nodded, "I steeled myself against the hope of his survival. But around the time he turned two and had already outlived the span of life granted his dead sisters, I couldn't help but hope; and as he grew and thrived, I came to love him above all else. All this around us, these works and all else connected with my industry became most paramountly his, rather than mine, as I dreamed of dynasty and started living as a family man, a father.

"And now," he said, looking his partner in the face with tearful eyes, "now, what is there for me? Five days a week, I run down to this office and sit here surrounded by the paper of my wealth and I feel like putting a goddamned match to it!

"What is there for me now, Gene? What's there to live for? What's there to work towards? I'm forty-six years old and I feel ready to die."

For a long while, the two men were lost in their thoughts. Finally, McIntyre came up with an answer for Silas.

"Look, Silas," he said, "I know you for a man who needs at least a challenge to live for and this business, oh, you might grow it a little more and tweak it here and there, but by and large, you've made it and it's done and it's pretty much old hat to you now. If I were you," he said, "I'd look for something completely different. — Have you ever considered going into politics?"

"Politics?"

"Yes," said McIntyre, "just a thought." As he left, Silas was contemplatively gazing out the window.

Back at Silas's funeral, McIntyre roused himself for a moment to audit the service, which was progressing, but slowly. An Episcopal burial service was underway for the ardent Congregationalist corpse, the officiating minister, Rev. Dr. Samuel N. Jackson of Burlington, having been designated by Silas to conduct the service. Rev. Samuel Jackson and his son, Rev. William P. Jackson of Dummerston, both accompanied Silas to the Holy Land a few years back, McIntyre recalled and once again retreated into his head.

Life Goes On

Of course, life went on, even for Silas. McIntyre seemed to recall that was the year Silas bought his big farm up on the mountain, a farm that subsequently produced a goodly percentage of the fodder for his animals. Throughout the summer, he continued the installation of his water system, connecting it up to a number of houses and stores. As many of his neighbors spent summer days touring his mill and farm, Silas started spending more and more time with his cousin Julius and more and more time at his office, too, sometimes working until surprisingly late in the evening. The only truly significant event in his life for quite awhile concerned the Union Church.

At a meeting on January 1st, 1884, the stockholders of the Danby East Village Union Society voted to sell the meeting house and lot at private sale for the purpose of paying the debts of the Society and voted to appoint G.S. Tabor, Agent. In August, Griffith paid $150 for a quarter of the Parsonage...meaning to convey all the lands and the Parsonage thereon.' Presumably, at that time, (although there is no official record of this), the building became "The First Congregational Church of Danby."

Silas was a big man by then. He owned virtually all of the Green

Mountain, besides countless other holdings elsewhere.

And then came 1885.

Beginning in April, Silas distanced himself from town as much as possible. In April, he went to Boston to buy goods for his and McIntyre's new store. In June, he was out of town for three weeks, part of the time traveling as far west as Nebraska. Within four days of Silas's departure from the community, Eddie Staples and his wife got on the noon train for Illinois and possibly Dakota, for a two- or three-month trip.

Libbie remembered all that as clearly as if it were yesterday:

They all left town to avoid the inevitable and I couldn't wait for them to leave, especially Silas!

Libbie

Reverend Jackson completed the burial service, Miss Minnie Bushee sang the "Holy City." The numerous eyes that turned to catch some response on the part of the widow, K.T. Griffith, were sorely disappointed.

For her part, Libbie ignored Minnie completely, just as she had largely ignored her former husband's protracted love affair with his handsome, thoroughly devoted employee when they were married. If you don't care for a man, you don't care what he does with other women, as long as he's reasonably discreet about it, which Silas had been.

After Harry, there had been nothing between them at all. What held Libbie to him in the years after Harry's death, was Silas's money, which Libbie enjoyed spending like water. After two years of increasing animosity, however, Libbie started talking divorce, the last thing Silas wanted. Especially because he was harboring political aspirations, he would have gone to great lengths to maintain the marriage, if only for that reason.

SILAS LAPHAM GRIFFITH

"They have had family difficulty for some time," William Pierce would observe in his diary two months later. It was a sufficiently lengthy period of matrimonial difficulties that the family Staples would have been well aware of. What Libbie's people thought about the situation varied.

Eddie, looking after his own skin as S.L.'s Superintendent, was dead set against rupture between his half-sister and his brother-in-law/boss. Libbie's oldest half-brother, George, on the other hand, felt just the opposite. As for her parents, Edwin and his second wife, Margaret (who had forced the girl into the marriage), they sided with S.L. and Eddie. They felt strongly enough about it so that substantial animosity arose between them and George, who supported his sister.

Usually, in situations like this, there is "a straw" which eventually breaks the proverbial camel's back. Aside from the innumerable accumulated causes which undoubtedly were responsible for the rupture, two different specific reasons have been volunteered by Libbie's kin as having precipitated the termination of the marriage, both having to do with Silas's philandering.

One version given as Libbie's reason for divorcing the community's most prominent citizen is that she happened to walk into the room where they did the wash to find her husband had pushed the skivvy over a big pile of dirty laundry and was going at her.

The other story put forth is that Silas came home from a business trip with "a disease" and his wife divorced him because of it.

In view of the widely held belief concerning Griffith's syphilitic affliction, it would seem appropriate to discuss the three stages of this chronic infectious venereal disease, the first two of which are contagious.

The first or primary state is characterized by an ulceration of the penis or lip. If untreated, it will disappear spontaneously, leaving no scar. The second stage arrives six weeks to three months later. The

145

patient develops a rash generally found on the palms of the hand or the soles of the feet. His lymph glands may have increased in size, and he might also have some highly contagious lesions in his mouth, and would run a fever. If untreated, the rash, glands, and fever disappear after a few weeks and the patient feels fine for a very long time thereafter, as the microscopic organism, the *spirochete,* is disseminated throughout the body, The organism may be deposited in any or all of the following places: the brain, the spinal cord, the thoracic aorta, and possible the stomach, kidneys, or bones.

Ten, fifteen, twenty or more years can pass in this latent stage, during which the patient feels fine. Then, bango! In its last stage, the patient becomes debilitated and dies.

If Griffith had contracted the disease during his short buying trip to Boston, both the first and the second stages would have been readily discernible and Libbie would not have waited until August to leave him.

Had he contracted the disease during his three-week business trip in June, this second stage could possibly have evolved during the two-month period between his return to Danby and the couple's eventual separation. But Libbie knew before Silas had even left on his extended trip west that she was finished with marriage. And she was determined to fully reap its last benefits during his absence. Once he was out the door, Lib started reaping. *What a divine shopping binge that was,* she remembered.

For months, already, Libbie had tested the outer limits of Silas's generosity. But there was always more to buy and oh, how she loved beautiful clothes and jewelry and dress goods and ornaments. She was an elegant, regal lady and she liked to dress the part.

For three solid weeks, without restraint, Mary Elizabeth Griffith, bought anything and everything that pleased her. Lacking her husband's overview of her purchases, she bought with unbridled extravagance, forcing her indulgences into already bursting closets and overstuffed drawers and, dutifully, as Silas had requested, placing all the receipts of her daily charges in an ever-growing pile on the middle of his desk in his study.

With her eyes sparkling with the joy of the hunt, careful to restrict her purchases to personal property, which, she had been assured by Counsel, was always included in the Alimony, Mrs. Silas Griffith was the salespersons' delight, the perfect customer, and oh, so lucky, to be married to such an affluent man, obviously smitten with his wife to permit her such lavish indulgences.

Silas returned home on the evening of June 21st. On the 23rd, the morning editions of the *Herald* and the *Globe* had notices, placed by Silas, forbidding anyone trusting his wife with credit on his account.

Elizabeth (Libbie) Griffith

> **NOTICE.**
>
> All persons are hereby forbidden to give credit to my wife Elizabeth M., on my account, as I shall pay no debts of her contracting.
>
> Danby, Vt., June 22, 1885.
> d16to63   **SILAS L. GRIFFITH.**

Newspaper notice regarding Libbie's debts

On August 26th, Pierce noted, "S.L Griffith and wife agreed to Separate today. They have had family difficulty for some time. She and Jennie go to Brandon, VT to live, and in September Mrs. S.L Griffith and daughter Jennie left for Brandon on the 4 P.M. train." Libbie filed for divorce immediately thereafter.

Neither Libbie nor her family held the rupture against Silas, but Silas was very angry indeed about it. Nor was Silas the only Griffith getting divorced. In October 1885, S.L.'s sister, Mary, went to Rutland to attend to her divorce suit against her husband, I. W. Kelley.

Shortly after, Eddie Staples and wife returned home and life in the community bubbled on as usual, savoring the latest scandal which centered about one Oscar A. Adams, who had been appointed postmaster in July, but very shortly, certain irregularities arose which prompted governmental charges against him, which proceeding dragged on from October through November 6th, when the case was closed and O.A. Adams left town and ran to his father's. On November 11th and 12th, Silas accompanied Bill Bond to Rutland, wheeling and dealing and pulling all the Republican strings he could, defying party lines, to aid Bond, a Democrat, to gain the postmastership.

The Trout Pond

"Say, Bill," Griffith asked innocently, as they were sitting on the train in Rutland waiting for it to leave for home, "I've been meaning to ask you. How's your trout pond doing?"

For many years, Bond's trout pond behind his house was his pride and joy. The town's first major fish culturist, Bond stocked his pond with trout supplied him by the town kids who earned a nickel for each trout caught in the streams around town and sold live to Bill Bond. Two of the youngsters involved in that enterprise were Gene McIntyre's boy, Cise, and Bill's son, Perry, close friends, just as their fathers were and, also like their old men, shrewd in their business dealings. It wasn't long after the two of them got into the trout-catching business that they became Bill's major suppliers - and oh, how his son's industry pleased Bill. Until he found out Perry's source of supply: McIntyre, laughing, had told Silas how one day Bond stormed into the Masonic Lodge, bellowing, "Do you know what our sons have been up to, McIntyre?! Would you believe," he'd said plaintively, "that Cise and Perry went out and caught my own danged fish from my own pond and were selling them back to me!"

"How's my trout pond doing?" Bond repeated. "Ah, come on, Silas," he begged, "Don't do that to me." Silas had his joke, but on November 25th, Bond was appointed postmaster and moved the post office to his store.

McIntyre may have laughed over the boys cheating Bond, but years later, after Silas had died, McIntyre's son, Cecil and his brother, became storekeepers for a bit. One time, Gene bought some goods from them, including, apparently, a sack of flour. And when his sons were charging their father, they charged him a little more than they did anyone else around town. When Gene found out about it, he was pretty mad. "Well, Pa, there's one thing about it," Cise said. "You know, we got to pay."

The Divorce

All manner of happenings compose the course of human events that affect people's lives and feelings. Gene McIntyre and Bill Bond

Divorce decree between Silas Griffith and Elizabeth Griffith suffered being misused by their children. But in addition to his vast personal hurt, Silas's whole life was altered irrevocably by the Bill of Divorce granted Libbie on March 23rd, 1886.

The divorce was granted to Mary E. Griffith on the grounds that Silas L. "hath treated said Mary E. with intolerable severity." And with the decree, she was given the right to remove herself and the belongings she had come with - and some she had gained along the way - from the House on the Hill that had been her marital home.

> ...All the personal clothing and wardrobe... materials for making clothes... all of the jewelry and articles of ornament... one small chair that was Harry's...one piano... tablespoons and nut picks, nine silver teaspoons, one half the napkins in the house,

the endless little things, the minutiae, the monuments of domesticity were all spelled out in the Alimony along with

> picture of deceased child Harry, but said Silas L. may take or have copies of this picture at his pleasure."
>
> "In lieu of other articles of furniture, Silas L. shall pay to Mary E. the sum of three hundred dollars in money. ... And that the said Silas L. Griffith pay to said Mary E. as Alimony the further sum of twenty thousand dollars.

Whereupon Libbie moved to Boston where she lived so high, wide, and handsome that she was cautioned by her father that she had to make the fortune she had gotten from Silas last.

And Silas officially started his bachelorhood in Maple Terrace, whose attainment had symbolized a future of unparalleled good fortune but had become a ghastly mockery of his hubris.

The house was full of Harry's absence. Its silence cried for want of his laughter and every piece of furniture, every room brought back memories. Every morning, from out his bedroom window, he'd wake to see his Green Mountain empire. What good is an empire without an heir? As time went on, he came to hate the house all the more for the happiness that had been.

Minnie Remembers

As the last magnificent sound of her rendering of the "Holy City" faded and Rev. William Jackson commenced reading the Scripture lesson, Minnie sat down and dabbed at her eyes, recollecting her life with Silas after his divorce.

How she had begged him to marry her. And he wouldn't even consider it.

"It's not that I don't love you, Minnie. You know I do. And you know I'll love you 'til the day I die. But I can't marry you."

"All of a sudden, after all these years, I'm not good enough for you!"

"You know that's not it."

"I think that's it exactly. All I'm good for is a quickie when you're so inclined, right here in your office. Never a night. Never a bed. Only on this stupid fainting couch! You don't even deign to take your socks off!"

"Minnie, I want to run for senator again. I'd already started greasing the political skids when Libbie upped and divorced me. How my adversaries are crowing, Will Otis up at the Corners, all of them, figuring I'm done for. But I'll show them!

"And as you well know, Minnie, in this day and age, a man doesn't get elected to office if he's married to his stenographer. I need a proper wife."

"I'm not proper enough for you!"

"You know what I mean! Minnie, listen. I'll take care of you as if you were my wife. And my marriage will adapt itself to us, or I won't marry, I swear it. But I won't..."

Oh, those awful rows! On and on and on.

The more Minnie nagged; the more Silas took to seeing other ladies to show her she wasn't the only fish in the sea. He was an attractive man, and he attracted women to him, like Katie Pierce, William's wife.

'88 was a bad year for deaths. H. G. Lapham died in Brooklyn at the age of sixty-six and Margaret Staples, S.L.'s mother-in-law died. Everyone went to that funeral, a large funeral at the house. Laphams, Staples, Pierces, Griffiths, a big crowd. The next day, Silas left for the National Convention at Chicago. The 4th of July brought a huge fireworks display, many large and noisy, held beyond the depot, on Griffith's land.

And the Bushee-Griffith rows continued.

"Silas, I want to be your wife!"

"I've told you, Minnie, it's impossible!"

So Silas became a little more blatant about his nocturnal romps. It soon became obvious he was playing a very wide field and that he was a very jealous man. It was fine for him to do as he pleased with another man's woman, but Heaven help a man who wanted a share in his. How the town snickered when one of his ladies was seeing another gentleman, and Silas hired some of the town kids to throw pebbles at the lady's bedroom window when she was entertaining up there.

And so it went. As time went on, discretion left. He flaunted his singleness. His field broadened. His escapades multiplied. The gossips loved it!

"Did you hear how the Italian women run into their houses and lock their doors when they see him riding his horse into The Job on the mountain? "

"No! Really?"

"From what I heard, there's plenty who don't lock their doors...".

He's running two Minnie's in tandem!"

"I was told he keeps the Italian men working while he takes their women."

"No, no. That's Eddie Staples."

Griffith's behavior reflected the mood of a man cut off from the love of his son, cut off from the stability of a twenty-two-year marriage and having to put up with endless aggravation from his common-law-wife, Minnie, who, rumor had it, occasionally gave him back some of the same medicine. It was a circus.

But, if nothing else, Minnie was a pragmatist. When it became obvious to Minnie that she wouldn't win the war, she figured she'd best insure the peace, so she applied herself to that.

Miserable. Sad. Sniffling. Tearful.

"Minnie for Heaven's sakes, stop it. Please. What can I do?"

"I'm just thinking, Silas, once you're married again... And I'm just like I am, a poor working woman with nothing to fall back on, no security at all, all alone in the world.... Do you recall? *(Sniff, sniff)* When you said you'd take care of me, as if I were your wife?"

"Certainly I recall it. Will a settlement make you feel better?"

"It might help."

"You know, Minnie," Silas said one day. "I really hate to see you so upset, so unhappy. So, what I'm going to do, I'm going to try a run for senator unmarried, and if it works, it'll be so much better for us, just to keep on as we have been."

In 1890, Griffith ran for senator of Rutland County. And lost.

After that, Silas applied himself mightily to finding a bride suitable for his purposes, Meanwhile he continued the escapades during the interregnum between marriages, which established him as a legendary womanizer and was given as a rationale for his alleged syphilitic condition.

The crowning incident of all concerned a woman Silas was seeing whom a Mr. Lincoln was also quite taken with. Everyone knew Silas to be a very jealous man, but nobody expected the extreme measures he took against Lincoln.

When S.L. found out Lincoln was two-timing him with his lady friend, Silas had some of his teamsters wait outside her Mt. Tabor home and when Lincoln came out, they popped their teamster whips right to him and almost killed him.

Thoroughly disgusted by her father's behavior, Jennie, who had grown into a beautiful, extroverted woman of twenty-five, eloped. She got on the next train to Washington, D.C., with her pet canary in its birdcage her sole luggage, always recalling with a smile Will's face as she stepped off the train that day.

On August 12th, 1890 Jennie married William Hatton Riddle. Bill Riddle, a man three years younger than Jennie, had been born in Philadelphia and, at the time of their marriage, was living in Redlands, Virginia, where his family had a farm, possibly a horse farm since his brother owned Man O War, one of racing's greatest horses. Riddle was not a man of great means, but when the couple's first child, Griffith Hatton Riddle, was born in February 1892, he was tended by a governess, Bessie Childs ("Auntie B.") who was brought over from Ireland to take care of him and, later to tend a second child, Marion Elizabeth. After his own remarriage, Silas made his peace with Jennie and her husband. Eventually he hired Riddle as his General Manager.

K.T. Remembers

Meanwhile at the funeral, as Rev. Jackson continued reading the Scriptures, the widow Griffith recalled the history that had brought her to this place she never wanted to come to.

Day dreaming, K.T.'s mind drifted back to her home at 605 Wood Street, where she had lived for over thirty years and where her parents, William Milezet Tiel and her mother, the former Mary Hastings, still lived with her brother and sister. The less than palatial house looked the same as it always had, but the neighborhood had changed from a lower-middle-class neighborhood to a working-class neighborhood, from which the better-heeled families she remembered from her childhood had long since removed.

The Tiels were respectable people, but they didn't have much. Her father made furniture with his brother, Charles, who lived nearby, and her brother, Willie, a clerk, didn't bring in much of anything. The sisters brought in nothing at all.

K.T. had never considered the house crowded when she was a child, but she had to admit that once she and Nellie and Willie were well into adulthood and still living at home, even apart from periodically having to board relatives for brief periods, they were uncomfortably crowded under the same roof.

Granted, it was cramped and hardly posh, but she loved her family and was close to them and there had been many good times, especially in '85 when Charles and Willie had lived at 209 East 84th Street in New York City. Later, Charles moved out of the Philadelphia house, leaving an extra room through '87, as Willie moved from job to job - clerk, to foreman, then watchman. Ah, that extra room...

While her parents suffered the embarrassment of two spinster daughters, the homely face that stared K.T. right in the eye every morning was her guaranteed ticket to freedom. She loved her life in Philadelphia, and a full life it was with its share of close friends, women friends, love poems, and closet lovers - forbidden fruit, and all the more exciting for it! The last thing she wanted was a husband and all that went with it and even her parents gave up nagging when she turned thirty-five.

K.T. figured she was scot free when one day her cousin, Charles, dear Charles from Easton, Pennsylvania, Charles M. who worked for Taylor Wharton Steel for fifty years, Charles proclaimed to her parents that he had just heard about a very distant relative, a Vermont tycoon with political aspirations, who needed an immediate wife. How in the world had he heard that?

"Oh, you know," replied Charles Mason Griffith, "the Griffith network is legendary."

"...Of course," Charles said to the Tiels, "I rushed right over, thinking how wonderful it would be for you if it worked out with K.T...."

One less mouth to feed and the space of one less body! A dream come true! K.T.'s parents needed no persuasion from Charles or his wife, the former Ella Greene. Convincing K.T. was something else again.

They all set upon her, pounding away.

If nothing else, her parents said, she should give some consideration to them and to her sister and brother, their comfort and support.

Was it too much to expect a little in return for all they had expended on her since her birth in 1855! Never had they begrudged her, but God knows they skimped for everything. Surely she could appreciate how their quality of life would improve with a little more space and how they would all benefit from a little more money to go around.

And was she too selfish to consider that if her wealthy husband might not see fit to settle a little on them, then she, as a rich man's wife, could surely find a way to give them a little something now and then, to make their life easier or perhaps even furnish them some real comfort or an occasional luxury.

And on. And on. And on the Tiels pounded on their recalcitrant daughter until she had no choice but to finally yield a little.

In no time, Silas, eighteen years her senior, came to call. He needed a wife, to whom he could promise a life of luxury. It was as simple as that. Her parents were thrilled. There was nothing K.T. could do to get Silas to back off.

"Think of something! "she demanded of her lover, during one of their stolen times together. "Tell me what to do," she begged. Together, after a great deal of thought and consideration, they came up with a plan.

"Silas," K.T. said, when next she saw him, "I've been giving all this a great deal of consideration, and, of course, I am deeply honored that you should consider me a suitable senator's wife. But I have this problem, you see..."

Claiming jealousy, K.T. flatly refused to occupy his former marital domicile. "I just couldn't bring myself to live in a house you had shared with another woman," K.T. told him regretfully.

"Oh," Silas replied, and played every aspect of that scenario around in his mind for a few moments, after which he turned to his intended with dancing eyes and a great smile and a bark of laughter and said, "Done!"

And so, both of them prepared for their life together.

Before he even returned to Vermont, Silas visited a number of Philadelphia's best stores, where he opened accounts and gave detailed instructions as to what Miss Tiel would be needing, after which his first order of husbandly business was to send K.T. on a shopping trip.

Back in Danby, he informed everyone of his upcoming marriage to a very proper, jealous, young Main Line Philadelphian.

"How young?"

"Very young"

("What do you suppose that's like, anyway, puffin' fifty-four into thirty-six?")

Immediately, Silas started tearing down the old Lapham place, Maple Terrace, tore it right down, thriftily burned it and its memories in his charcoal kilns and on its site, in its stead, commenced erecting a fine new home with a conservatory to grow the flowers he loved so dearly (as had his mother, Sophia, whom he had adored). His new dwelling was to be ready for occupancy by the first week of September, upon the couple's return from their month-long honeymoon.

A scant ten days before his wedding day, Silas deeded half his cemetery plot to his in-laws by his first marriage, for the Staples family to use for their perpetual burial ground. It was at once an appeasement and an eternal bonding of the two families as well as a virtual guarantee that at least throughout eternity, Lib would not be far from him — an outrageous connivance that ultimately would result in his two wives being buried back to back, not fifty feet apart.

After a last reassurance to a weepy Minnie Bushee, Silas prepared for his departure to Philadelphia.

K.T., for her part, was spending as much time as possible with her sweetheart, swearing tearful assurances that it would be a very different thing, that she hated the very thought of it, and that she could be counted on to make frequent trips back to Philadelphia to see her parents and, of course, her love.

The Second Marriage

Back at the funeral, as the congregation suffered in the sweltering church, Rev. Jackson finally completed reading the Scripture and a quartet rose to sing, "There is a Green Hill Far Away." The widow Griffith, sweltering in the church, remembered well the equally sweltering morning of August 1st, 1891, when she and Silas were married at 10:00 A.M. at 605 Wood Street in the presence only of relatives (her relatives) and a few close friends of her family's. The rooms were decorated with flowers and potted plants that were already drooping from the heat when the Rev. Dr. James Shingley brought the brief ceremony to an end. With barely time for a piece of wedding cake and a toss of rice, the couple was off on the noon train of the New York and Chicago Ltd., on the first leg of their extended honeymoon.

Twelve years and two days ago, to this day of his funeral, was the start of her indoctrination to her marriage to Silas. And, of course, his indoctrination to his marriage to her. Early on, on that honeymoon, they had laid down the ground rules that would govern the years to come. Although Silas seemed to delight in poking fun at this rigid product of urban middle-class morality that would have done Queen Victoria proud, he hadn't forced himself on her at all, for which she was most grateful. For quite a while, K.T. assumed that Silas didn't care much for that sort of thing, and for quite a while, she reflected, the arrangement had been mutually beneficial.

While she had maintained her utter composure, her first sight of the elegant home Silas had built for her took her breath away. She could hardly believe such a commodious house had been built just for the two of them, albeit with sufficient guest rooms to permit her family and others to visit there for days on end. She had never dreamt people could live so luxuriously.

And the help! Maids and a laundress and, once they started serious entertaining, a chef! (Silas had discovered Barnum on one of his trips and had hired the superb chef at a goodly price, to come to Vermont and work for them.) And then there were the grounds and the gardens and the carriage house and the stables and the horses and the buggies, all taken care of by experienced help. But of all of it, Silas's favorite was the expansive greenhouse, which he delighted in and where he indulged his passion for flowers.

He spent $1,000 to $1,500 yearly on his greenhouse and his professional gardener and his florist, and delighted in the joy brought to others when he gave his marvelous flowers away. They went to Rutland Hospital, the Old Ladies' Home, and, on Sabbath to the church that on Easter received a display of lilies that would have cost $500 to $800 if bought at some city florist. His flowers also brightened innumerable sick rooms and funerals and, later, decorated the Senate in Montpelier.

Silas got such an enormous kick out of those extraordinary blooms that he shortly started exhibiting in Flower Shows. "I believe that in the culture of flowers, all credit should be given to the Supreme Maker and that I, as a grower, am simply an agent in His hands to do His will," were the words K.T.'s departed spouse would spout when his flowers captured first honors at flower shows.

Married Life

Indeed, K.T. recalled, Silas had his share of enjoyment and delight after his marriage to her. But once the initial awe of being a rich man's wife had worn off, K.T.'s life after her marriage to Silas had left virtually everything to be desired.

Any thought she might have had that Silas's countless relatives and their wives would greet her with open arms and ease her into the social life of the community, she found, wasn't the way of it at all. And, as Silas once again immersed himself into his work, she was left with virtually no companionship whatsoever. She counted the days between her trips back home, to her parents and her lover, while Silas picked up past business and plotted his future.

As his business had grown bigger, Griffith had trained several trustworthy employees in its conduct. And when it got to a size that it became utterly impossible for him to give his personal attention to every detail, he divided it into departments with a competent man in charge of each, which gave him time for other endeavors. These key men had all been with him for many years. His cousin Louie Griffith was his head bookkeeper and office manager. Honest and thorough, Louie made sure the books and everything else were in order at the Head Office. O.O. Nichols was the lord of the Depot. And on the mountain, there were Eddie Staples, Harry Ralph, and Ellis Millard. With these men in charge, and Gene McIntyre in and out, Griffith could easily turn his attention elsewhere.

To give him credit, K.T. admitted that shortly after their honeymoon Silas had tried to involve her, to some degree anyway, in her new home. Not only had he introduced her to the minister of the Congregational Church, but he had urged the Reverend to encourage

K.T. to join Ladies' Aid and Christian Endeavor and the like. Silas had also toured her around his Works and had introduced her to the majesty of the forest. If he thought it would captivate her, though, he was much mistaken.

With no pressing business but with a new mistress in his house, Griffith turned to actively pursuing politics. He saw grand entertaining as the means to further those ambitions. So to that end he started planning the construction of a vast lodge up on the mountain. It would overlook Lake Griffith, which they used to call Buffum Pond, a fifteen-to-twenty-acre body of water surrounded by creeping vines and honeysuckle.

The site, as described by a future visitor, was some four or five miles from any human habitation, in the midst of unbroken woods of thousands of acres of hill, mountain and valley, nearly 2,400 feet above sea level.

With the hope of commencing work in spring of 1893, Griffith drew up plans for a lavish lodge that would contain twenty or more fully furnished rooms where a party of twenty or twenty-five people could

K.T. Griffith

be comfortably housed and entertained. In addition to the house, there would be a large barn and a boathouse, all occupying the site which loomed some 1,400 feet or more above the South End of Mt. Tabor.

Before any of that could start, however, he needed a road.

To access the site (and also to open up new cutting areas in that vicinity), Griffith outlined plans for a road over such steep terrain that Harry Ralph looked at him in amazement. "Do you know what that would cost?" he asked his boss. "We're going to build it anyway," was Griffith's reply. So, he set Harry to the job at once upon his return to Danby in September. So when the choppers were sent out into the woods in October 1891, some of them started clearing a road course. As soon as it was warm enough in the spring of 1892 for him to start, Harry supervised the road's building by his road crews. It was a hard, hard road to build. Steep. High on the mountain with sharp drop-offs. Could it have been finished by winter 1892?

Maybe. If so, at the very earliest, construction of the Lake House didn't begin until it was warm enough in 1893 to start the job. With the best possible effort, then, the Griffiths would have been married about two and a half years before they could start using their lavish home away from home. Meanwhile, the couple entertained on a smaller scale in their new home in town.

On one occasion, some big customers couldn't get over the size of the blooms of the floral displays and wanted to know the secret of their culture. So Silas called one of his gardeners, an Italian man, to the dining room, to tell them.

"What makes them grow so large?" the guest asked him. Of course, the gardener was nervous, being in the house, and not speaking English too well. So when he heard the question, he didn't quite know how to answer it. "Fertilizer," wasn't part of his vocabulary, and if "manure" was, it didn't come to mind. So finally he blurted out, "Eets-a-plenty-o' sheet, that does it." and when the men didn't understand him, he got excited. "You know, *sheet, sheet,* plenty o' *sheet*" and while the men were still trying to figure out what he meant, K.T. stalked out of the room. A very proper lady, K.T. Griffith. Nobody said "shit" in front of her.

One can but imagine the compatibility level between this eternally composed, rigid, overly proper woman and Silas, but in his eyes she served the purpose for which she had been married.

Sundays, the couple went to church. Although Silas was known to be punctiliously prompt, the Griffiths always arrived at Services a little late, just late enough so that Silas, with K.T. stately, ramrod straight on her husband's arm, could march in solitary grandeur down the aisle, before seating themselves in the second pew on the right side, immediately behind the deacons.

Nonetheless, nightly in her bed, K.T. clutched a treasured memento from her last trip to Philadelphia, crumpled from constant handling:

She Is Coming
My dear one now is whirling, whirling
Rapidly towards love and home;
Sweet the meeting and the greeting
When safely she at last has come.
Tho' wide the distance still divides us,
Each hour shorter grows the space;
And my heart is filled with gladness,
For I soon shall see her face.
My loved one now is coming, coming!
Slow the lagging hours drag by;
Loud my heart is beating, beating,
Impatiently I wait and sigh.
Nearer, nearer still, and nearer,
Shorter doth the distance grow;
My darling to me swift is speeding,
Ah, we soon shall meet, I know!

Timber Baron, Timber Bandit

Meanwhile, life was going on as usual.

As various legal documents would allege, in November, two months after his return home, Griffith started cutting over various timber lots that one Martin Foley claimed belonged to him, an action that would result in one of the most spectacular cases of alleged timber banditry in the history of the industry.

Meanwhile, the cutters were cutting for the road to the future lodge and, lacking any other immediate project, Silas turned his attention to the culture of trout, establishing a facility at the South End of Mt. Tabor, a hamlet about three miles from Danby Borough. He was immersed in this project in September of 1892, when Aldrich v. Griffith intruded.

The case of Edgar H. Aldrich and Barney W. Aldrich v. Silas Griffith, which most spectacularly accused Silas of relocating the Wallingford-Danby town line, had started on its way through the lower courts shortly before Griffith's wedding. Whose land Griffith had cut depended, simply, on where the boundary line was between the townships...

As a newspaper reported:

> ...plaintiffs gave evidence which tended to show that the true line ran in a straight line from a marble post in the railroad embankment, at the northwest corner of Mt. Tabor, to a spruce stub at the northeast corner of the same line. Both sides agreed that the marble post in the railroad embankment was the true northwest corner of the town of Mt. Tabor

> and that the northeast corner of that town had been a matter of controversy for many years; and that in 1858, a petition was pending in the Rutland County Court by the town of Mt. Tabor against the town of Wallingford to have the dividing line between the towns established and that at that time two lines had been surveyed and marked, more or less, both starting from the marble post, one running in the general direction of the spruce stub and the other to a stone monument more than a hundred yards farther north and while Wallingford has ever since claimed the spruce stub as the northeast corner, Mt. Tabor's officers and people insisted that the stone monument was the northeast corner - in which case all cutting complained of would be in the town of Mt. Tabor, and the verdict would go to the defendant.

There are lots of stories that Griffith's men allegedly moved numerous boundary lines in the night to suit his purposes. But in the instance of the Wallingford-Mt. Tabor boundary line, it seems quite farfetched, seeing as how the disputed stone monument as the rightful northeast corner was the cause of controversy between the townships for over thirty years before Docket # 126 had come before the courts. In the September Term of 1892, the county court found for the plaintiffs, whereupon Griffith appealed, kicked the case up to the state Supreme

SILAS LAPHAM GRIFFITH

Court, and went back to his trout hatcheries at the South End.

A news clipping, believed to have been published in early 1893, establishes the South End as one of Griffith's mill villages, with its sawmill, store, post office (Griffith, VT), blacksmith shop, school and chapel and tenement houses with more houses to be added. Concerning the fish hatchery, it envisioned the completion of the project within in three years at an additional cost of $15,000 and adds that

> a mountain road from the hatchery to [Lake Griffith], 1000 or more feet above, was built last summer... opening up timber land and the development of the fish industry.... As soon as weather permits, Mr. Griffith will build...another house on the mountain, on the shores of Lake Griffith, for a keeper to protect the trout there. This lake, by the way, will figure in the experiment in the breeding line that are to be soon undertaken.

Apparently, Silas didn't want the world to know how commodious a house he planned to build up at the lake for his "trout keeper."

Although the road that was installed was to be used to open up timber land, as well as to provide access to the lake, we can be certain that Silas did not expend such large sums to reach a trout tender's bungalow.

In actual fact, as it happens, there were two roads built to the lake. A visitor described them: The news clipping reported that the first, built in 1892,

> was a considerably steeper grade [than the second road, built in 1896], and there is an S curve which makes it a less desirable road to lumber over. ...Looking back to see the teams coming behind, all double, with brakes on the wagons, I thought what would be the result should the brakes refuse to work or harness break, but happily we all reached Griffith [the South End] in safety, and spent a pleasant hour in looking over the fish hatcheries there.

This calamitous road building effort, a far cry from the awesome, direct approach Griffith had envisioned, had been built, it turns out,

> during his [Griffith's] absence a few years ago [by] an engineer who had been in his employ for thirty years...

It's surprising that the grades of this road were too steep and its curves too sharp to properly haul lumber; and that this road, which the lumber baron would seem justified in rejecting, had been built by Harry Ralph, a master road builder whose gentle grades are legendary.

It is also of interest that this road was sited very close to Martin Foley's timber holdings, which were allegedly being cut over at that time. . . .

Who would have been Harry Ralph's overseer in Silas's absence? Eddie Staples. As foreman and overseer of the mountain, Staples had full charge of the whole or a large part of cutting the wood and timber; it was also his duty as Superintendent to become acquainted with many of the lot lines.

A breath of good luck came Griffith's way in the January Term of 1893, when the Supreme Court of Vermont, in the case of Aldrich v. Griffith, 66 VT. 390, overturned, over-turned the ruling of the lower court and ruled in Griffith's favor. Apparently swayed by the officers and people of Mt. Tabor who insisted that the stone monument was the northeast corner and therefore the cutting was all in Mt. Tabor. It is of interest that the Selectmen and other officers of Mt. Tabor in 1892 were Edwin Staples, M. Barrett, B.J. Griffith, D.C. Risdon, C.L. Sowle, L.J. Griffith and Harry Ralph.

But those were frustrating days for Silas. The unforgettable road to Lake Griffith filled his head with visions of a mountain of winged $$$ bills, blackening the sky as they flew off in the air.

And then, there was the matter of Eddie, Eddie Staples, the thermometer man, the ruling King of the Mountain. Staples was tough and independent, and he did things his own way, ways that were not always Griffith's way. When Eddie had started working for his brother-in-law, he was easier, nicer in those early days. But he changed as the years went on and Silas didn't like the changes, neither in his attitude nor in his deeds. It was easier to look the other way and put up with it, but matters went from bad to worse. Staples did a number of things Griffith didn't approve of, some of which got his boss in considerable trouble.

There were those who felt that Silas was a decent person but that his help were crooked and that a lot of the petty thievery that went on he wasn't personally responsible for. But he got the cuss for the devilry they were up to. There's no question the buck ends with the boss; there's also no question but that plenty went on.

One time, for example, a drummer, a peddler, walked with his valises from the West Side, around Danby Four Corners, halfway up the mountain to peddle his wares there. It was winter. Snow. An awful hike. And of course, he was foolish to even attempt such a feat since the policy was to buy only from Griffith's stores. But the peddler persisted. When Staples apprehended him on the road, he pulled his pistol out and removed the guy's valises, dumped them in the snow, scattered his merchandise, and sent the drummer hiking back without them. But, of course, the drummer knew. Like the fella who found tobacco charged on his bill and complained, "I didn't buy it here." "It was there. You could've had it," was the reply. The drummer should have known better. Still and all, there was no reason for Staples to pull a gun and ruin all his stock.

The day came when O.O. Nichols was yammering to Silas about something Eddie had done, and Silas had it. That did it. Griffith had a belly full, and he told Staples so, told him off, faulted him. So Eddie quit. Left. That's when S.L. found out who the real king of the mountain was.

When did Staples leave? On October 4th, 1893, he was still a resident of Mount Tabor and the town's Auditor. But on March 3rd, 1894, during the Proceedings of the Board of Civil Authority of Mt. Tabor, C.L. Sowle was appointed town auditor to fill the vacancy occasioned by the removal of E.L. Staples from town. This point of fact was substantiated in the first known reportage of a trip to the Lake House. That trip took place on Memorial Day 1894 by a group invited by the Danby Grand Army of the Republic Post. The report notes, among other things,

> [Griffith's] large establishment on Mt. Tabor...is under the general management of Charles Sowle, who at one point was "our Charlie" and clerked ...at the hotel. The boys would hardly know Charlie. He is all business and has the merited confidence of his em-

> ployer. Also of interest are the following random comments in the piece: employees all respect him [Griffith] for his liberal pay and honorable dealing....His help in the woods and at the mill get all the way from $1.25 per day to $1,000 per year, house rent, garden and fuel free. ...The liberality of this man's hands...
>
> At an expense of nearly $8,000 he brought water to the village and for a nominal consideration supplies the town. ...His office near the depot is fitted with all modern appliances, ...including a typewriter.

There is no mention of fish hatcheries at the South End, but there is mention of "carriage roads" through the forest and, at Lake Griffith,

> a fine boathouse and first-class boats... in readiness for guests or patrons.

but, in this case, apparently unused.

> Domestic ducks and geese...provided for and protected by the keeper. [And about the fish in the lake,] One of the pleasantest features of this lake is the generous supply of genuine speckled trout that inhabit its waters. Under

> the fostering care of Mr. Griffith, they will soon increase in size and numbers until they will furnish a rich supply for the table. In this matter, he takes great pride and an experienced man cares for them and has a close eye for poachers.

Nor did the Club House impress them overly:

> In a few years, this wild-wood place will command...admiration of all... fortunate enough to be invited ...and enjoy the generous hospitality of its worthy owner.

All in all, a very lackluster tour. Not even a mention of refreshments, nor of Mrs. Griffith's presence. Perhaps their host was having an off day. Perhaps the hatcheries had suffered a setback. Perhaps it was that the Works were suffering the loss of Eddie or perhaps it was the monumental row between the Griffiths that changed their amicable arrangement forever.

Troubled Times

Back at the funeral, the interminable service continued. "...Always a charitable man, Mr. Griffith believed that it was not only more blessed to give than to receive," droned the Reverend, "but that there was more pleasure in giving than in receiving, and to that end, in the last years of his life, Silas Griffith entertained a party of some fifteen or twenty senior gentlemen of the town, for two days and one night at his lodge on the mountain."

Mr. Griffith, in his early sixties, was one of the youngest of the group, that ranged in age upwards to eighty-eight years. During the days, the group fished from the shore and the boat landing, and at night played euchre and other card games, smoking and enjoying social conversation. Without money and without price, chewing gum, matches, good cigars, pipes and tobacco were made available in addition to the fine food served . "The 'Boys' Club,' outing was looked forward to with pleasure, and always, with the hope that they would all survive another year, to participate in the fun - a celebration ended for all with Mr. Griffith's passing..."

As the good Reverend kept going on and on and on about S.L., his social intercourse and contributions to church and charity and so forth and so forth and so forth *ad nauseum*, K.T. Griffith remembered that "monumental row" all too well...

```
               CONTENTS                     TOGETHER . . . . . . . . . . .
               ========                     DOST THOU REGRET . . . . . . .
HOW I LOVE THEE . . . . . . . . .           GOODBYE . . . . . . . . . . .
HEART'S DESIRE. . . . . . . . . .           MY LOVE IS FAR AWAY. . . . . .
A LOVE MESSAGE. . . . . . . . . .           THE MELANCHOLY POET. . . . . .
NO LOVE SO FOND . . . . . . . . .           FAREWELL . . . . . . . . . . .
SWEET VIOLETS . . . . . . . . . .           I THOUGHT THAT LOVE WAS DONE .
LOVE'S OFFERINGS. . . . . . . . .           MEMORY . . . . . . . . . . . .
A LOVE BALLOON. . . . . . . . . .           THE SAD HEART. . . . . . . . .
LOVE'S VALENTINE. . . . . . . . .           YEARNING . . . . . . . . . . .
LOVE'S CHRISTMAS CHRISTMAS GREETING. . . .  DRIFTING APART . . . . . . . .
DOST THOU LOVE ME . . . . . . . .           ALONE. . . . . . . . . . . . .
SOMETIME. . . . . . . . . . . . .           PARTED . . . . . . . . . . . .
SHE IS COMING . . . . . . . . . .           LOST LOVE. . . . . . . . . . .
SOON WE SHALL MEET. . . . . . . .           HEART'S SORROW . . . . . . . .
WHEN WE MEET. . . . . . . . . . .           TIRED. . . . . . . . . . . . .
HOW SHALL WE MEET . . . . . . . .           MISCELLANEOUS. . . . . . . . .
I'M WAITING FOR THEE. . . . . .
```

K.T.'s Book of Poetry

K.T. had been in Philadelphia on one of her frequent visits when a radiator valve in her room leaked to the floor below and needed immediate attention. In her haste to leave, she had taken less than her usual care to put away her most personal things. So, when Silas had gone to her room to locate the source of the trouble, he had come across the brown, leather-bound volume entitled *Heart Throbs,* that contained a compilation of mimeographed love poems, authored by one Laura M. Ford, published by Comfort & Co. in Philadelphia in 1893. Curious, he had glanced through it.

As the Table of Contents indicated, the work had started in the heat of passion and ended sometime after the affair was waning, for the long-distance relationship was counterproductive to its sporadic satisfactions. With no notion that the compilation were poems that had been written and presented to his wife, with a shrug and a wince at K.T.'s choice of literary matter, Silas was about to set the volume back on her night table when a single sheet, also mimeographed and clearly typed with the author's name on the same machine as the bound selections, fell to the floor from the pages of the riffled volume and he read the poem, *Wounded:*

> *Wounded*
> 'Twas such a trifling thing, dear heart,
> And yet the hurt was deep;
> You did not see the tear-drops start,
> Though even now I weep
> As I recall your careless speech,
> Which from indifference sprang-
> Not dreaming it my heart would reach
> And cause a bitter pang.
>
> I see your glance of calm surprise;
> You ponder, and you smile;
> A kindly light gleams in your eyes:
> You wonder all the while
> What thoughtless words you now have said
> To wound this heart of mine;
> What added grief you now have made
> To cause me to repine.

SILAS LAPHAM GRIFFITH

'Twas only that you chided, dear,
And thought me selfish grown;
You did not guess the reason why"
If you could have but known
That what seemed selfish on my part
Was only love's desire!
I sought but comfort for my heart,
And did not know it would "tire."

But ah, dear heart, you did not, know
What would have made my bliss;
You did not understand; and so
You thought it all amiss.
'Tis over now! I'll dry my tears;
The ache will pass away.
Thus it has been through-all the years
'Twill come another day!
It takes so little love to wound,
And loving over-much
is why my heart must respond
To every tone and touch.
One tender word your love to prove,
And all the world is bright:
One chilling frown from you I love,
And sunshine turns to night.

You did not mean to hurt, you'll say;
It may be you were glad
To have me with you on that day,
And yet you made me sad.
I cannot tell you, dear- NO! No!
You could not understand!
Forgive me, love-we'll let it go.
This heart I must command.
—Laura M. Ford.

With a blast of fury, Silas accosted K.T. when she got home.

"How *dare* you!"

"There's nothing to discuss. It's been over for some time."

"Nothing to discuss!"

"Nothing at all."

"I forbid you from ever, *ever* again..."

"I'll not embarrass you, Silas, and I'll perform all my duties. But I'll do as I please. And what are you going to do about it, Silas? Are you going to divorce me?"

With a hint of a smile, K.T. saw her late husband as he was that evening, shaking with fury and the frustration of impotence.

Business Problems

Nor was Griffith's marriage the only problem in his life. Under Charlie Sowle, his business was suffering. So Sowle became a memory to be briefly replaced by Ellis Millard, the woods boss, as Superintendent, but that didn't work out either. Griffith soon realized Eddie Staples was indispensable. As it became increasingly clear that Silas couldn't run the Works without him, hat in hand, Griffith went out west to hire Staples back.

Gloating, Staples heard him out and finally Eddie said, "Well, I might come back. But only under two conditions,"

"And what are they?"

"For one thing, if I do come back, you'll never again tell me how to run my mountain. And for the second, you'll have to pay me $4 a day to have me."

$4 a day! Unheard of high!

Nonetheless, Silas paid. And with Staples back, Griffith's problems with the Works on the mountain ended for a while, anyway. But to oversee his entire far-flung empire of holdings and also to enjoy his grandson, Griffith Hatton Riddle, who had been born in February of

1892, he hired his son-in-law, Bill Riddle as his general manager and then S.L. once more turned his attention to the matters closest to his heart.

The Lake House, in its spectacular setting, with its wide veranda, built for large scale, impressive entertaining, was finally ready to serve its purpose. And while its awesome approach was not yet complete, still it was a fitting stage for the magnate to parade his triumphs before his guests and show off the large barn and boathouse on the site, as well as Lake Griffith that was rapidly filling with speckled trout from his hatcheries below.

As the Griffiths started to entertain, Bill Riddle was starting to work his way into his new position. He had been much impressed with his father-in-law's Head Office with its state-of-the-art telephone system with thirteen instruments that connected each mill to the main office. How handy the system actually was proved out the day a big, rugged Italian man came down to collect his pay on the 30th of the month and he complained he'd been underpaid.

"This is all we can pay you," Riddle told him. This is what Ellis sent in for you." Well...

"I'll killa-the son-of-ma-bitch, killa the son-of-ma-bitch!"

"Well, you'll have to settle with Ellis," Riddle told the man.

So the Italian went out of the office and headed up the mountain, about a four mile walk, screaming all the while, "I'll kill 'im!"

Riddle got right on the phone, pretty upset, and he said to Ellis, "This big fellow is coming up and he's going to kill you. You'd better gather some men around you and protect yourself."

And Ellis said, "All right...."

"I tell you, this is serious. This guy is all upset. He's in a killing mood." And again, Ellis said, "All right, all right."

Riddle pleaded with him some more and finally hung up. Well, Ellis didn't wait for the man to confront him in the office up there. Instead, he walked down the road a-ways about the time he thought the Italian would get there and he stood behind a tree with a stick of four-foot wood in his hand. And when the man arrived, Ellis stepped out and laid him right on the ground. Then he waited for him to come to and get up ,and he said to the Italian, "You collect your pay and then don't come back here anymore or this is just a sample of what you're going to get."

A rough business, indeed, but Riddle was a quick learner and he became a great help to Silas in many areas over the years,

Meanwhile, construction on the second road to the Lake House, the direct approach Griffith wanted, was well underway, but it was an awesome undertaking. As one article reported:

> In building this road, Mr. Griffith struck a line from top to bottom and said, "We will build the road here," and he fought it out on that line. No deviating from the course on account of ledges or solid rock to cut through or deep chasms to fill; no going around, but going through and over. This second road to the lake was about four miles long and ascended one of the steepest, most rocky and inaccessible mountain sides to be found in Vermont, this description suggests very hard climbing but the party rode over a road on which any lady might safely drive a team so far as grade or smoothness are concerned. The resulting road was smooth, dry and solid, almost the entire length of it being

Building the road from the South End to Lake Griffith
Harry Ralph in sweater

corduroyed on the upper end wherever the soil was too soft.

To build a road over a way so steep and rough that it was almost impossible for a man to climb on foot, in one place it was necessary to blast about twelve feet of solid rock off the top and side of a ridge of several rods,

> All this stone was used just below in filling a gorge fifty-six feet deep and backed up against the mountain on the other side. In another place, the mountain side was so precipitous that it was necessary to drill into the rock and drive in iron rods to hold the logs on which stone work is based. For over three miles the road is dug right out of the side of the mountain, much of the way it being necessary to blast it out on the upper side, piling the stone on the lower. In one place, the road is blasted out of the side of an almost perpendicular ledge and on the lower side the mountain side seems to be nearly a hundred feet below.

How much Griffith spent on road building to the lake varies with the amounts he supplied to various publications:

> $12,000 for the second road, $27,000 - total for the two roads (The Southern Vermont Mirror, Danby, Biography)
>
> $18,000 "for a road built solely for Mr. Griffith's lumber business" (The Rutland Evening News, during his senatorship)
>
> $30,000 for the second road. "Between the two roads, Mr. Griffith spent about $50,000 for about seven miles of road." (The Burlington Daily Free Press, 1898, during his senatorship)

Foley v. Griffith

The 1890s were costly years for Griffith, a good deal of the problem coming from an enormous increase in the Mt. Tabor tax rate. Then on November 15th, 1895, Martin Foley sued Silas Griffith. Foley! What was he doing to Griffith's aspirations? His plans! His fish! Finally, a grand Lodge in which to entertain people who counted, men he needed for the senatorial race ahead. And then Foley came along, intruding on his time and energy—and reputation. Just when he needed him least!

Just what was the suit all about? According to Martin Foley v. Silas Griffith, Docket #2306, Silas Griffith.

> broke and entered the property of the plaintiff...then and there with force and arms as aforesaid, having no privilege or right and without leave or license, cut down and carried away forty million spruce trees of the plaintiff of the value of twenty-four thousand dollars; and also, with force and arms as aforesaid, carried away from thence four million feet of spruce lumber of the plaintiff then and there lying, of the value of twenty-four thousand dollars...

Forty million trees, four million feet of lumber!

> ...and also, with force and arms aforesaid, cut down and carried away forty million other trees...

A forest! Eighty million trees. How many men would it take how long to cut down, with axes or cross-saws, eighty million trees?

Ah, Foley... That was a humdinger! With fond recollection, Judge Joel Baker recalled Docket #2306, probably one of the most celebrated legal actions in Rutland County. For four years it would occupy the courts, outliving the Plaintiff, Martin Foley, and enduring through a particularly public period during Grifffith's life when he could least afford the notoriety it brought him. As a judge, Joel couldn't represent Silas directly, but wherever possible, he was behind the scenes and what a romp it was.

Especially considering its timing, the case would undoubtedly have been settled out of court, for there had been all manner of dealings between them and, according to the papers of the case, Griffith had promised to pay Foley certain sums on demand "for the use, rent and occupation of his premises," yet, though often requested, he neglected and refused to pay them.

It's more than possible that Griffith was feeling a little pinched. Most of his wealth was tied up in real estate. Plus, it had been a period of massive expenditure between the roads, the trout hatcheries, his new residence, the Lake House, and the 300% increase in the Mount Tabor tax rate, of which, one source estimates, Griffith's share was two thirds of the entire town tax. Never one to maintain large cash balances, on at least one occasion he had borrowed a large sum of money from John B. Griffith to pay funds necessary to proceed with a lawsuit.

Martin Foley must have felt Griffith was at least temporarily strapped, because a scant week after the Writ was filed, Foley's lawyer attached Griffith's teams, his mills and business holdings in Mt. Tabor for $25,000 and his home and personal property in Danby for an additional $25,000.

Almost apoplectic, Silas had raged to Baker, "Those attachments! That did it! The frustration. The aggravation. The press! All of Rutland County thinks it a great joke, Martin Foley suing me! To go up before a jury with a case like that. And I can't lose, I can't lose and win

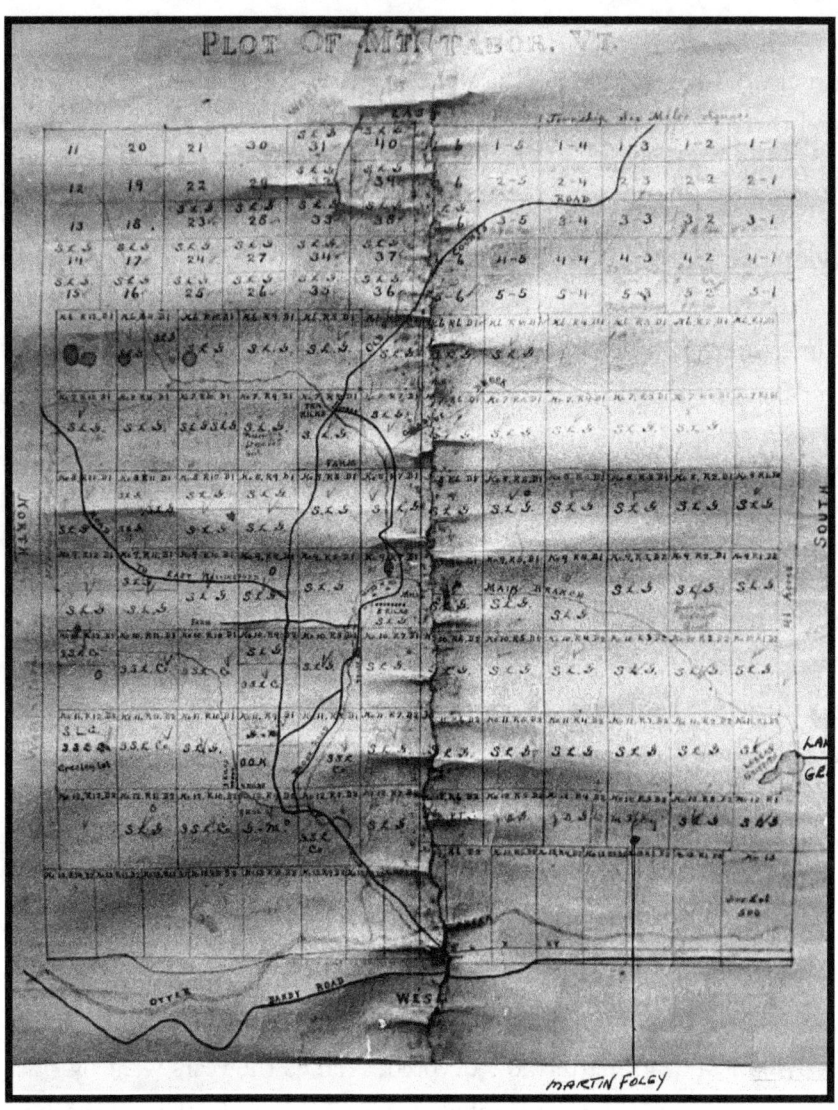

Plot of Mt. Tabor

an election! I can't! How to put Martin Foley out of business *fast* is right at the top of my agenda. And as for you Joel, you work with my lawyer and you see to it that he does everything to bleed Foley dry!"

Actually, in the Foley action, instead of using surveyor Croft, who usually did his work and whose lines might have wandered a little here and there in accordance with his client's wishes, Bates was the surveyor of record on Docket #2306.

Minnie Troubles

Nor was Martin Foley the only cause of Griffith's distress The day came when Minnie Bushee poured oil on the fire of his already flaming fury. When all was said and done, Minnie had no one to think about except Minnie and she did a lot of that. It seemed to her forever since she had started ministering to Silas, and whatever forays she had occasionally undertaken with other admirers were inconsequential and short lived, a little fun, just right for her then-circumstances. But times had changed. Silas was once more a married man and how it hurt her to see his proper wife, Mrs. Hoity-toity Grand Lady Griffith, go through the moves and roles required of her, acting as hostess to his important guests, marching into church on his arm on Sundays, accompanying him here and there, the paragon of propriety, living the rich life, living the life that should have been hers.

Meanwhile, Silas, pushing sixty, had attained a delicious balance of stability between wife and mistress, that it seemed he would enjoy for the rest of his life. But Minnie wasn't getting any younger and she was tired of fun. She wanted stability in her life, too, a husband, not a married lover, no matter how devoted. And as the years went by since his marriage to K.T., she wanted to hurt Silas back, the way he hurt her, knock away some of that stability he so took for granted.

I'll give him back some of his own medicine! she thought

Minnie was a smart lady. So, with malice afore thought, Minnie took a lover, a very special lover, indeed.

One day, after a particularly frustrating session discussing Foley strategy with his attorneys, Silas couldn't wait to reach the sanctuary of his private office. With relief, he unlocked the door to the room that was Minnie's and his little home, their place, to which only he and Minnie had a key. But there, in their inner sanctum, in his private office, he walked in on Minnie, defiling their couch, their green plush fainting couch, with his cousin, Louie Griffith, his head bookkeeper and Office Manager.

A moment to be remembered, that was!

"Before you fire me, Silas, I quit!" said Louie as he stormed out, pulling up his trousers en route. Meanwhile, Minnie had just looked at him, with tears rolling down her cheeks. "Now you know the hurt you've caused me, Silas. I want to be married, Silas. I should've been your wife..." *My God, what a mess!* Cuckolded by his common-law wife, violated by his inviolate cousin and employee!

L.J. Griffith had hardly left town for Batavia, Illinois when Silas replaced utterly honest, indispensable Louie with his cousin, Wilbur Griffith, Julius' son, who would prove to be quite different in character.

In no time at all, it was Town Meeting day again on Mt. Tabor, March 3rd, 1896, with L.J. Griffith notably absent forever from the roster of officers of the town of Mt. Tabor, a position he had so prominently served in the past.

Tax Time Again

As always, setting the tax rate was part of the business of the meeting. If the Mt. Tabor taxes were already grievously high, they were about to get even higher.

Silas Griffith is held personally responsible for pushing through the tax rates in Mt. Tabor. He is blamed for it and damned for it. How can a man force a town's vote? When most of the voters are one's employees and the vote is taken by a show of hands, that's how.

Why is he said to have done it? Because it benefitted Silas Griffith. Griffith had power enough to raise the poll tax to $20, which many farmers couldn't pay, so they sold their farms to Griffith. Some said, too, that he did it to pay for roads and bridges. Ohers opined that he did it to put Martin Foley out of business.

An alternate reason for Mt. Tabor's excessive taxes and one that Danby, as William Pierce put it, "was too selfish to do anything to aid in the undertaking" was for the building of the Lebanon Springs Railroad, as set forth in some pre-election press in the *Editor Sentinel* in 1898:

> The high taxes in Mt. Tabor are the result of a bonded debt contracted years ago to build the Lebanon Springs railroad in the state of New York, which, together with accrued interest, has taken over $80,000 from the pockets of taxpayers, and for which Mr. Griffith is in no way responsible; he having fought successfully to keep his own town from bonding when he had but little interest in Mt. Tabor, now has to draw his check for two thirds of the big tax in this town. If he has outstripped his neighbors in an honorable competition in business, it is due to his superior judgment and foresight rather than any control which he has over the vote or finances of this town.

If, in fact, Griffith did engineer the increase, aside from the amount of his own tax bill, it cost him dear politically and would seem to have been better postponed until after the senatorial election. In any case, the 1000 cent tax rate had been continued in 1897, before dropping to 500 cents in 1898 and 1899.

How did the residents of Mt. Tabor handle these onerous taxes? Most probably paid the normal poll tax and suffered no consequences, or, by agreement with Griffith, "You pay half and I'll pay the other half." Others simply moved out of town, establishing residence in Danby and then moved back to Mt. Tabor - a course taken by Ellis Millard and O.O. Nichols, among others. Some couldn't avoid the taxes. One man's uncle didn't pay the tax and found the amount docked from his pay.

The Ladies

Needless to say, life did not stand still in Danby while the Mt. Tabor tax issue was raging next door. S.L.'s women were, each of them, completely absorbed in taking care of Number One.

In the years since her marriage, K.T. had become well-adapted to the role of a rich man's wife and had investigated various avenues to fulfill her own life. Slowly, she had interested herself in church affairs and other suitable functions and was researching the requirements necessary to join the various women's prestigious Societies such as the D.A.R. and other comparable organizations.

Minnie, for her part, became seriously embroiled with Jay Bromley who had the Box Shop. (Silas couldn't fire him because Jay didn't work for him.) And though Minnie knew it killed S.L. to have to share her with Jay, she knew he surely loved her, for he swallowed his bile and gave Minnie his love to the very end, and even gave Jay his business. But Bromley refused to deal with Griffith at all, and it was Bill Riddle who mediated between them and got Jay to do whatever work was required.

Even now that he was gone, Minnie had to admit that Silas had treated her very honorably. He'd kept his word. Financially, he settled on her the exact same $20,000 he'd paid Libbie in Alimony—a fortune, for a wife's usage. And while she had sizzled a little, hearing about the proper Main Line lady he was going to marry, one look at K.T. was enough to prove he'd certainly kept his word about making a marriage that would not interfere with their love affair.

A Jury Trial

Throughout it all, Foley v. Griffith, Docket #2306 marched inexorably forward, until, in the September Term, 1897 of the Rutland County Court, the matter was tried by jury.

For three weeks, the jurors were bombarded with conflicting testimony about the value of the timber cut, which differed materially between the parties, Foley claiming damages of $24,000 and Griffith stating $1,000 or less as the value of the timber cut. More than one hundred deeds were introduced to demonstrate ownership; conflicting surveys and plans to demonstrate lot lines (many of which were disputed); and, last but not least, boundary lines having to be determined by the age of markings on trees, by counting the grains in the wood.

Legend reports that Griffith had gotten on reasonably good social terms with Foley while his help moved the line and, in fact, in the Foley action, a large part of the original markings had disappeared and the true location of the original survey depended on the study of remaining fragments of marks. Presumably, in such a situation, it would be relatively easy to "move a boundary line."

Legend further has it that Martin Foley not only sued Griffith for cutting over his land, but also for relocating the Wallingford-Mt. Tabor town boundary line, but this legendary blending with the Aldrich action is patently untrue. The Foley action was sufficiently notorious on its own without this embellishment.

SILAS LAPHAM GRIFFITH

The trial lasted three weeks and resulted in a disagreement of the jury and a continuance of the cause. Griffith's Motion for Continuance and Affidavit, dated March 8th, 1898, reached the courts in the March Term of 1898.

Portions of the Affidavit read as follows:

> I, Silas L. Griffith, ...on oath depose and say: That I expected to be ready for trial at the present term, ...and I am informed by my counsel and believe that...I cannot safely go to trial again without the testimony of Edward L. Staples, who now resides at Morrison in the state of Illinois. ... That for twelve years, Edward L. Staples was in [his] employ, much of the time as foreman and overseer on the mountain in Mt. Tabor and had full charge of the whole or a large part of the work there of cutting this wood and timber. That as such Superintendent it became his duty to and he did become acquainted with many of the original lines in this survey. ...Agreed to come and testify ....asked him to come,... received no answer. ...That said Staples left this defendant's employ and went West to live before this suit was brought.

Really?

Eddie Staples had started his employment with Griffith in January 1883. A full twelve years of service would have required his employment through January 1895. At the end of '93 or the first months of '94, Charles Soule was appointed Auditor of Mt. Tabor to fill the vacancy of E.L. Staples, who had removed from town. No mention of Staples appears again in the Mt. Tabor Records.

But Staples wasn't away long, nor did he move west at that time. Ed Staples is in Danby's Grand List of 1894, having removed to his family's farm at Danby Four Corners, where Ed is also on the List in 1895, and "Staples" is listed in 1896 and 1897, although omitted in 1898 and 1899. The Original Writ of Docket # 2306 was dated November 15th, 1895 and the case was tried in the September Term, 1897.

Griffith's Affidavit goes on to state that on the advice of counsel, he cannot safely go to trial without the testimony of his surveyor, Mr. Bates. And he believes that Bates would come now if he was able to do so and is confident he will come at any time "when he recovers from his present illness"...

Appended to the Motion for Continuance were a number of sworn statements including one from Everett E. Potter, M.D. of Pownal, dated and sworn March 7th, 1898:

> I, Everett E. Potter...am the family physician of Daniel T. Bates...and am attending him at the present time.
>
> He is now suffering and has been for some nine days from congestion of the lungs caused by a severe cold, which renders it very imprudent and dangerous for him to go out of door for some time to attend to any business.

Oh, the shenanigans!

The day after Griffith's Motion of Continuance, with its appended Affidavits, was the beginning of the court's 1898 March Term.

To wit, this deposition (here paraphrased)

I, Edward Foley... on oath depose and say — That I am a son of the plaintiff... and that the plaintiff himself is of advanced age,... in feeble health and unable to give personal attention to the preparation of said cause.

I came to Rutland on Monday evening, March 7th, . . . to assist, ...and at about 8:00 P.M. ...was notified by George Lawrence, of counsel for defendant, that a motion for continuance would be presented, but he gave no information as to the cause either to me or to Mr. Howe, plaintiff's counsel. Thereupon, plaintiff's counsel went with me to Mr. Lawrence's office to make inquiry as to the cause of the motion for continuance. I did not go into the office, but remained in the vicinity and very soon after plaintiff's counsel left, I saw Mr. Lawrence going in great haste to the Telegram Office, where he wrote a message.

Plaintiff's counsel then informed me that the defendant's counsel would seek a continuance on account of the alleged sickness of Mr. Daniel Bates of Pownal and I was therefore requested by counsel to go to Pownal as quickly as possible to see Mr. Bates and ascertain his condition.

I left Rutland by the midnight train and observed that Mr. F.S. Platt of counsel for defendant was a passenger. Mr. Platt got off at Bennington and I also got off at Bennington, believing that Mr. Platt knew the whereabouts of Mr. Bates, while I did not. At Bennington, I procured a conveyance and drove to Pownal to the

> residence of Mr. Bates and found that Mr. Platt had already arrived. I saw Bates and conversed with him; he appeared to be in good health and said to me his health was good. Upon my inquiring, he told me he had been out every day... about his usual work and business and that he intended to do the same on that day, which was Tuesday, March 8'. Mr. Bates said that he had a cold, but did not claim that he had been or then was sick in bed or confined to the house and repeatedly said that he was "all right."
> (Sworn to March 9th, 1898)

Apart from their gall at rousing Bates in the middle of the night, for a man who didn't know Bates' whereabouts, Foley found his home readily enough without chasing Platt there in plain view. And why Foley's Affidavit waited until the 9th, when he had his information shortly after midnight of the 8th, is a puzzle. Surely, it would have had more impact had it arrived earlier. Instead, the Motion for Continuance beat it.

And on March 9th, 1898, Daniel P. Bates himself swore that although for the past ten days he had suffered from a severe cold, he had managed to attend to his business until the day before yesterday he felt so sick he had to give up and was presently confined to the house and advised by his physician not to leave his house for a number of weeks to come, and feels entire unwell and unable to go to Rutland, a statement reconfirmed by Everett Potter, M.D. and verified by one Henry S. Goodall, M.D. Of Bennington, both physicians' statements sworn on March 9th, 1898.

The paper storm from Docket #2306 arrived like a hurricane, filed in August, for the September Term of the Court.

SILAS LAPHAM GRIFFITH

On August 15th, Plaintiff's Motion for a Continuance arrived. Designated the 7th paper of the Court in Foley v. Griffith, Foley objected on the grounds that assistant judges do not constitute a quorum, and moved for a continuance until Judge Start would be present. By the 25' of August, six additional court papers were filed, five of them between August 16th and 17th:

```
Defendant's Application Order for a Struck
Jury (#8)
Plaintiffs Objection (#9)
List of 48 Names (#10 )
Certificate of Names Stricken Off (#11)
List of Twenty-four Special Jurors (#12)
Special Venire (#13)
```

The trial was scheduled to start on September 14th, opening the September Term of the Court. There would be five additional documents in 1899, for Docket # 2306, eighteen, in all, a thick packet of skullduggery, best forgotten. "Get rid of it," was Sile's terse directive to Joel Baker, when the matter was finally concluded.

Sitting at the funeral a few years later, Joel remembered taking care of that, thanks to an obliging courthouse clerk, who assured him that the papers of the trial had been permanently misplaced and the jackets of the progression of motions and objections and legal diversions had been hidden well away in the dusty archives, sometimes mis-indexed or mis-filed. "It would take a real ferret to chase them down," the clerk had assured him with a wink. "The story those jackets told... That guy, Griffith, he was a *crook!*" the clerk said, shaking his head, "He bought out juries!" And then, with a laugh, "I bet I'm not the first one to say that about him in these hallowed halls."

ANN K. ROTHMAN

Running for Office

> S.L. Griffith, one of the candidates for senator in this county is the most unpopular man in the county if not in the state,

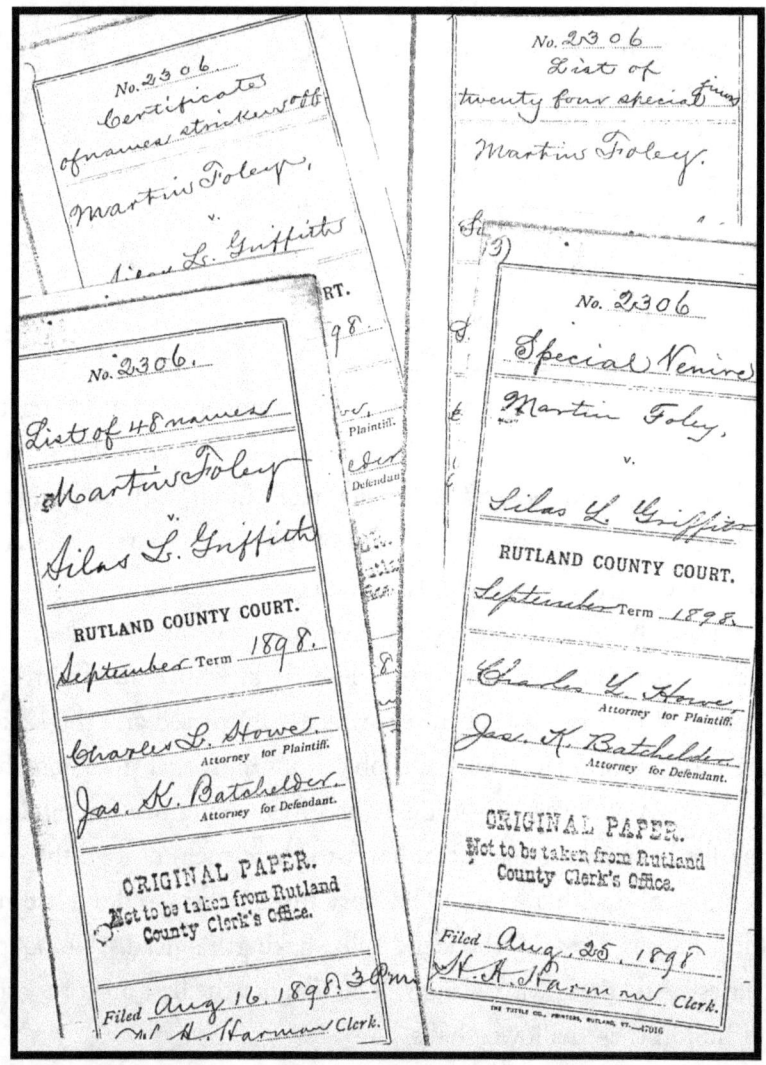

Legal documents

trumpeted the *Poultney Journal* in a muckraking vendetta that took up much of their editorial page on September 2nd, 1898. Meanwhile Silas continued campaigning in great style at the Lake House, entertaining a party of sixteen which gained some good press for his trouble: There were the J.D.S. Packers and Dr. and Mrs. T.A. Cootey, and the Tarbells, Trasks, and Allards, and the L.T. Fletchers and the J.E. Fletchers and the Milton Whites. And after a tour of the grounds and flowers and hatcheries and roads, they arrived at the Lake House, where K.T. and her friends made them welcome. Then, chef Barnum sounded the foghorn and the party sat down to a beautiful dinner, after which they went boat riding and fishing. Nearly all caught something: Mrs. Fletcher caught the largest trout and Dan Allard caught a duckling. It was great fun, all reported. And that evening, there was vocal and instrumental music, and good old hymns. Griffith sang and told a few stories, and Jud Packer held his sides in laughter as if in pain. It was grand. They left the next day.

Without question, Griffith needed all the good press he could get. There had been remarkably little election news in the press, which had filled its pages with reports of the Spanish-American War, which had broken out in April and was over by mid-August, after which the up-coming election got wide coverage.

Shortly before Election Day, the following letter was forwarded to all the papers for publication:

> APPEAL TO REPUBLICANS
> TO THE REPUBLICANS OF
> RUTLAND COUNTY:
> The undersigned republican voters of Danby and Mt. Tabor, invite your attention to the following facts relating to the candidacy of S.L. Griffith

for senator:

Mr. Griffith secured the nomination in the county convention through delegates who pretended to represent Danby, but who were never elected by the republicans of that town. This delegation was chosen at secret caucus, no notice of which was given to the public, and at which there were only a few persons present, including Mr. Griffith. A caucus was held in Danby to elect delegates to the county convention, which was regularly warned by the republican town committee, and at which a large number of republicans were present. This caucus elected delegates who were opposed to Mr. Griffith's nomination, but they were unseated by the county committee, and the Griffith delegates were admitted, in spite of a written protest signed by a large majority of the republican voters of Danby.

We believe that Mr. Griffith ought not to be elected to the senate of the state of Vermont; that the same reasons which caused his defeat in 1890 apply with even greater force today, and that the true interests of the republican party in this county and state demand that he should not be

> elected to that office of trust and honor.
>
> We, therefore, appeal to our fellow republicans in Rutland County to unite with us in voting for Mr. S.M. Rising of Pawlet in the place of Mr. Griffith.
>
> Signed by eighty-eight
> voters from Danby and
> six from Mt. Tabor

In an editorial, the *Rutland Herald* stated that they printed the letter as an advertisement,

> because we hardly consider it of enough importance to print as news. As we understand the matter this opposition to Mr. Griffith represents simply a local feud and does not concern the general public. Mr. Griffith was nominated in the convention fairly, would unquestionably have been nominated if both the Danby and Mt. Tabor delegations had gone against him, and he will unquestionably be elected.

But the opposition fared substantially better with the *Poultney Journal*, editor Humphrey starting off his bray with the cautionary header:

> DO NOT BE HUMBUGGED
> Some prominent republicans in this

county claim that a paper ballot is not legal. Let us urge everyone to pay no attention to such caviling; it is only a bluff intended to disenfranchise the voters who vote for any other person than those on the republican ticket. They have tried every dodge known to sharpers to compel the election of S.L. Griffith and his compeers. They claim that writing is the only way. This we deny and defy them to point to any such law... set your mind at rest. The law contemplates that every man should vote for the man of his choice. Do not be humbugged. Cast your vote for S.M. Rising and elect an honest man.

And after going on at the *Herald* for being so flippant over the protest of one hundred republican voters (having puffed up ninety-four signatures), and making the point that the Herald, ...which assumes to be fair to all men, ...closed its own eagle eyes [because] ...Mr. Griffith is a stockholder in the Herald association and the truth should not be spoken at all times.

One hundred good republicans of his own town are protesting against his election on the grounds of unfitness,

> not that he is an imbecile but that he is a dangerous man to be placed in office. His method of conducting his campaign shows the character of the man. His favorite scheme is to invite delegations from different parts of the county to visit his place whom he dines and wines in the most lavish manner. A temperance man himself yet he does not hesitate to furnish his political friends all the good things to drink they can hold.

Humphrey felt that was such a dastardly thing to do that he threw it in twice and also the statement that Griffith loaded these emissaries with "boodle," a claim he rehashes further on:

> The emissaries that scour the country from one end to the other on his behalf are not in it for their health, nor do they go with empty pockets, but are generally prepared to place money where it will do the most good. It is a campaign of corruption so far as Mr. Griffith can make it and if the republicans will not rebuke him as he was rebuked in 1890 it may safely be stated that money saved him. Will the honest republicans of Rutland County stultify themselves by electing Silas L. Griffith? The workingmen of the county and every man who is not bound

> to [sic] much to party should be sure to cast their vote for S.M. Rising, an upright citizen and a friend to the workingman.

It was a bitter fight, that election, all the worse because the battlefield was his home town of Danby. The opposition to Griffith's candidacy, "the Otis Post Office faction," as it was called, originated not in the village, the Borough, but in Danby Four Corners, up in the hills. Will Otis, who had the store and the post office up there was at the bottom of it. The fact that Will's older brother, old H.F. who got the farm, thought the world of Sile, didn't do a thing to lessen Will's enmity, for there was a good deal of feeling between the two brothers and their opinions about things were often diametrically opposed.

Will Otis was a popular man up there, a sort of *de facto* mayor of those parts, and he was also an ambitious man, an incumbent in collusion with the Democrats, an alliance formed solely to effect Griffith's defeat. When Griffith won the nomination in the county convention in June, oh, he was mad. So, he mustered his troops, his sons and cronies---the "best men of the Republican party," to paraphrase Humphry—and they wrote up that letter, the Appeal to Republicans and forwarded it around to all the papers. Early in the campaign it was agreed by this faction that in the event Griffith's nomination, the Republican vote of the town should be turned over to the Democrats.

And then, right in the middle of all of it, a few days before Election Day, the local papers ran another header:

> **THE FOLEY-GRIFFITH CASE NOT TO BE TRIED THIS TERM**

The trial of Foley v. Griffith, Docket #2603, scheduled for September 14th, a few days after Election Day, was again postponed, this time for an entire year. And regardless of whatever machinations defendant Griffith might have undertaken to accomplish another delay, this time, without question, it was Martin Foley who was responsible: He died.

A few days later, this sharply abridged article hit the papers:

> SENATOR ELECT S. L. GRIFFITH
> HOW HE TRIUMPHED OVER HIS ENEMIES
> IN RUTLAND COUNTY, VERMONT
> MT. TABOR, September 12,1898
> EDITOR *SENTINEL*:
>
> The battle...for a straight republican ticket having been fought and fairly won, ...letters and telegrams of congratulations are now pouring into his office by the score, and he is really the happiest man in town.
>
> ...During the progress of the campaign and when those kicking republicans, gangrened with jealousy and envy, had worked themselves up to a white heat, the services of the *Poultney Journal* were called in and Mr. Griffith was pitched into in true pugilistic style. After being divested of all his good qualities, he was put through a smut mill, but came out bright as a new cent.
>
> The clerks, mechanics and common laborers whom he has had in his employ from five to twenty-five years,

> attest his popularity as a friend of the workingman.
>
> In the total republican vote of this town, 101, his majority was 100, the largest vote ever polled in the history of the town for a single candidate.

One hundred votes, the most votes cast for any man in any office, for senator; more votes than any one person had received in any of the prior ten years of elections, as far back as was checked. How many votes had the other three men running with him received? Ninety-four votes each. And in Danby, Silas carried the Republican vote two to one.

Imagine the almost unbearable joy of the man at having won his hardest battle and having achieved his final ambition; and imagine his almost unbearable loneliness for having no one to share it with.

There, before him and for him, a great victory celebration, a torchlight parade under a fine September evening sky, with his mountain the backdrop of a procession over a third of a mile in length, reaching from the depot to Main Street, consisting of sixty-five horses and their riders bearing torches and transparencies, followed by a drum corps and five hundred footmen, and the hills ringing with their rejoicing.

All that for the son of David Griffith, Jr., a poor farmer. All that accomplishment, all those people surrounding him, the center of it all, and he alone in their midst.

A thousand citizens from Danby, Mt. Tabor and adjoining towns, witnessed and joined in the parade. Supporters and employees joined to pay their respects and to celebrate his victory. It was all crowned by an elaborate display of fireworks upon the hillside, contributed by Mr. Griffith's workmen, adding a further brilliancy to the occasion.

Later that evening, at his residence, the successful candidate received his friends' congratulations on his better than 2,500 county-wide majority. Finally, after the last cigar had been handed out and the last back slapped and the last toast made and the final hails and hearties had been exchanged, the guests had left and the Griffiths were alone in the House on the Hill.

Sile nodded good-night to K.T., went to his bedroom, and crawled between the cold sheets. He thought about the women in his life, who, if choice be given him, he would want to share his bed with, this night. He considered Minnie, for whom he cared deeply and certainly loved in a way, but that was very different now that he was sharing her with Bromley. And right before he fell off to sleep, his mind drifted to the all-too-infrequent moments of true intimacy he had shared with Libbie, his true love.

The following week, Silas and Eugene McIntyre left for Iowa to purchase three carloads of horses to be used on their Works.

Senator Griffith

There was a change in Silas in the years after that, lacking battles to fight or aims to achieve.

Within the ranks of the senate, he was, for the first time, a member of a body of men with whom he had much in common. And he blossomed and mellowed with enjoyment of the collegiality, the congeniality, and in Montpelier, he furnished marvelous blooms from his conservatory, winning him a resolution of appreciation and thanks. The flowers brightened up the senate chamber, where he good-naturedly sponsored his self-serving Fish Bill, Griffith's Bill, Senate Bill #23, which would allow the sale of trout from private hatcheries during February, March and April and would give him "quite a bonus" —a bill that gained little if any publicity in Danby.

Understandably, Silas avoided the Foley trial, which was on the Court calendar for the September Term of 1899. On the 9th of August, he re-instituted his paper storm with a List of 48 Names, followed

Legal documents

the next day with a Certificate of Names Stricken Off and A List of 24 Special Jurors. On September the 6th, a Venire was filed for Special Petit Jurors, that was followed by a Notice on September 19th, 1899 that Docket # 2306 was settled and discontinued without costs.

Cuba

A trip to Cuba by the Griffiths was a highlight of Silas's senatorial service.

| **REAL CUBA** |

was the bold header from an undated Burlington paper for an article of surprising length.

> ```
> State Senator Griffith gives the Pub-
> lic New Light ...Penetrated the Heart
> of the Island and Saw the Natives at
> Home – His Solution of the Cuban Prob-
> lem
> ```

was the sub-header of the piece which commenced with a letter from Griffith:

> ```
> It being New Year's, and not being
> where I could make children happy in
> Danby and Mt.Tabor, I thought I would
> see what I could do in Manzanilla.
> I procured about 100 (centavos)cents,
> and gave each child I met begging, one
> centavo, and wished I had more pen-
> nies.
> ```

It says something for Griffith's vitality at the age of about sixty-three, that this report of the Cuban trip states that Silas made the journey

> for the purpose of learning the opportunities for the successful investment of American capital in timber lands," and the article goes on to note that "should be stated here that the report sent out by a writer in Washington that Sen. Griffith had purchased 3000 acres of timber land in Cuba is entirely false. He looked over some tracts but has not made any purchases as yet.

Griffith's approach to problems is revealed in his solution of the Cuban question. Not at all enamored with military administration for Cuba and feeling that the soldiers there are too anxious to "whip" the Cubans whose real nature they don't understand, Griffith said his way of dealing with the Cubans would be "first to give the Cuban $25 for his rifle and ammunition and as capital to purchase tools to begin the cultivation of his property. Give him to understand that if he has been industrious that at the end of three months, he will be loaned another $25 and so on until he has been allowed $100. This sum is as good as $1,000 here and will give every honest Cuban a chance to start in life again. Having secured his gun and ammunition with the first $25 we would have the Cuban disarmed and with the remaining $75 conditional upon an industrial life, we would have the Cuban bound to a useful life for a given period and so well started in the industrial pursuits that it would be unnecessary to 'whip' them again, and at less cost than a continued military occupation of the island."

And then there is the humor of the man:

While on the boat to Cuba, Griffith took considerable pleasure in hearing the various speculations about sea sickness.

"You would think," he wrote, "to hear the passengers talk, they all expected to be seasick. None have been sick - a disappointment to a lot of tourists.
When I left my stateroom to join Katie (Mrs. Griffith) for dinner, I found her chewing gum for all she was worth, and knowing she never used it at home, inquired the cause, and strange as it may appear, she replied: To prevent seasickness...
...Some of the lady passengers started the report that this was a sure specific for seasickness and inside of half an hour you should have seen the women on this ship chewing gum... One woman of the group was an old lady, without teeth. Her jaws had a sideways motion and at times her chin would nearly touch the end of her nose, but this had no effect... Katie with the rest - they kept on chewing...

The Funeral Draws to a Close

"...Increasingly, at the end of his life," droned the Rev. Samuel Jackson relentlessly, Silas Griffith took his greatest pleasure doing unto others, giving back to the people of the town and the community he loved, to the family, as it were, that he was a part of. "To make heaven for others is heaven enough for him," Jackson said, believing that the heaven that is in store for him after the breaking of the 'silver cord,' is the heaven he made on earth.

"...For his neighbors, the citizens of the town, who have clamored for a library for the past fifteen years, plans for a fine Library have been drawn to hold the books lovingly collected by the late William Pierce of this community and others who tirelessly accumulated volumes in the old Reform Club for the enlightenment of the public..."

ANN K. ROTHMAN

The Rev. Samuel Jackson rambled ever onward.

"During the early months of 1901, Mr. Griffith toured the Mediterranean and the Holy Land. A tour of the Holy Land is usually an unrelentingly sober experience, but even there Silas Griffith's sense of fun came forth as he haggled the use of an Arab's garb for an amusing photographic memento of himself in that costume.

"But his thoughts were ever on the betterment of the lives of others.

"When Mr. Griffith was in Palestine, after his visit to Jerusalem and Bethlehem, it occurred to him that he would give the children of Danby and Mt. Tabor just such a Christmas tree as he believed Christ would have given them, were he on earth and in this place, an intention brought to fruition on Christmas Eve 1901, when he initiated the practice of holding a grand party in this church...

Silas in Palestine

SILAS LAPHAM GRIFFITH

"On that first occasion, three spruce trees that reached nearly to the ceiling were mounded with upwards of 500 presents for the 140 children present from Mt. Tabor and the Borough, from whence he drew his work force. On these occasions he always invited and urged all children to be present, regardless of religious preferences or whether or not they ever attended church, his earnest endeavor being to bring all children together at this time, rich, poor, Catholic, Protestant. ...If any distinction must be made in the distribution of gifts, he endeavored to favor the poor, believing that on this day of the year above all others, there should be on earth Peace and good Will to men...."

"I say, "whispered one of the senators who had arrived so early, to his associate, "How much longer do you suppose this chap can go on?"

"Not much," replied his companion grimly, mopping his sweaty brow. "He's already at 1901. How much more could Silas have done for the town between now and the day he died?")

"...and while in Bethlehem, the headquarters for the manufacture of rosaries and crosses," the good Reverend rumbled onward, "Mr. Griffith purchased a rosary for each of his Catholic friends and on Christmas gave them the rosary and with it sent a letter, extracts of which I would like to read here today...

...I purchased some rosaries, and to make them the more interesting and appreciative, I purchased them near the entrance of the Church of St. Mary, a church that stands on the spot where it is supposed Christ was born. I brought them with me until I arrived at Rome, and when there took them to the Vatican and had them blessed by the Pope.

With this letter I send one of the rosaries which please accept as a slight token of my friendship and as a Christmas present.

Hoping that the future years of your life may be numbered by the beads of this rosary, and wishing you a Merry Christmas, I am,

Your friend,

S.L. Griffith!

("A Catholic friend of mine got one of those and found the letter offensive," whispered one woman to another. Well, I asked her, "Why?" and she explained that there are fifty-three beads in a rosary plus six Our Fathers-totaling fifty-nine beads in all, although a devout Catholic counts them omitting the Our Fathers. "I'd feel he was putting a limit on my life," she said to me.

"People are funny, "her companion replied, shaking her head. "They believe what they want to believe. I've heard some Catholics say he disliked Catholics, and that phrase might well be responsible for them touchy ones feeling that way.")

"...In answer to the question, 'Can a Christian, through benevolences atone for his sins and save his soul?' *No!* is the answer," bellowed the Reverend, finally winding down. "...although this is a common belief, prevalent in all societies and classes, it is not the Bible's teaching... A person cannot make up for his sins by benefices.

"True giving is giving out of gratefulness to God, wanting to give, as Silas Griffith gave... God reads the heart..."

Finally, a prayer was read. A hymn, "Fear Not, I Am With Thee," was sung. The benediction was pronounced, and the audience left the church to Chopin's funeral march, rendered on the organ by Mr. Engels. The casket and remains were borne to the hearse by a group of Griffith's long-time employees, including Eddie Staples who had been back in town on the family farm since 1900, since the Foley trial had been settled. And, of course, Harry Ralph, was included among the pallbearers, all of whom had worked for Griffith for more than twenty years.

As he was performing this final task, Harry considered the changes the last years had brought. Word had gotten around that at one point Silas had asked McIntyre to buy a parcel of land in Peru and sometime later asked if he had done so, to find that McIntyre had bought it all right, but he had bought it for himself, and, sure enough, in

1901, 100 acres of Peru land had been sold to Warren McIntyre in one of those deals. All Harry knew was that by 1902, McIntyre had no separate property interest in the area except residential. But Harry lamented the absence of Louie Griffith from the group of bearers, although he'd read in the *Mirror* that Louie had done real well for himself in Batavia, Illinois, where he was the head of the extensive coal and lumber firm of Griffith & Hunter, where Cecil McIntyre had taken a position. And then there was O.O. Nichols, who would surely have been one of the bearers, had he not died in 1899, at the age of forty-two. The doctor in town had diagnosed the case as appendicitis, for which they were just beginning to operate at Rutland Hospital, and the doctor recommended 'Dolph go up and see what they could do, although they were losing quite a few patients. 'Dolph had been in pain for several days and he decided to give it a try, so he walked to the station and when he got there, he realized he didn't have his hat, so he started back to his house to get it. "Don't go back, that's bad luck. If you forget anything, go without it. Don't ever go back," he was cautioned. But he did go back and he got his hat and went to the hospital and had the operation and *pffit!* He died. His oldest boy, Nelson, who was fourteen, quit school to support his family. A smart boy. Good at figures. Honest. Clean. Griffith realized that the family was going to be in severe financial straits, so he handed a Bill of Lading to Nelson and said, "Can you figure this up, boy?" Nelson figured it right up and handed it back up to him. "Yes, sir," Griffith said, checking it over, "that boy can do it. Yes, sir, he can do it." And he gave him a job in the Head Office, the youngest one in there. Harry sighed, wondering how that family would make out now as he trudged down the aisle through the church.

A fighter, that's what Silas Griffith was, even his detractors admired him for that. He kept on expanding to the very end. In 1901, in one of the largest transactions in southern Vermont, he purchased

6,600 acres, mostly in the town of Stratton. A news item went on to note that he was, at that time,

> ...the owner of 50,000 acres... Nine mills... largest private fish hatchery in New England.

All too well, Harry remembered that although Silas got sick in June of 1902, he was again conducting business by October, and two months later was expanding yet again. As reported in the December 12th issue of the *Mirror,* with his associate Charles Sowle of Groton Lumber, he had purchased six million feet of spruce logs and planned the erection of a mill in the spring to saw the same into marketable lumber, still going on, despite the painful demise of his beloved fish hatcheries, adding to his other Vermont real estate holdings in Mt. Tabor, Danby, Peru, Winhall, Stratton, Dorset, Sunderland, and Ryegate besides his half interest with McIntyre of holdings in Arlington, Peru, and Ludlow.

Then, the December 26th issue told how Mr. Griffith would visit California. And right after he'd left on his trip, the January 23rd issue of the *Mirror* reported that the Groton Lumber Company he had purchased a scant month before had been sold by his financial manager, Wilbur Griffith. And it was rumored that just about all his timber land holdings were on the block.

Funny business, thought Harry Ralph, as he walked the casket into the rain and put it into the hearse, followed by the honorary bearers, the survivors of the Boys' Club.

Funny, funny business.

Norse Lodge (old Foley Homestead), Danby, VT

Mount Tabor Landslide due east of Norse Lodge (old Foley Homestead), 1930s

ANN K. ROTHMAN

Steam Sawmill at Griffith

Horse-drawn logging

The William Pierce Home (now The Quail's Nest Bed and Breakfast)

Ship on the Hudson River

Union Church, late 1800s

K.T. Griffith (center) and friends at Lake Griffith

SILAS LAPHAM GRIFFITH

Abandoned Griffith Village

Readying lumber for shipping

ANN K. ROTHMAN

Eva Stafford at the Griffith office

Griffith office interior

Dozens of volunteers who pitched in to raise a new barn at the farm of Joseph Bales in 1910

Charcoal kilns

ANN K. ROTHMAN

Equinox Hotel, early 1900s

Loggers sawing down tree with crosscut saw

Lumber on sled

Cathedral Church of St. David's, Pembrokeshire, Wales

Former Pierce Store now the Masonic Lodge

Griffith mansion decorated for Danby's 150th celebration

SILAS LAPHAM GRIFFITH

Griffith mansion

K.T. Griffith in the mansion's music room

ANN K. ROTHMAN

Silas Griffith on the mansion's front lawn

SILAS LAPHAM GRIFFITH

View of the north side of Griffith mansion

The Griffith mansion rebuilt for K.T. Griffith

ANN K. ROTHMAN

The new Griffith House replacing Maple Terrace

Interior, Silas Griffith greenhouse

Danby fireworks

Riddle family gravestone

Chapter 4
The Cortege

IT WOULD BE REPORTED that in addition to the hundreds who viewed the body, hundreds more attended the funeral. Many, with heads bowed, stood in the rain outside the crowded church, where they remained until the service ended. And then the long procession slowly wound its way through the rain and the mud to Scottsville cemetery, a ways north of the village.

Friendship and Animosity

En route to her late husband's final resting place, K.T. Griffith recalled her time in Vermont during what would prove to be the last years of Silas's life. She thought about how slowly, oh, so very slowly, she had put down her own roots in this place to which she had been wrenched from her beloved Philadelphia. In time, by becoming active in church affairs and Christian Endeavor and the like, she had made a few friends, among them, young Vera Griffith (Silas's niece, William's daughter). But overall, the town never accepted her, wouldn't give her the time of day. Finally, in the fall of 1899, after eight hard years of loneliness, she had been accepted into the D. A. R., the Daughters of the American Revolution. At that point, her life had been completely transformed.

At once, she had been thrust into a social whirl of women's functions and doings, *"do's,"* as they were called. There were teas and luncheons and all manner of other affairs that took up her time and finally offered her the opportunity of socializing. She even gathered together a group of out-of-town ladies, acquaintances that she could entertain at the Lake House for various functions including jamborees.

It was at one of the do's that she had met Emma Rising from Salem, New York. Emma was the daughter of Silas's senatorial opponent, Seth Rising. Recognizing one another's names, the two women began to talk. After commiserating with the girl over her father's electoral loss, K.T. added, conspiratorially, that her personal choice would always be "a friend of the working man," as Seth Rising had been termed. Soon, the two women had gone on to other subjects. K.T. learned that Emma was a primary school teacher. As the months went by and their acquaintanceship turned to friendship, K.T. eventually inquired of her young friend how it was that such an attractive girl was neither engaged nor married. To which Emma had unhappily blurted out that some years back she had hoped to marry one Jay Earle Brown, but he had ended up marrying someone else. "Oh, my poor dear!" K.T. had replied.

After a substantial period of time had passed, their friendship grew to be a very close friendship. K.T., in her mid-forties, found Emma, a delightful, thoroughly captivating young woman in her early twenties, an oasis all the more refreshing after so many interminably parched years.

From the very beginning of her relationship with Emma, changes in K.T. brought increasing strains on a marriage already held together primarily by tenuous stands of obligation and necessity. As a crowning blow, Silas's published account in the Burlington paper about her chewing gum on the boat to Cuba to avoid seasickness infuriated K.T.. The result: a dreadful row.

"You humiliated me! You mocked me!" K.T. cried.

"That's called 'joshing.' What kind of a person are you?" Silas answered. "Not only can you not laugh at yourself, but I've also never seen you laugh at all. You are completely devoid of humor!"

"I find your abundance of it disgusting and common!" K.T. retorted. You're utterly lacking in the dignity befitting a man of your means and station."

"K.T., whatever else I may be, I'm a Vermonter, a Danby man and proud of it," Silas replied. We're down-to-earth, forthright people of humor and we don't much care for airs. Personally, I find your unrelenting primness and propriety pretentious, especially considering your antecedents, and I will mock you for them until the day I die!"

And he had, infuriating her at every opportunity with an endless barrage of the type of straws that eventually break camels' backs.

The animosity between them increased over time to the extent that both she and Silas went their own ways whenever possible.

As her carriage continued its lurching progress to the cemetery, K.T. realized that it was about a year ago that Silas had taken ill, not long after the Boys' Club outing in June. As reported in the *Mirror*:

> **The inherent humors that have troubled him more or less all his lifetime has culminated in erysipelas.**

This was a serious disease, she knew, one that in very extreme cases could be life threatening. For a few weeks Silas had been very ill with a fever. During the worst period of his illness, he was attended by a specialist from Rutland as well as Dr. Grinnell, their local physician. But by the end of the month, he was much improved and had been able to sit up some. And within a fortnight he had been out on carriage rides nearly every day with his nurse, although he was forbidden to engage in conversation with anybody for fear of contagion.

As reported in the July 11th *Mirror,* Silas, determined to rid himself of the humors in his blood, if possible, had entertained a party of specialists from New York, Brattleboro, and Rutland. They met with Dr. Grinnell at the Lake House, where Silas expected to remain for several days. At the same time, K.T. was there with Vera Griffith and a friend of hers. Hardly in the mood for company, especially that of two young schoolgirls, Silas had been less than overjoyed, K.T. recalled. The women left the next day, while the doctors and Silas were still in residence. His aggravation over her visit may have generated the edict from the physicians that Silas, improving very slowly, sojourn for a while with the utmost quiet. So, Silas decided to stay at Lake Griffith for at least two weeks longer, for there was no more beautiful spot in Vermont in July than the rambling lodge with its staff constantly ready to tend to visitors—and above all to him.

Bill Riddle and a customer came up for a brief visit one day the following week. Among other news, he reported that Gene McIntyre's son, Cecil, had been replaced as foreman at the depot, having resigned the job for a position with Louie Griffith's firm in Batavia, Illinois. Hunter & Griffith, manufacturers of lumber and charcoal, had offered him an option to take a half interest in the business.

Trouble came, however, when K.T. had arrived to stay at the Lake House with her guest, Emma Rising. Silas erupted.

"I can entertain my friends up here, too, Silas," K.T. had said. "This is my house as well as yours, and there's plenty of room."

"No house is large enough for that. You're a brazen woman, K.T.,"

Silas had said, as he stormed out of the room.

A few weeks later, as reported in the August 8th *Mirror,* Emma, K.T., her sister Nellie (who had come from Philadelphia for a month's visit), Silas's sister Mary, and a Mr. Porter took a carriage ride to West Pawlet. They dropped Emma off at her relatives' house, where she would stay for a while before returning to Salem. In the paper, Charles Baker omitted to state how long Emma had remained in Danby prior to this departure. Whatever the duration had been, Silas, who had been steadily improving, taking trips to Rutland, and entertaining at the lake, fell ill with exceedingly painful boils under each arm, abscesses that had to be lanced thirty times.

The September 19th *Mirror* observed that

> **Mrs. S.L. Griffith accompanied her sister, Miss Nellie Tiel, on her return home to Philadelphia on Thursday for a two or three week stay. She will also visit Atlantic City where Mr. S.L. Griffith is enjoying the salted breezes of the Atlantic coast.**

Whereupon Silas, muttering about a possible future trip to California, cut his stay in Atlantic City short and was back at work by the end of September. There, he entertained a proposal to go into the production of acid from wood. And he considered how best to supply Washburn-Moen Mfg. of Worcester, Massachusetts, the 1,000 cords of firewood the firm requested to enable them to protect poor people of that city against a threatened fuel famine. By the end of October, Silas was well enough to take a ten-day trip to southwestern Iowa to buy a carload of horses for his Works, and he was fitting up a meat market in the village.

It was the beginning of November when he returned from Burlington in fine spirits. There he and his florist, Mr. C. Hass, had attended the flower show, where they had won two first prizes in competition with Dr. Webb for the chrysanthemums and roses he had exhibited. At this point Silas had broached the subject of Thanksgiving.

"I thought you should know, K.T., that I expect to invite Bill and Marion and Griffith, of course, to the house for Thanksgiving."

"You can do as you please, Silas, but we're already having company for Thanksgiving."

"We are? Who?"

"I've invited Emma Rising to have dinner with us."

"Not with *us,* K.T.," Silas had said in a fury. "Be sure Baker knows who that girl is visiting!"

> (Miss Emma Rising of Proctor was a guest of Mrs. S.L. Griffith for Thanksgiving.)

Indeed, Emma and K.T. were the only two people at the table on Thanksgiving. It was an awkward affair that cast a pall on K.T.'s time with Emma, who was very disturbed about her "unwanted guest" status. Emma swore she would never again come to Danby when Silas was in residence.

Deep in Projects

More than ever, Silas buried himself in projects: For his work, he commenced erecting another kiln and a two-family house on Depot Street. And in the beginning of December, it was announced he was expanding in Groton in partnership with Charles Soule, having purchased six million feet of spruce logs and planning the erection of a mill in the spring.

To further proficient singing primarily among the young people of the community, Silas was the chief promoter of a singing school. He provided the necessary funds for all wishing to take advantage of instruction, a philanthropic byproduct on the part of a man who enjoyed singing with the kids in the choir in the church.

In another effort to rid himself of the skin eruptions that had troubled him on and off throughout most of his life, he left for New York on December 19th for a conference with several physicians regarding his case and future treatment. He returned with a preparation for painting his face that the doctors thought would be efficacious. The hope was that it would cure his facial inflammation. To avoid frightening his friends with his appearance, he was to apply it before retiring at night and wash it off in the morning. It is possible that the physicians gave him some of the local application for the treatment of erysipelas recommended by one R.V. Pierce, M.D. in his *The People's Common Sense Medical Adviser* (1895), to wit:

"...the inflamed surface may be covered with cloths wet in the mucilage of slippery elm. Equal parts of sweet oil and spirits of turpentine, mixed and painted over the surface, is an application of unsurpassed efficacy."

Silas being Silas, determined to become a well man again, couldn't care less what his friends thought. So, he appeared on Christmas Day with a complexion "that much resembled the aboriginal Red Man." as Charles Baker put it. K.T. had been spared the sight, having passed the holidays with her family in Philadelphia, not planning to return to Danby until the second week in January.

Particularly with Charles Baker's weekly items in the Personal Mentions and Local Brevities of the *Mirror* listing most comings and goings, there was no way that anyone who read the paper could avoid knowing that the Griffiths' marriage was in trouble. It was clear that Mr. Griffith and Mrs. Griffith assiduously went their own ways.

SILAS LAPHAM GRIFFITH

When it was reported that Silas, on the advice of his New York physicians, would make an extended trip to California with the intention of remaining in the mild climate there for a period of three months or more, K.T. couldn't have been happier at the prospect of being rid of him. So, when it was announced that he was expecting to leave Danby the first week in January, K.T. made it her business not to arrive back in town from Philadelphia until January 9[ii]. That just happened to be the day that Silas started for California with his close cousin, Julius.

> ...the former for his health, the latter for pleasure and companionship of the former...

Once home, K.T. had made immediate plans to leave the following week to visit Emma for a few days to work things out for the months to come, months without Silas!

Off to California

Back at the funeral, a few carriages behind K.T., Julius Griffith was thinking of the splendid time he and Silas had had together at the beginning of the year. He especially remembered Silas's sigh of pleasure as the train started its five-day journey to the west coast.

"Ahhh, I feel better already," he'd said. "It's a pleasure getting away from all the aggravations of home. Takes all the tonnage off your shoulders. You know, there's always something," Silas remarked, as he patted his pockets for a cigar. "Take drinking, for example. The beginning of December I sent out notices to my different lumbering jobs that I'd have any intoxicated persons arrested. I don't like using the power of the law on those unfortunates who are slaves to drink, but I had to do something to find out who was furnishing the liquor. And I made it quite clear I'd prosecute him to the fullest extent of the law. And by golly, I got him, too," S.L. said, lighting up a cigar and puffing up a storm with great relish. "The fella left town in a hurry a couple of days later."

"I took care of that, did everything else I had to do. I signed a new will three days ago. And I instructed Wilbur to sell out my holdings."

"You did? You're feeling that bad?"

"No, no, no. My health is the least reason for it. You know, Julius, I'm really looking forward to having a good time out in California. The change is going to do me a world of good."

"You ever been to San Diego before?"

"Can't recall as I've ever been to southern California. Spent a fair amount of time in Washington State, though, especially up north in Whatcom County. Up until a couple of years ago, I'd go up yearly and visit Bellingham Bay, a lovely spot. I've picked up a fair amount of property up there over the years, about $40,000 worth, I'd guess. An M.J. Scouton of New Whatcom represents my interests there, an awful nice man. For some time now, he's been sending me a freshly caught salmon once or twice a year, about a twenty-pound fish. Once he shipped one to me by express during hot weather as a test of the express company's ability to transport fresh fish such a long distance and deliver it in good condition. The express people changed the ice twice en route and the salmon arrived in prime condition."

"When did you get into investing up there?" Julius had asked.

"In '93, I started buying mortgages," Silas said. "In '97, I started buying all kinds of property and I incorporated the Griffin Shingle and Lumber Company. Besides acreage—I've got mills and machinery and all kinds of stuff, even a coal mine...."

"Griffin Lumber?"

"Why, yes. Out there I'm not too fussy about using 'Griffith.' No point in the left hand knowing what the right is doing. Besides, it could save me tax-wise..."

"Chauncey and Martha are up there too, aren't they?"

"Yes, indeed. They're in Aberdeen, Washington. There's quite a number of Griffiths up there by now, I imagine...."

And so it went.

As Julius recalled, they touched on just about every subject under the sun, especially, that favorite of all, the practice of medicine.

"...Seems to me the best of them don't know what they're about," Julius opined.

"Quacks, that's what," Silas said. "The profession is loaded with them. Why, look what happened with Garfield. He was shot on July 2nd and the reports on his progress came through almost daily. Why, through the 12th of August he continued to improve, or so the doctors said. Even with the President of the United States, people felt there was a good deal of quackery around him. By the 17th of August, he was much worse. By the 27th he was lying at the point of death and though he gained a little here and there, he died on September 20th. Quacks, the lot of them!"

"And those patent medicines... We sell them and sell them. You ever look at the alcoholic content in those!"

"Why, they're guaranteed to cure just about everything or your money back," Silas laughed. "Hard to collect on a money-back guarantee when you're dead. About the only thing they don't claim to cure is rotten teeth."

"You know what they say, Silas, 'A man who's been a butcher can become a dentist, but a man who's been a dentist can't become a butcher.' You know, Dr. Grinnell charges $1 for every tooth he pulls, but if a man doesn't cry, he pulls them for free. Sensible people have one pulled at a time when absolutely necessary, but me, I had my whole jaw cleared simultaneously," said Julius, shuddering at the recollection. "And having endured that," he went on, "there was the aggravation of their replacements. I received my teeth by mail from Edwin Griffin.

We had to send them back to Rutland to Griffin to have them fixed. And then I had to go to Rutland to have them repaired. This went on and on, time and time again until I decided not to pull any of the teeth I had left. And my tooth difficulties hung on for spells up to ten days in length while I grunted away with the tooth ache and took a sweat until the tooth ulcerated and it broke and it was better..." Julius shook his head.

"I sure hope the climate out here will clear up this skin condition of mine," Silas said as they approached their destination. "I'm already feeling better."

"Anything special you have in mind to do?" Julius inquired.

"Yes, as a matter of fact," Silas replied. "Once I see if I like it out here, we're going to go house hunting."

"House hunting! "Julius was shocked.

"Yep. I'm going to buy me a place out here. Quite aside from the fact that it will be a pleasure to avoid those Vermont winters, I need a place far, far from home to install K.T., get her out of town. After all these years, she still hasn't been accepted in Danby. All those parties and gatherings and excursion groups to Rutland that you'll see in Baker's Personal Mentions and Local Brevities never include her, not unless she's visiting her family or they're visiting her or maybe that social butterfly Vera's got her in tow on rare occasions. Aside from that, her social life is barren as the Sahara, except for frequent listings, always the same, 'Mrs. S.L. Griffith and Miss Emma Rising of Proctor.' Why, she even had the crust to have her to the house for Thanksgiving! Her cavorting with that young woman is ruining my reputation, and I won't have it. People are muttering. I figure a house on the west coast should put an end to it."

By this time, they had alighted in San Diego and settled in at the home of Julius's nephew, Theron P. Griffith. (Theron's father, Peleg, also was in residence.) They had barely settled in when news reached them from Danby that Wilbur had sold the recently purchased Groton Lumber Company for $30,000. "Good," Silas had grunted.

But, Julius recalled, having started to unload on the east coast hadn't deterred his cousin's interest in real estate on the west coast.

As Theron daily plied his way to his job at G. W. Marston's store, where he was the manager of the men's furnishings department, and as K.T., on January 16th, left for Proctor, where she would be the guest of Emma Rising for a few days, Silas was gleefully absorbing the scene in San Diego, otherwise known as the City of Destiny.

Headlines in the *San Diego Union* proclaimed

> **SAN DIEGO'S BRIGHT OUTLOOK**

and went on about the city's expected gradual appreciation in real estate. Meanwhile full-page ads from Folsom Brothers touted lots in their Fortuna Park addition, a splendid tract of land overlooking Mission Bay where they were "practically giving away" the first 100 lots at starter prices of $20 each. Proclaiming their present worth as $150, articles predicted a future value of $300 to $500 each "when the boom starts in strong". After the starter lots were sold,

> `our price for lots will be $50 each, payable $20 down and $5 a month for six months without interest or taxes and with life insurance clause.`

Silas practically giggled, Julius recalled. He devoured every edition, every page of the *Union*.

He read the news of great mineral deposits in the Sierra Nevada range, belts of gold and gold mines and gems through San Diego County and in Klondike country. He read with interest plans for a transcontinental railroad. He observed the large number of lodges and fraternal organizations and societies in the city. He became familiar with the names of the two attorneys who handled the biggest cases and were prominent in the Chamber of Commerce. (These two— L.L. Boone and Eugene Daney— were featured in the news on a regular basis.) And he even read the comings and goings of the prominent residents in the Personal Mentions.

"Do you realize, Julius," Silas remarked one day with glee, "there are even more Griffiths out here in San Diego than there are in Danby, and I don't even know them!"

And in the February 4th edition, page one, he read,

| **VERMONT NO LONGER PROHIBITION STATE** |

"I guess that was inevitable," Silas had commented. But his reaction to a wire that arrived from home some weeks later was hardly as restrained.

"Good Lord!" he exclaimed, horrified, after reading its content. "My store was wrecked and my clerk, Arthur Hebert, was seriously injured from a terrific explosion that shook just about every house in the center of the village!" he informed Julius and Peleg who were in the room with him when he got the news. "It appears," he explained, "that there was a gas leak in the acetylene gas plant that lights the store and the meat market. Arthur thought he smelled gas and opened the door and the gas rushed into the north front room and ignited by coming in contact with the fire in the stove. It blew out a large part of the north wall and blew Arthur out through the hole, right onto the street. He's got a back injury and was badly burned on the face and hands and is in a good deal of pain. But he's expected to recover without loss of sight, thank God. As for the building, the front windows are out along with the goods that were in them and a lot of goods were damaged. They finally got the fires out with pails of water from the nearby houses. They're in the middle of doing an inventory and getting in touch with the insurers. —That Bill Riddle is handling it all," Silas sighed, "Don't know how I'd get along without him…"

Julius and Silas had met people as they'd gone here and there with Peleg—and with his son Theron, when work permitted him to join them. To Silas's delight, his name had been proposed for membership in the fraternal order of the Masons of San Diego! And all the while they had toured around with real estate brokers, looking for a house. Finally, in early March, Silas said, "This is it" of a property situated near San Diego in National City in the Chollas Valley. He was especially taken by the approach to the property and its abundant variety of flowers.

"This here's the 'Palm Hill' ranch, also known as the 'Bowen ranch' after its former owner," their broker, Fred Samborn, had announced. "It's also called The Palms," he said as they turned onto a 700-foot-long highway lined, on each side with towering palms. "It's a fruit ranch," Samborn was saying, "See the fruit trees on either side of this driveway. There are twenty-five acres here of fruit-bearing, nut, and ornamental trees," and, consulting a list, the broker started rattling off specifics: 350 navel orange trees, 420 lemon trees, 44 tangerine trees, 28 mission olive trees, 27 peach trees, 15 prune trees, 14 strawberry-guava trees, 12 apricot trees, 10 Bartlett pear trees, 6 apple trees, 6 pomelo trees, 4 lime trees, 3 fig trees, 2 plum trees, 2 quince trees, 2 walnut trees, 1 persimmon tree, 3 mulberry trees, 300 Logan berry, 51 date palms, 27 fan palms, 6 rubber trees, 1 pepper tree, 4 camphor trees…" And all the while Silas was sitting there with this little grin as they reached the residence at the end of the drive. "That's the craziest looking tree I ever saw," Silas remarked with a laugh, pointing to a pine of some sort to the left of the house. "Looks like a shorn poodle's tail. What is it, anyway?" "Oh, that's a Norfolk Island pine," Samborn answered as Silas walked around. The house was of moderate size, unpretentious but handsome.

Palm Hill Ranch

Sided with cedar shakes and lattice trimmed with a large wrap-around porch, it was set on a slight rise and had a magnificent view overlooking San Diego city, the bay, the Coronado Hotel, and the ocean. After a tour of the house, whose hardwood floors were liberally sprinkled with imported rugs and furniture valued at $3000, Silas asked, "How much?" In no time, he bought the property, valued at $30,000 with its span of horses, two wagons and an excellent Jersey cow, from one David Nangle of England,. (Nangle was a world-renown owner and breeder of fast horses.) News of the sale made the pages of the *San Diego Union* (March 11th, 1903).

> The Bowen Ranch bought by S.L. Griffith...Mr. Griffith came west to escape the cold of his eastern home and to regain his health which

has been somewhat impaired by long and useful labor in the business, political, church life of his former home. Though here but a short time...he decided that this was the place where he wanted to spend at least the winter months of his remaining years... The long acquaintance of Mr. Griffith with Senator Proctor and other politicians and leaders of the Green Mountain State will have the effect of turning their attention this way...

Silas Griffith in California, "the picture of health"

At once, Silas had sent for K.T. to join him immediately and spend the rest of the winter with him in California. As well as Julius could recall, she arrived on the 18th of March, and he departed for home the following morning.

Now back in the present and having reached the cemetery, Julius made his way to the Griffith plot. He held in his mind's eye the picture of Silas taken outside Theron's front door, with his bow tie askew and his fedora at a rakish, debonaire tilt. He'd looked so vibrant, so alive that he practically jumped out of the photograph. A man in fine spirits, a seeming picture of health. Yet four months later, he was dead. It was inconceivable.

Chapter 5
The Burial

AT THE CEMETERY "Let us pray," intoned the Reverend, thus starting the burial service that would consign Silas Griffith to his final resting place.

Emma, Emma, Emma K.T.'s mind sang, *I told you not to despair. I told you, promised you, our time would come...*

When Silas's wire reached her, demanding that she join him at once, K.T. was with her family in Philadelphia. (She'd left Danby on February 13th with plans to also visit relatives in Wilmington, Delaware, and Montclair, New Jersey.)

The Tiel family was astounded to see their relentlessly imperturbable K.T. in a mindless fury. Not only would her departure for California impinge upon and foreshorten her treasured private time, but the thought of being cut off from Emma and her family for endless months on end was intolerable. What it came down to was that apart from a few D.A.R acquaintances, her family, Emma, and young Vera were the only friends K.T. had in the world. All too clearly, she remembered those first dreadful years in Danby and she simply could not, would not go through that again.

Briefly, she considered disobeying Silas's edict, but however much her family wanted to maintain their constant, frequent visitations rather than have K.T. removed to the west coast (the other end of the world!), they insisted she obey her husband. They reminded her that "obey" was what she had sworn to do at her marriage twelve years before. It was her duty as a wife, essentially a chattel to her husband. "The local paper published the fact that your husband was sending for you to join him," her father said. "If you don't go," he pointed out, "your marriage will be over, and you will never be able to show your face in Danby again or be with your friends there. Instead, you would be with us once more, for I very much doubt Silas would give you one cent for essentially deserting him"

Of course, he was right. And if truth be told, after twelve years of living the rich life, the thought of moving back to 605 Wood Street was not a desirable option. So K.T. went to California.

Palm Hill, also known as The Palms

SILAS LAPHAM GRIFFITH

"Well, K.T., welcome to your new home," an exceedingly relaxed, well-looking Silas had greeted her as she alighted from the train. And after seeing Julius off the next morning, she and Silas left for The Palms.

"Isn't this marvelous!" Silas remarked enthusiastically as they journeyed on and on and on down the palm-lined driveway, finally ending in the middle of Nowhere. To the transplanted city girl, she might as well have been dumped in the middle of the Sahara Desert, so isolated was this place, so removed from shops or church or even neighbors! As much as she had detested being wrenched to California, her hatred for this new house of Silas's was limitless.

K.T. at Palm Hill

"C'mon," he had said, once she had settled in, "I'll give you a tour." And with camera in hand, he parked her beside a palm tree and chanted the photographers' classic "smile for the birdie." K.T. had tried to hide her feelings behind her usual mask of impenetrable composure, but her clenched fist demonstrated her fury. Silas's jibing inscription of the memento tells its own story.

Soon, K.T. was reading the *Union* too:

> L.L. Boone, the attorney in the Gay divorce suit threatened the sheriff with $150,000 damages suit when he wanted to serve a warrant for John Gay's arrest.

My word! There's a lawyer to have on your side, K.T. thought. Meanwhile Silas was feeling very well indeed and looking better every day with the color in his cheeks from the California sun. He left K.T. alone as he went upon his daily business of investigating various investment possibilities in this place of endless opportunity, which, of course, included a little real estate speculation here and there.

"See here," he said, one day, thrusting before her eyes a snippet from the April 20th *Union* under

> **REAL ESTATE TRANSFERS:**
> Theron P. Griffity et ux to Silas F. Griffity, property in Ex- Mission, $10.

"$10?"

"Certainly, $10. Everyone does it," Silas said airily, as he pulled out a clipping he had removed from the March 19th *Union*.

SILAS LAPHAM GRIFFITH

> **SAME HERE**
> An evil is manifested in the writing of "$10" as a consideration of deeds for real estate when the actual value of the land often runs into the thousands. The "ten dollar transfers" do Los Angeles a big lot of harm, for they make the totals of daily deals much smaller than what they truly are, and make the town look as if the real estate business is a small affair when the truth is the opposite. When the federal law required the affixing of revenue stamps the absurdity of the "ten dollar transfers" was often plain, for while the transaction might lie on the deed, they could not afford to lie to Uncle Sam. Why not tell the truth? Nothing is gained by such deception. It hurts the town. Stop it.
> -*Los Angeles Journal*

"Just an evil person, that's what I am," said Silas, with a laugh.

"And *Griffity.*" Silas chuckled.

"What did you buy?" Again, Silas laughed. "Actually," he explained, "the transaction took place on April 3rd. That's the date I bought this place here, The Palms, from Theron and his wife, eh, K.T. Griffith. He bought the place from Nangle for me for $5,000."

"Why? Why all this deviousness?" K.T. asked, shaking her head.

"...and then," Griffith continued with a twinkle, "four days later, up in Washington, The Griffin Lumber and Shingle Company bought some more machinery - they've been collecting that up there."

"I know nothing about your affairs!" K.T. protested strongly.

"You'll find out everything, my dear, when I'm dead and buried. You do figure, after all, in the will I drew before I left home," Silas grinned. "Oh, I meant to tell you. If you've any plans to have Theron and his wife over for dinner, you'd best have them soon. She's leaving with the children for St. Louis next week to spend the summer with her family."

"Lucky woman," K.T. sighed. "I don't suppose, Silas, that you'd let me go to visit my family?"

"Of course not, m'dear. A wife's place is by her husband's side," Silas nodded emphatically.

I hate him, I hate him, I hate him, K.T.'s mind chanted, as she calmly nodded her acquiescence as he left the room. And, with a sigh she turned her attention once more to the *San Diego Union,* her sole companion. In the May 17th paper, her eye happened to catch on some news from Imperial that one Dr. T.R. Griffith was appointed health officer for Imperial by the county supervisors and will likely enforce a thorough cleaning up of the town.

Around that time, Bill Riddle had dinner with them and stayed overnight on his way home from a business trip. After Bill had told him about his trip and had conveyed Scouton's regards, Silas had said, "You know, I think I'm going to install a bottling plant at the foot of the mountain and sell that vile tasting stuff from that mineral spring. It appears to me that anything that tastes so foul must cure something. I'd like you to please get started on that project, you and Wilbur." "I'll take care of it," Bill replied, and penciled a note himself.

"Tell me, Silas," Riddle had asked over the dinner, "when can I tell everyone you're returning to Danby?"

"Well, Bill, I'll tell you," Silas had replied, "when I left, I told everyone I expected to be back in June, in time for the Boys' Club outing. But, just between us, now there's no reason, really, why the Outing couldn't be postponed until July. Hopefully nobody will die for a month's extension. I'm having a swell time here and I'm feeling so awful good, that I hate to rock the boat. So, put them off kindly, I wouldn't want to hurt anyone's feelings. I promise, you'll be the first to know when I'm ready to head home..."

For her part, K.T. couldn't wait to leave. Nightly, she dreamt of Emma and her parents, and daily she occupied herself by devouring the pages of the *San Diego Union*.

> ...The Easter Hat is flat and *wonderfully adorned* either with lace or feathers. Feminine styling is the rule this season, in both dress and hair...

Silas, too, read the paper carefully, but for its business content:

> ...Yuba Well, drilling for oil...

> TO DRY LUMBER IN SAN DIEGO
> According to a publication in a trade paper published in San Francisco, Eureka has taken an 8 year contract to clear land and ship the lumber to the eastern market... Mills of Humbolt county...Hammond Company, Minor Mill & Lumber Company and Eastern Redwood Company...
>
> J.P. Morgan quoted as remarking that it was his opinion that in ten years time the city [San Diego] would be

> larger than either San Francisco or Los Angeles...
>
> A new town is about to be laid out 5 miles south and 1 mile East of Imperial...

K.T. was so desperate that she was reduced to reading the Local Brevities besides everything else:

> J.J. Brenner will be tried at El Cajon tomorrow on a charge of running a gambling joint. Eugene Daney will defend him.

K.T. read articles on "leprosy caused by fish," or a local gunfight.

> **A TEXAS DUEL**
> EL PASO, TEXAS, JUNE 6TH
> ...another Texas duel last night at Eagle Lake, when City Marshall Kinard and Wil McDow shot each other to death... Kinard was trying to quiet McDow when McDow shot him through. Kinard fell dying but raised himself and shot McDow. As he fell McDow said, "We are both done for, let us die friends." They shook hands and died.
>
> **COUNTY CORONER SUES COUNTY**
> JUNE 7TH, 1903
> Dr. A. Morgan, county coroner, whose

bills for several months past for holding inquests have been cut down considerably by the Board of Supervisors upon the advice of the District Attorney, yesterday brought suit in the Superior Court against the county for the full amount of his bills, which aggregate $588.25 for the three months of February, March and April... The Supervisors allowed the bills for $311 but Coroner Morgan refuses to accept this amount. District Attorney Carter contends that inquests were not necessary in all the cases in which they were held.

AN ANSWER TO CORONER'S SUIT
JUNE 14TH, 1903

District Attorney Carter says he held a number of unnecessary inquests.

His answers says, "action of coroner was unauthorized by law and an abuse of that official discretion vested in him as coroner for the county of San Diego."

He named cases where none were killed, died as a result of suicide, none suddenly died under such circumstances as to afford a reasonable ground to support his or her death had been occasioned by the act of another

> **by criminal means.**
> **He went on to state that the coroner's actions served no other purpose than to enlarge his bill for costs.**

"Well, I'm all for saving money," Silas had observed when he'd read the piece, "but it appears to me that being penny wise could prove pound foolish there. Incidentally," he went on, "I got news that Bill and Wilbur are in Boston to arrange for bottling and carbonating apparatus for that bottling plant I mentioned to Bill last month."

Looking for a neutral topic, K.T. asked, "How would you like to celebrate your birthday, Silas? The 26th isn't very far off."

"I've been thinking about that," he responded. "Quite a few people I've been talking to are going down to Tijuana to go to a bull fight they're having there on July 5th. They tell me there's a reputable place down there to stay - The Tijuana Hot Spa Hotel, owned by a P.L. Carle. It was built in 1885, supposed to be quite nice. It might be fun to give it a try, go down there."

"To a bullfight?" K.T. was shocked.

"At least to the hotel," Silas said. "They've got these mud baths. Might do me some good. Lord knows, I've tried everything else."

"If that's what you want to do."

So right before Silas's birthday, they went down to Tijuana, then a lazy little Mexican town. Unfortunately, they found that the hotel was fully booked for the bullfight. "There is another place down here that also offers mud baths, if you don't mind, eh, roughing it. I doubt they'd be full," the hotel clerk sniffed haughtily.

"Well, we're down here. Why not?" Silas said.

In any case, the Griffiths indeed roughed it. And surprisingly, they stayed for a while, at what might best be termed a "rustic spa." It was apparently managed or owned and largely run by James and Ethel Cienfuegos, whom the Griffiths photographed in profusion. Their lat-

SILAS LAPHAM GRIFFITH

Camp in Mexico

ANN K. ROTHMAN

Snapshots in Mexico

er inscriptions on the photo prints told their own tales of their memorable stay at the place, where it would seem they were the sole guests.

Silas presumably passed a good part of his days buried in mud, tended to by James (Jim) Cienfuegos, his improbable "nurse" as K.T. termed him. K.T., meanwhile, passed at least part of her days horseback riding. Sometimes she rode with Jim, sometimes with Ethel, whose picture she snapped in a particularly alluring pose outside the cook tent. It was probably Ethel who confided to K.T. that Jim had stolen their white horse!

"Stolen?" K.T. gasped, for horse thieves in the States had been hanged for less. Ethel simply shrugged, saying that just to live, they had to take a little here and there, when an opportunity presented itself.

Hot springs in Tia Juana, Mexico

It would appear from S.L.'s pungent photo inscriptions that he was considerably less complacent about the whole Tijuana experience than K.T.. One must assume it was K.T. who in some way forced the issue of bringing Ethel back to San Diego when they returned home. How long Ethel stayed as K.T.'s guest at The Palms, while the photographs were sent out for developing and were later inscribed, is not known. But Ethel did go to San Diego where she spent at least one day bathing with K.T. at the exclusive Coronado Hotel. Meanwhile, Silas went out hunting, as reported by the *Rutland Herald*,

| **a fortnight before his death.** |

This would have been on or about the 7th of July, the starting date of the 1903 California Deer Season, which ended on the 15th of the month.

Sudden Death

Fourteen days later, the one-time third largest lumber producer in the nation died.

According to the *Mirror,* the first news that Silas was seriously ill was a telegraphed message K.T. sent to Wilbur Griffith on July 18th. This was followed by another dispatch the next day, saying that Silas appeared to be near the throes of death.

At least during these last days, Silas's mind was sufficiently lucid for him to summon to his bedside L.L. Boone, Esq. He dictated a codicil to his will to Boone, one of San Diego's most prominent attorneys. The typed codicil was signed on July 20th and witnessed by Eugene Daney, Esq., an attorney of about as much stature as Linden Boone. Theron and Peleg Griffith attended the signing but did not act as legal witnesses to the codicil. San Diego press reported that, "the end came peacefully and without pain. He had passed a fairly comfortable night with his mind unclouded and seemed cheerful and resigned. Early this morning he was taken worse and lapsed into unconsciousness from which he never rallied." Silas Lapham Griffith died at 5:12 P.M. on July 21st, 1903.

SILAS LAPHAM GRIFFITH

At 66th birthday party in Mexico

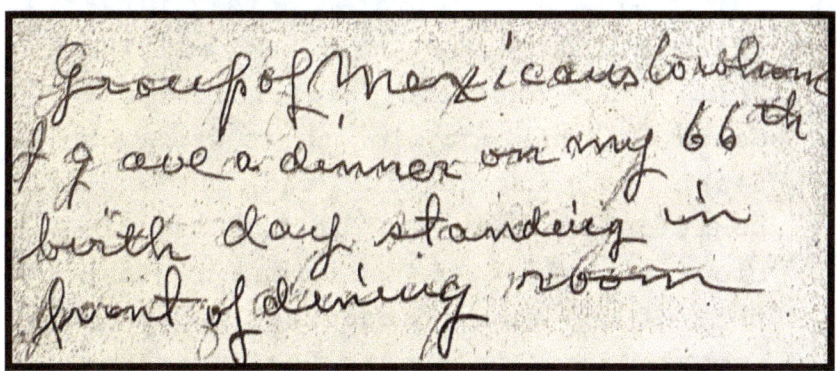

What Happened?

As she waited for Wilbur's arrival, K.T., less than clear-headed, telegraphed to Danby not one but two different versions of the circumstances that led to Silas's death. Charlie Baker published both on the front page of the July 24th *Mirror*.

1 | After fixing a date in June for his return to Danby, Mr. Griffith decided to go down into Mexico, to some noted hot springs, and he did so. Here he took what are termed mud baths - that is, was virtually buried in the hot mud of that locality for stated periods. We are told that this treatment was detrimental to his condition, rather than beneficial - in fact, it left him in a state that made it impossible to then withstand the fatigue of the long journey home and his sufferings increased till death released him.

(He was well enough to go deer hunting.)

2 | Mr. Griffith celebrated his sixty-sixth birthday, on June 26th at "The Palms," his handsome California residence. On this occasion there was much feasting and rejoicing and the supposition is that Mr. Griffith injudiciously partook of too great a quantity of the good things that had been prepared for his guests. At any rate, his condition immediately became unfavorable, in consequence of which the trip to the Mexican hot springs was decided upon.

SILAS LAPHAM GRIFFITH

(But the Mexican dining room photo inscribed by Silas proves the site of his birthday dinner. Why did K.T. lie?)

K.T. awaited Wilbur's arrival before making final funeral arrangements. Her first thought was to have the funeral at The Palms, but instead the services were held at Johnson's and Connell's chapel on D and Seventh Streets in San Diego, with the Reverends W.E. Crabtree and Abbott officiating. Silas's body was shipped home, after one E.M. Fly, M.D. had certified on the Physician's Certificate of Shipping Permit, that he had attended Silas L. Griffith, the decedent from May 1st, 1903 to July 21st, 1903. Noted also was the cause of death as *Pityriasis Rubra* which was contracted at Danby, Vermont.

The funeral was reported in detail in the August 7th, 1903 issue of the *Mirror,* with the following addenda to Charles Baker's reportage:

> **TRIBUTE FROM A BUSINESS COMPETITOR**
> In this connection we are pleased to print a character sketch of Mr. Griffith from the pen of Mr. M.J. Hapgood, who on account of his continuity to Mr. Griffith has had exceptional advantages to study his life.
> Probably no other name has been as prominent in southeastern Vermont for a great many years as that of Silas L. Griffith. In many places and in many respects, his name has been a household word. Now that he is dead it is well for us to calmly consider some of his most prominent traits and the means by which he obtained his success and

prominence.

The youth and boys of today can well learn a deep lesson from his life. His early advantages were of the most meager character, and schoolmates of his tell how his scholarly qualifications were extremely limited. Mr. Griffith was a person who made full use of all his opportunities - and that is the whole secret of his success. He had no vantage ground from which to start, but he ever used what strength was in him to the best and fullest purpose. He was a man who had a distinct aim for all his actions, who knew where and when and what to strike and who never expended his strength in beating the liar. He was a man intensely practical. He loved terseness and brevity and sought to reach the kernel of things by a direct thrust at the center.

Mr. Griffith as an antagonist was a foe worthy of any man's steel; and the harder the contest, the keener his enjoyment. His phrenological bump of combativeness was highly developed; and he had little respect for a man who would not stand up for his rights, even as against his own interests. Business with him was a game - to see which party would win - and it must be admitted that more often than otherwise he was himself the winner.

Hospitality with him was a study - a part of the routine of daily affairs. I doubt if anyone in these parts has been able to bring it down to a finer point, and to cause guests to feel more at home and perfectly at ease in their surroundings - just as though they themselves owned it all. His parchment diploma of Doctor of Hospitality was well earned.

Mr. Griffith was able to pass that supremest of all tests-he was a public-spirited citizen. Even his friends were surprised at the utterly disinterested course of his actions during his senatorship. His political convictions were honest and no influence could induce him to swerve from them. Besides, he was keen in his insight into character.

On the whole, thoughtful persons must acknowledge that Mr. Griffith's death is a great loss to the community. His example as a man of wide-awake ideas alone was worth much. Although like all persons of decisive actions, he had his faults, but his virtues predominated. And it can safely be

> asserted that had he lived, the ensuing years of his life would have been largely devoted to matters of public welfare. His character and methods were so forceful and unique that it will be a long time before his like, or anything near his like, again appears among us.
>
> As the real intent and purpose of his heart, God alone only knows and must be the judge. As for me, although often the mark of his missiles as well as the recipient of his favors, one shining fact alone offers all due proof for my conviction. He loved the flowers well nigh to a passion. Even his office table was always decked with them, and there was no business care so absorbing as to long distract his attention from them. Flowers and music! Such love dwells not in hearts of baseness. Amid such companionship ill will and hatred cannot thrive.

One additional article of interest also appeared in the August 7th Mirror:

> **FOR DISTURBING THE PEACE**
> After the arrival of Mr. Griffith's body last Friday night, a number of Italian employees gathered at the

house of Mr. John Christian, where they drank intoxicants and feasted a large part of the night - as is their usual custom when a friend dies.

Heretofore such observance has usually taken place in the settlements of their own countrymen, and no objection has been raised. On this occasion, however, they greatly disturbed the slumbers of some near neighbors who are not accustomed to such affairs, and in consequence Mr. Christian was arrested and hauled before Justice Herrick upon complaint of Grand Juror Parris. The trial was put over from Saturday to Monday, when Mr. Christian pleaded guilty to disturbing the peace and was given the minimum fine of $5 and costs.

ANN K. ROTHMAN

Chapter 6
The Aftermath

SETTLING THE ESTATE The storm of community speculation over the cause of Griffith's death continued seemingly endlessly long after his funeral.

A man can't die of a skin disease!" some said. "He died of *syphilis,* that's what he died of. Anything else on the Death Certificate was just a polite way of putting it," others argued. But many did not accept the venereal disease theory as the cause of his death, and its inexplicable suddenness troubled quite a number of people. Silas's niece Vera Griffith, for one, couldn't understand why there was such a mystery surrounding his passing. To the end of her days, she asserted there was no obvious reason for his death.

The amount of money Griffith had amassed was another matter of endless discussion. But word quickly traveled around town that the community would receive not the smallest inkling of information right away and that it would be months until some word about his bequests would become known.

The information the community was most interested in was news about the future of the business, which continued operating after the funeral. A brief article in the August 7th *Mirror* reported that

> ...Until the will has been probated, Mr. Rice tells us it is the intention of the executors to continue the same as near as possible.

Which announcement generated a communal sigh of relief, and slowly life in the community regained a degree of normalcy.

At the end of August, K.T. Griffith, with her mother, sister, and brother went to Lake Griffith for a short stay. Her brother left about a week later, but the women, apparently, stayed on.

The Bequests

In September, the public bequests of S.L.'s will were finally published,

> ...but all efforts to learn anything relative to the private benefactions of the will have only met with discouragement from the executors,

reported Charles Baker in the September 13th *Mirror*. He noted that the executors of the will, Wilbur H. Griffith and George L. Rice, Esq. were also named custodians of the various trusts.

TOTAL ALLOCATED FOR PUBLIC BEQUESTS:	$105,000
Bequeathed for the erection and maintenance of a library on a lot donated for that purpose	$51,000
Bequeathed to the Cemetery Association	$11,000
Bequeathed to the Congregational Church	$23,500

INCOME OF THE TRUST TO BE USED FOR:	
Christmas gifts for the children of Danby and Mt. Tabor regardless of their church or denomination	$2,500
Established for the purchase of shoes and clothing for needy children at Christmas time	$2,000
Bequeathed to Danby and Mt. Tabor schools	$15,000

PRIVATE BEQUESTS:	
one third of the estate was to be held, in trust, for Jennie Riddle and her children (the same percentage K.T. would get), plus an additional bequest to his daughter, outright	$5,000
To his grandchildren, Griffith and Marion	$3,000 ea.
To his brothers, Charles and William	$2,000 ea.
To his sister, Mary	$10,000

While Minnie Bushee sang at all manner of recitals and kept company with Jay Bromley and visited family, and K.T.'s family remained constantly in attendance, court appointed appraisers busied themselves making an inventory of Griffith's Vermont holdings. They counted horses (155 horses, $125 each) and mowing machines and ox yokes and cords of wood and cords of bark and lumber and household furnishings and office furnishings and stock and tools of the various blacksmith shops and real estate (in Mt. Tabor, $106,980; in Stratton, $109,210; in Peru, $62,700; $44,980 in Sunderland; $19,200 in Danby and so forth and on and on) and merchandise in the various stores, etc. It was an enormous task. When finally completed and evaluated, the appraisers reported a total value of $562,154.13 for Griffith's Vermont real estate, equipment, goods, and furniture.

The Superior Court of San Diego, California, was also involved in the legal process. On September 2nd, 1903, pursuant to the commission issued out of the Probate Court of Rutland, Judge Norman H. Conklin called before him several gentlemen to testify concerning the codicil Silas executed the day before he died, which had been drawn in California by Linden Boone, Esq.. Among them was Theron P. Griffith. After having been duly sworn, all vouched for Griffith's clarity of mind and that he acted without duress, menace, fraud, or undue influence. Notably absent was Griffith's nurse, witness James Scott, who left for London shortly before having to testify.

A Busy Life

As the wheels of Probate continued and Wilbur Griffith skittled around collecting Quit Claims and the like, K.T. was busy too. Even with family visiting, she became the president of the Ladies Aid Society of the Congregational Church. Finally in late December she returned to Philadelphia with her mother. She would stay for several months.

December found Wilbur in California, probably on Estate business but also doing some personal real estate dealing, paying $1.12 to redeem land sold to the state for delinquent taxes. In Danby, when Christmas rolled around, there was no money for the Christmas party gifts, nor would funds from Griffith's bequests become available for several years. Only the children attending Sunday School received presents.

In March 1904, the last meeting of the commission for examining and allowing claims against the Estate of S.L. Griffith took place in

Advertisement for the sale of Palm Hill

SILAS LAPHAM GRIFFITH

Vermont and in San Diego, with L.L. Boone acting as attorney. The Letters Testamentary were proved and recorded. Meanwhile, K.T. remained in Philadelphia, having been appointed treasurer of Danby's Christian Endeavor in her absence. It wasn't until April that she returned to Danby, accompanied by an aunt. In May, she learned from a beaming Wilbur Griffith that "The Palms" had been sold to a J.W. Hartshorn for $8,000 - a tidy $3,000 profit over its cost. ("The fella muttered something about possible future development," Wilbur told her.) As for her personal activities of note, K.T., with a few others, attended a Christian Endeavor convention at Rutland and pledged $150 to retain the pastor of the Congregational Church, matching Silas's last subscription.

The widow Griffith would seem to be a changed woman from the K.T. Griffith of yesteryear. To judge from Charlie Baker's incomplete listings, it would appear the widow had "married the church." For all the frequency of time spent with her family during S.L.'s lifetime, since his death she clung to them unnaturally; indeed, judging from the *Mirror's* lack of other reportage, she exclusively depended on the Tiels for company. Family and church, church and family, were all that ostensibly occupied her time.

The constant former comings and goings and visitings and stayings between Emma Rising and herself were ancient history according to Charlie's empty columns. Nor was K.T. ever reported, as formerly, in the company of Vera Griffith or Silas's sister, Mary. But if her life was indeed that barren in Danby, why didn't K.T. sell the House on the Hill, and once the estate had been settled, move from the town that had never accepted her to her beloved Philadelphia? There the extremely rich widow could live like a queen and be near the Tiels, to whom she was so devoted. What held her in town?

And then, what was happening with Griffith's other Vermont holdings that had been reported for sale in July of 1903, with options being held on many of his timber properties? Not a word about that was published either, nor was there a jot written about the job on the mountain, or about Bill Riddle or any accidents that may have occurred. The *Mirror* reported nothing at all about any of that. It was as if Charles Baker had been gagged in all respects concerning Griffith business, as the months rolled inexorably by and the process of Probate continued.

In June 1904, ending a year of mourning, K.T. came out of social isolation. On the 24th, Baker duly reported Emma Rising as a guest of K.T.'s, soon to be joined by Mrs. Tiel and Nellie who would be spending the summer with K.T. in Vermont. It was August before Emma left for Schenectady, ending a six-week visit in Danby.

Carriage rides to Rutland seem to have been one of K.T.'s favored ways to pass time, sometimes with her sister and/or mother or a visiting relative from out of town. Except for Emma's visit, K.T. enjoyed no other reported social intercourse except with her family. She otherwise filled her time with church activities like the soap bubble party held by the Ladies' Aid, of which organization she was president. Once, briefly, K.T. visited friends in Massachusetts.

Selling the Lumber Business

September 1904 brought the disappointing news that although there were numerous other prospects, an expected sale of all the timber lands of the Griffith estate had fallen through. Riddle explained that, expecting the sale to be consummated, roads and other details had been neglected.

```
  ...the executors...are now prepar-
  ing to take up lumbering operations
  again, reported Baker, ...although
  much time has been lost that is usu-
```

> ally devoted to timber cutting, and it will be impossible to carry on operations this winter or anywhere as large a scale as for the past few years. ...Little or no work will be done at the South End this winter.

Christmas 1904 was less than happy for the community's children, for once again, for lack of distributed funds from the Griffith Trust, there was no money for the Christmas Party. And for many of the workers, the prospect of getting through the winter without a job was bleak, indeed.

In January, Nellie and Mrs. Tiel left for Philadelphia accompanied by K.T. and Silas's sister, Mary, both of whom would go on from Pennsylvania to West Palm Beach, Florida. They'd winter there until May, leaving behind a grim winter in Danby. In March, Griffith's estate stopped logging for the season and discharged a number of men, who doubtless missed Silas sorely. At about the same time as Danby's Imperial Marble Quarry became the Danby Marble Company, Inc., the S.L. Griffith & Co. Store was robbed of $5 in pennies and nickels, a watch from a display and a pair of mittens, which the thieves had dropped. Some in town were desperate. But there was news that another company was negotiating for the timber lands.

In May 1905 K.T. and Mary Griffith arrived home for the summer, with Mrs. Tiel and Nellie coming soon. Emma, having apparently moved from Proctor to Gardner, Massachusetts, visited K.T. in July and again in September and December. She finally returned to Massachusetts in January, after spending a few holiday weeks in Danby with K.T., who remained in town that winter.

The December 15th, 1905 issue of the *Mirror* carried the welcome header,

GRIFFTH TIMBER LANDS PROBABLY SOLD

and went on to report that negotiations with a New York State concern had sufficiently progressed that it was deemed best to cease the cutting of timber as the negotiations continued.

Accompanied by family, K.T. interrupted the long February days with a sleigh ride to Tinmouth to visit friends. At the same time the sale of the timber lands to the Emporium Lumber Company (based in the Adirondacks in New York State) became an assured fact. By mid-March the firm was getting ready to commence operations at the South End, which plant they expected to keep busy all summer. Edwin Staples, their local manager, was in charge of their local affairs. Eddie soon proclaimed that the company expected to maintain Lake Griffith and restock it with fish and would shortly begin work to install a short-track railroad to better transport logs.

Over the coming months, K.T. left for a four-week stay in Philadelphia with her mother and sister. Minnie Bushee and Jay Bromley finally tied the marital knot and settled in Springfield, Massachusetts.

At the same time, Mr. Sykes, the owner of the Emporium Lumber, arranged to have a standard gauge one-to-two-mile railroad track installed at the foot of the mountain. An engine was brought in to transport the cut trees and logs skidded down the mountain to the South End. There the logs were dumped into the pond, which washed them off to some extent, making them easier to saw. After they were sawed in the big steam mill down there, they were loaded onto the Rutland Railroad cars on the siding behind the mill. In early May it was announced that the "South End" had been renamed "Sykesville," a plan that was shortly squelched by Mr. Sykes.

It was reported that Wilbur Griffith bought a fine span of horses, naming one "auto" and the other "mobile" after the newfangled, fashionable, costly automobiles just coming on the market! And Harry

SILAS LAPHAM GRIFFITH

Ralph moved down from "Griffith" to the South End. Meanwhile, K.T., her mother and sister returned from Philadelphia, to be joined by Emma in June for her usual month-long summer visit. On Main Street, William leased the Griffith Store (with an inventory of $16,000 to $18,000) to Eugene McIntyre and his sons, Cecil and Edward. Eugene was having a great time in July 1906, driving people around in his red town car, sometimes to Manchester, sometimes to Danby Four Corners (a trip he made in a record fifteen minutes), and sometimes touring to Lake St. Catherine and Bomoseen. His automobile made quite a record that summer, killing two dogs and causing a runaway.

Change after Change

Meanwhile, the probate process went forward. On July 30th, 1906, the Superior Court of Whatcom County, Washington, listing various properties, compared them with the original Decree of Final Settlement and issued the Order of Distribution to Wilbur Griffith, Executor. Wilbur granted those properties to one George C. Fisher on October 8th, 1906. On the same date, Katherine T. Griffith additionally granted other lots to Mr. Fisher. Five days later, Griffin Lumber & Shingle Company declared bankruptcy.

As funds for Griffith's public bequests were finally released, it was announced that work on the Library was expected to start in September. This brought new life to Main Street while the month tolled the death knell for the lumber job at "Griffith" on the mountain, which had closed down. The few people left there to finish sawing had moved away, ending the life of a community that for many years was the largest settlement in the town of Mt. Tabor. By the end of September, only one family remained, waiting to find a new home. The post office was discontinued, the steam mill abandoned, the buildings dismantled—all of it left for the devouring forest.

Townspeople discussed all that for a bit until those subjects were replaced by the incident which occurred at the new jail in town. Intended as an awe-inspiring object for evil doers, the building was instead the site of a party. Passers-by saw three or four drunks singing, dancing, drinking, and otherwise carousing within the structure with much merriment. Some thought it funny; some found it shocking. Editor Baker urged the town to speedily install the building's door.

Christmas, '06 brought the first Griffith Christmas Party to the Congregational Church since Silas's death, commencing a marvelous and well-loved tradition that would continue forever.

Gone. All Gone.

As K.T. celebrated the holiday with her family, Bill Riddle severed his connections with Silas's estate and opened his own wholesale lumber business in Rutland. Eventually, when the Griffith estate auctioned off remaining holdings, he purchased all the property on the west side of the railroad tracks - the feed mill and elevator, the Box Shop, dry kiln, lumber sheds, office building, four charcoal kilns, store houses and the like "at ridiculously low figures." A year or so later, he sold the buildings to Emporium.

The last trace of the golden years ended. Emporium continued their operation, hiring Nelson Nichols as a bookkeeper. And, on Main Street, the new Library building was being built.

Spring brought Emma Rising to visit with K.T. and her family, who now seemed to be in permanent residence in Danby. For her part, K.T.'s former intense involvement in church affairs would seem to have diminished to next to nothing over the past year. Instead, she was occupied with her seriously ailing mother and her brand-new black Franklin touring car in which she was chauffeured about. But it was Mrs. Tiel who occupied her time and her thoughts, for the lady's health deteriorated quickly until death released her in September. The funeral was held at the Congregational Church, after which the remains were shipped to Philadelphia.

No longer occupied with her mother's illness, K.T. once more plunged into church affairs, shortly becoming elected treasurer of the Congregational Church and Society and preparing for Emma's holiday visit, as 1907 gave way to the new year.

Griffith Memorial Library

The Memorial Library

Without question, the most visible monument of Griffith's philanthropy was the handsome S.L. Griffith Memorial Library that had risen on Main Street. It was dedicated with great ceremony and fitting exercises in the Congregational church in March 1908. Mayor Walter J. Bigelow of Burlington delivered the principal address. Reverend H.J. Mallet of East Dorset also spoke. And music was furnished by Brehmer's orchestra of Rutland and the choir of the Congregational church.

Built according to plans drawn up prior to Silas's death by architect Charles E. Page, the library was constructed at a cost of $14,000. The one-story building with a pressed brick body, blue marble foundations, white marble exterior trim, and a red slate roof was a dignified, impressive, lasting monument of the benefactor's generosity. Its two ells, each measuring approximately 47 x 28 feet, were lit by gasoline from a gas plant, on site, for this purpose. Inside, it was a welcoming, delightful place with two curly-birch finished reading rooms on either side of the rotunda, one for adults, one for children, each with a red brick fireplace. Its original stock consisted of six thousand books. On the opening day, the interior of the building was decorated with beautiful floral adornments: cut flowers, palms and flowering plants in profusion from the greenhouses of its donor's widow.

In his lengthy address, Mayor Bigelow said no other town in Vermont of less that 1000 population could show such an institution as the new library. "If we consider the whole endowment of $51,000 and the lot," he continued, "we find but six libraries in the State of Vermont better endowed," and proceeded to name the Middlebury College library, St. Johnsbury Athenaeum, Fletcher Free Library at Burlington, Billings Library at the University of Vermont, Haskell Free Library at Derby, and Kellogg-Hubbard Library at Montpelier.

In conclusion, he said, "It is not the mature men and women of today in Danby who will find the greatest value of this library, but the boys and girls who are just coming to years of understanding."

Within a week, 150 library cards had been given out and 200 books had been checked out.

But the true value of the library in its early days, and the history of its coming is set forth in a lengthy piece written by the late Sarah Alice (Boyce) Nichols when she was about ninety-two years of age. (c.1926). Mrs. Nichols was brought up a Quaker and when that religion died out in Danby, she became a fervent Spiritualist.

SILAS LAPHAM GRIFFITH

The history of a library in Danby started way back, she wrote: ...the old reform club, founded before the Civil War, was mostly due to the efforts of William Pierce and a few co-workers who devoted much time, effort and money to its establishment. A few neighbors would come together every Thursday evening, compare notes and experiences, read papers laboriously written after long hours of toil, and lay traps and plan inducements to interest the young people. After awhile they began to collect books.. .. They were freely loaned to anybody would read and return them. It was slow work, but the thing held, and the broadness of mind which distinguished the enterprise from its inception was very alluring.

[Many] people were interested in the reform club and the little library and, in spite of the many discouragements and set backs, it grew. Judicious selection of books catered to all classes. Lines of demarcation were obliterated. All classes joined hands to support it and it was a power for good. When Mr. Mears took charge of the Congo Church he gave it judicious and powerful support. In the selection and purchase of books he was invaluable. His sermons and his daily life brought comfort to mourners. He united or recognized the union of the seen and unseen worlds.

Then, with Mr. Griffith's post-mortem endowment, it became what it is; the

Total cash on hand at the time of Griffith's death	$17,851
Balance from a Minnesota Estate (which no one appears to have known about)	$8,474
Five Minneapolic mortgage	
Chicago lots	$5,000
Balance from his Washington Estate including warrants	$35,326
Balance from the California Estate (presenting the proceeds from the sale of "The Palms" which had actually been sold for $8,000. The executors may have put it in at the lesser amount to save taxes, but what happened to the $2,811 balance?)	$5,188.40
SALE OF LUMBER:	
Arlington	$201,998

Danby and Manchester, cash which figure included $270,000 of mortgage bonds of Emporium Lumber Company, the firm that bought Silas's Green Mountain kingdom.	$469,339
Silas had no money at all invested in securities, but he had five insurance policies one of which, for the amount of $1,664, had the initials L.M.G. after it, presumably meaning that Libbie Mary Griffith was the beneficiary. Indeed, a rare man was Silas Griffith. He must have loved her dearly.	$47,484
SOME OF THE PAID CLAIMS ALLOWED BY THE COMMISSIONERS WERE AT LEAST AS INTERESTING:	
Inheritance tax paid on the public legacies of $105,000 approximately .0155%, but the inheritance tax rate jumped considerably for non-charitable legacies. The rate of tax paid for the legacies of Jennie Riddle, her children and Silas's three siblings was 5%.)	$1,630
Expended on freight at Danby, Manchester, Arlington and Dorset	$52,692
Labor at Danby, Manchester, Arlington and Sunderland	$275,631
There were also barn expenses, store expenses, repairs and sales expense on real estate and general expenses.	
SPECIFIC EXPENDITURES INCDED:	
Taxes	$12,853
Insurance	$10,314
Attorney's Fees	$3,926
Court Fees	$1,256
Funeral expenses	$1,329
1908 DanbyTaxes	$354
Executors fees paid to w.B. Griffith and george L. Rice, executors	$41,400

pride and blessing of the people and a lasting memorial not only to Mr. Griffith but to the brave, devoted men and women who laid its foundation years before many of its beneficiaries saw the light of day.

In May 1908, the Accounting of Griffith's Estate would be filed and allowed by the Hon. Thomas P. Robbins, Judge of the Probate Court of Rutland. Of the $1,439,226.62 total, some of the items listed are of particular interest:

All told, the paid claims allowed by the Commissioners amounted to $733,571, leaving a net estate of $705,654 according to the Court's figures. After deducting $10,000 for the Danby homestead which had been willed to K.T., $695,654 was left in the hands of the Executors for the family to fight over, and fight they did, as the *Free Press* proclaimed to the world:

> **GRIFFITH LEFT $695,654.73**
> Contest over Distribution of Lumber King's Estate Reveals Its Size... the largest estate that the probate court of this district has handled for several generations. The appellants are Charles H. And William B. Griffith, brothers of the deceased, and Mary E. Griffith, his sister. The defendants are Mrs. W.H. Riddle of this city, Katherine T. Griffith, Wilbur H. Griffith and George L. Rice of Rutland. The most prominent lawyers in the county are associated with the case...

The issue was the Court's interpretation of the codicil.

While the family was embroiled over the amount of their respective shares, the community scoffed over the now public figures. "He had twice as much as what showed," was the general feeling around town, but Perry Bond, Bill Bond's son, laughed hardest."Why," he said, "Silas sent me up to northern Washington to sell some lots for him on a harbor. I sold two lots for nothing," he told, "but the fishing up there was so good I wasn't in a hurry to leave so I held off selling the other lots and enjoyed myself, and while I was there fishing, they discovered gold in Alaska. After that, I sold the other five lots for $300,000 each; made him a million and a half right there and fixed it up in great shape so he wouldn't have to pay out the taxes." Considering the holdings Silas had around Bellingham Bay, Chuckanut Bay and Agate Bay, that's one story that might just be true.

But what happened to all of that hidden money will never be known.

Then there were tales about the executors being less than honest.

And K.T.? She continued living in the House on the Hill, where she had a housekeeper with a daughter who lived in the house with her and a man who would drive her around in her black Franklin automobile. With a party of friends, she would drive to Pawlet and Manchester; with Nellie, she would go to Boston, Philadelphia, and Atlantic City. But the former numerous particulars mentioned in the *Southern Vermont Mirror* had gotten to a point where they barely dribbled forth. The format of the paper had changed over recent years and Baker had moved his plant from Danby to West and Evelyn Streets in Rutland. The enormous header on the March 26th, 1909 issue said it all:

The Last

THE EDITOR EXTENDS GOOD WISHES TO
THE MIRROR READERS AND
THEN "SCUTTLES"
THE JOURNALISTIC SHIP

That was the end of the *Mirror*. The town shrugged and kept on living.

K.T. kept on just as she had been. How long her sister lived with her isn't known.

Emma and K.T.

The town's later recollection of Emma is that, as a teacher, she was hired by K.T. to tutor her housekeeper's daughter. And it was recalled that she moved into the House on the Hill as K.T.'s companion in the mid-1920s. The reality—that the women's close friendship goes back to 1902—seems to have been lost to time, along with the fact that it was in 1913, when K.T. was fifty-eight years old and Emma was thirty-six, that Emma moved into the House on the Hill. At that point, the House on the Hill, said to have been painted dark green, became known as the Haunted House.

Nobody saw much of the two women. Keeping very much to themselves, they were always together for the next twenty-six years until K.T.'s death.

As to K.T.'s background, one family had heard she had been a New York City actress, dancer or singer, but only Anivol Colvin who became her long-time driver and who refinished furniture, had been told her father was a furniture maker. With pride, K.T. showed him a bedroom set her father had made that she had brought with her to Danby. But even so, Anivol, along with just about everyone else in town, deemed her Main Line Philadelphia society. And K.T. certainly acted the part; she was a lady to her fingertips. In one anecdote it was said that Anivol was fond of snuff, and although Mrs. Griffith never said a word about that, he felt he'd better give it up. So he switched to cigarettes. What she did insist on was that he wear a dark blue suit when he chauffeured them around.

Without question, K.T. liked the finer things in life. Although she was termed "not frugal, but *careful*," and *"close,* but not stingy," her buggy whip had silver handles with K.T.G. engraved on it. And K.T.G. in gold leaf decorated dusty rose walls in her dressing room. On the ceiling were gold leaf wreaths that matched the wreaths on the ceiling in her bathroom, which was also embellished with gold leaf.

In 1914, a year after Emma moved to Danby, a Massachusetts man named Pete Ackert arrived in town with his large family. Ackert soon purchased the big hotel that had been Bill Bond's. During Bill's ownership, the ell of the hotel that migrated south along Main Street housed a restaurant, shops, a livery and a boxing stable. But Pete was a ferner by occupation. Fancy ferns were widely used in floral arrangements and at funerals at the time, and there was much demand for them. Pete bought the ferning rights up on the mountain from Emporium and his children and anyone else who needed work in town harvested them. They were stored in a cold storage plant built by Ackert for that purpose. The plants were bound twenty-five ferns per bunch, packed in wooden cases, and held until the winter shipping season when the fancy ferns were shipped to florists across the country. As long as Pete was in business, he was a mainstay of the local economy.

The Family

In the outside world, the years had brought maturity to Jennie Riddle's children, Marion and Griffith. Silas's granddaughter, Marion Riddle, was the product of a "nursery childhood," brought up by the governess "Auntie Bea." She attended the Bremmer School in Boston, at the foot of Beacon Hill and then went to Miss Bennett's [finishing school] in Millbrook, New York. Marion was the last U.S. debutante to be presented at the Court of St. James's in England, before the practice was ended by the war.

Bill Riddle died around that time, leaving Jennie, a very beautiful, very popular young widow, living in Boston. She was quite a toast of the town with lots of escorts, but she chose to remain unmarried. Jennie was at ease with everyone, an extroverted lady, and a theosophist who practiced the Bahai faith. It would seem she favored her eldest child, Griffith ("Griff").

Life Goes On

Around 1916, K.T. made a memorable gift to the Masons of the town. Although they had wounded her late husband by denying him membership, she gave them the old Stone Store that had been built by Jesse Lapham and occupied for many years by William Pierce. In April 1917, the name selected for the Danby chapter No. 83 of the Order of the Eastern Star was "Katherine," in honor of K.T.'s gift of the building to the Marble Lodge No. 76, F & AM.

Over the years, K.T. contributed an assortment of gifts to her adopted home. Thanks to her, a large, beautiful cast iron fountain for watering horses graced the intersection of Main and Depot Streets. When one of the town stores was robbed, she furnished money to install streetlights and keep them on all night in the village. And she was interested in the school. Over the years she contributed equipment for studying general science and chemistry.

The Flu Epidemic of 1918 claimed many lives in Danby, among them woods boss Ellis Millard and his brother, who had become the proprietors of the store on the northwest corner of Main Street and Brook Road. But November 11th brought the joyous blasting of every siren and whistle in town, splitting the air with the glad tidings of an Armistice in World War I.

In 1919, William sold the S.L. Griffith & Co. Store building to Abe and Pauline Rosen for $1,000. In the same year, probably for economic reasons, the Emporium Lumber Company closed out their whole operation. Nelson Nichols, who had become their supervisor for the past few years, moved with his wife, and children from the South End to the Borough, where Nelson became the proprietor of the general store vacated by the death of the Millard brothers the year before.

Occasionally, the village was blessed with a visit from Minnie and Jay Bromley who would arrive in their fancy car. "Mrs. Perfect Bromley" bragged about the fine home they had built from the money Silas had given her. At the same time, K.T. expanded socially, becoming a member of the Daughters of the Society of 1812, and the Vermont Society of Colonial Dames. On Main Street, amidst bunting and bands, a Civil War monument of a soldier standing on a tall marble column was dedicated, a gift of Eugene McIntyre, himself a veteran of the war. At the time of its installation, it was placed in the middle of the road at the juncture of Main Street and Mt. Tabor Avenue (where cars constantly bumped into it).

Over the years, town talk, the fuel that ever drove the community, often meandered to the subject of the women in the House on the Hill.

"Well, what I heard is that this fella went up to the garden to meet with Emma and he found K.T. with the minister. "

"So what? The woman's always with the minister, she's so involved with the church."

"Emma says K.T.'s about the nicest woman she ever met."

"What do you expect her to say? "

"Have you ever noticed how it's K.T. who does all the talking, and Emma never says a word?"

"She keeps her kind of like a slave up there, keeps her up at the house."

"Emma comes and goes."

On and on, and among themselves, the town women, mostly, and very quietly, speculated on the nature of the two women's relationship. But after a while, a ripple of news traveled throughout the community: Rumor had it that K.T. told Emma, "I'll give you all my money if you promise not to marry." And Emma had agreed not to.

SILAS LAPHAM GRIFFITH

Although K.T. is remembered as giving benefits on the lawn, none remembered her better than Anivol and no name except the ubiquitous Emma comes forth as a friend of hers.

On their occasional travels, Anivol chauffeured the two women. Occasionally, they visited Emma's family, sometimes Emma went alone. Whenever they went on long trips, Anivol always ate with them at the table. Once they went to the Chateau Frontenac in Quebec; another time they went to a Centennial in Philadelphia where they stayed for four weeks with Anivol's wife as their guest. If Anivol's wife chose not to accompany them on a jaunt, she always received a nice, sterling silver remembrance. Not surprisingly, Anivol found K.T. a good person, good to work for.

Of course, the town kids had their own way of looking at things. Those who remembered Silas loved him, as a "jolly good fellow," but found K.T. pompous and were scared of her; others thought Emma more uppity than K.T.. The youngsters kept a healthy distance away from them, and when Halloween came around, no trick-or-treaters approached the House on the Hill.

The Family Continues

By the 1920s, Silas's grandchildren had married and started families of their own. Marion ("Mollie") married Jerry Tone, a society man who was actor Franchot Tone's brother. Although possessed of extreme charm and wit with a marvelous sense of humor, Marion was introverted and lacked confidence in herself. She felt she was an unloved child since her brother, Griffith, was her mother's favorite. While Mollie went through her childhood lonely, Jennie favored Griff, who grew into a charming man. And it was on Griff, "who went through two fortunes," that Jennie showered money. For many reasons, including their differences in religion and temperament, there was an unfortunate rift between Jennie and Marion, who kept more with her husband's family. Marion is believed to have had but one daughter, Mary Riddle Tone.

Griffith, a charmer and a great spender, had two wives but had only one child, a daughter, from his first marriage, to Bessie Grumbine. Their daughter, Marilyn Elizabeth Riddle was born in Newton, Massachusetts in 1925.

Goings On in Town

The 1929 stock market crash played special havoc with the trust funds under Wilbur Griffith's management. They were already depleted from his injudicious investments. Indeed, he lost a tremendous amount of the estate in the stock market and told Nelson Nichols how bad he felt and how disturbed he was over losing so much. At one point, he had to personally chip in to add to the Christmas Funds so there would be enough to provide Christmas to the youngsters of the town.

Never more than during the Depression did Silas's Trusts for the children mean more, though, for during those hard, hard years, the big orange and the present they got under the Christmas Tree in the church, (often a box of candy and clothing during those years) was, for many, their sole gift. To the homes of the very poorest children, a note was sent, inquiring about the sizes needed for long underwear or stockings or shoes. And the clothing they received from Griffith's post-mortem generosity was a Godsend.

Silas's name came up frequently during the Depression. Never was he more warmly recollected and genuinely missed. Remembering "the old days," the town appreciated that he tried to be kind to people. His thoughtfulness in always trying to keep work for his men year round, was constantly reiterated. When the snow got too deep up on the top of the mountain, they remembered, he'd always try to have a job for the men down below. He'd keep logging jobs at the foot of the mountain so that they could work all winter. He might not have paid much, but many considered him a good man to work for. His practices, like jumping his workers' bills in the stores, writing them off when they couldn't pay, were well remembered, especially during those Depression years, especially when the Marble Company staged a lock-out.

There had been a wildcat strike at the marble quarry, generated by the Communist chauffeur of a North Dorset man. The Company took that as an excuse to close down and they kept closed all winter and oh, it was hard and there was trouble. When the quarry finally reopened in the spring, the Company let go some of their older workers. One of them, an active man of sixty-five had a wife who had been spouting off about old Griffith and when she got all done, her husband said, "By Jesus, I'll tell you one thing. If old Silas Griffith was on Earth today, by Jesus, I'd have a job." He said, "He kept old fellas down there watching coal kilns at night that just barely hobble. When they got a little old, he didn't just turn them off. He found work for them." And his wife shut right up.

Then, various acts of arson started taking place. In May of 1934, Pete Ackert's Hotel was torched and, of course, the huge old building went up like a tinder box. It was the biggest fire anyone had ever seen, and the only town fire extinguisher they had to fight it with was a small, hand-operated chemical machine that had to be pulled. Before the engines came from Manchester and all the surrounding towns to help, people kept the fire from spreading by wetting the surrounding buildings down with hoses. Even with that, Rosen's store (which had been Griffith's store) started to char and some of the other neighboring buildings started to singe. There were no hydrants in town, so when the Rutland and Manchester crews got there, they put their pumpers close to the Mill Brook and ran their hoses across the road. And right in the middle of that, just as the Rutland firemen were stringing up the hoses and had gotten the pump going, along came the local mail carrier, old, *very* old Warren McIntyre. By then he was as numb an old coot as could be found, driving his old Model T, taking the mail down to the train. That was his job; he was fixed on doing it.

By then in his eighties, Warren was beyond the point of being bothered by obstacles in his path. Oblivious to the world around him, he constantly bumped into the Civil War statue in the middle of the road; on this occasion, he blithely thumped his car over those hoses and broke one. Of course, the firemen were ready to kill him. Didn't bother Warren any. He got out of his car. Ignoring the inferno and the uproar, he puffed on his pipe. Stood there and faced them off. "You know," he said to them sternly, "It's a federal offense to hold up the U.S. Mail!"

Pete Ackert died the following year, and the proprietorship of his fern business went to his son, Mortimer, who expanded from ferns to cut evergreens for Christmas.

At this point, the Civil War statue Gene McIntyre had donated to the town was moved to the lawn where the hotel had stood, where it wouldn't interfere with traffic.

On Halloween, especially during the 1930s, the older kids played a lot of pranks, some years more than others. A favorite pursuit was toppling over the fountain where the horses drank. One year they put a small buggy on the roof of the barber shop. Another time, they climbed up the statue of the Civil War veteran and they put an old thunder-mug (a piss-pot) on the soldier's head, with the handle pointing to the front and they tied quite a pretty flowered apron on him. Looked kind of cute. The following morning, the spectacle drew all manner of reviews. The kids found it hysterical. Some of the adults found it quite amusing; others clucked their tongues, thought it was awful, a terrible thing, a desecration. But everyone waited around with their different opinions, until Cecil McIntyre stopped in, as he always did, at Nichol's Store. Now, Cise was partial to White Owl cigars.

He didn't smoke them; instead, he'd bite off a piece and chew it. He spat quite a lot. That morning, when he glanced up at the statue, he stopped right dead in his tracks, mad. He stormed into Nichol's Store, furious, and spat two or three times and said, "If I could find the fellas that done that, I'd have them prosecuted to the full extent of the law!" Some wondered what the full extent of the law would be for putting a piss-pot on a soldier's head and tying an apron around him.

What Happened to Them All

By this time, Silas's generation was all but gone. In 1931, Libbie died at the age of eighty-six years and nine months and was buried in the Griffith/Staples plot in Scottsville cemetery.

K.T. was in her seventies by then, a sentimental lady who would give sterling silver spoons for a baby shower and who liked to see the brides and grooms from her window. She'd even request the brides to please stand forward, so that she could see them better. In 1934, at the age of seventy-nine, she legally adopted Emma Rising as her daughter. Suffering from apoplexy since 1937, K.T. died in 1939, at the age of eighty-three. She was remembered throughout the community as a decent, quiet, kind, nice woman, excessively sober, prim, proper and completely lacking a sense of humor. No one ever saw her laugh or cry. She was unchangeable, her composure absolute. No one said a word against her.

A modest newspaper piece reported that afternoon funeral services were held at her home, the pastor of the Congregational Church officiating with a minister from Springfield, Massachusetts. Floral tributes were received from the various organizations she was a member of or had contributed to besides those sent from neighbors and friends. Anivol Colvin, Cecil McIntyre, and Nelson Nichols were among the pall bearers. Interment was at Scottsville Cemetery, in the Griffith plot. (And as a result, both of Silas's wives were buried back to back....)

K.T.'s Estate amounted to $261,463. Fred C. Spencer of Rutland was appointed executor and trustee.

To her daughter, Emma Rising, K.T. left a total of $90,273 including the house and the residue of her estate. A total of $18,000 was earmarked for various Danby public bequests. In all, the bequests totaled $150,273, the remaining balance after paid expenses of the $261,463.

After K.T.'s death, Emma Rising married her old flame, Jay Earle Brown, by then a widower. Her marriage must have surprised her family, since "Emma never had much use for men" some said. As for Brown, he was universally castigated by Emma's family who considered him a "treasure hunting low-life rapscallion."

Respected by her family as a businesswoman, Emma was deemed a "shrewd" and "careful" person. In town, no one said a word about her except for one gentleman, who said she was a "beautiful woman" who had sent his daughter to Boston for singing lessons and sent another girl to Boston for schooling. (These two girls might have been the recipients of K.T.'s $3,000 bequest to Emma for the education of specified children.)

In 1949, Silas's grandson, Griffith Riddle, died in New York City and was interred in the Griffith family plot in Scottsville Cemetery.

Emma died of cancer in March 1953, leaving a gross estate of $237,968.

Silas's daughter, Jennie, a long time Massachusetts resident, lived for many years with the family retainer, Bessie Childs, as her companion/housekeeper. At some point in her old age, Jennie moved to the Tones, an institution in Brookline, Massachusetts, composed of two very separate and different parts. One part, where Jennie lived, was an exceedingly posh establishment, a nursing home consisting of private homes and apartments. Jennie chose to live in a lovely second floor apartment where she maintained a beautiful, private home with her own furniture. There she was visited by family. All of Jennie's remaining money was expended on her maintenance at the Tones. The other portion of the institution, well separated from where Jennie lived, was for the mentally insane, which was certainly responsible for an ugly rumor passed on by Cecil McIntyre's wife, that Jennie had died destitute of congenital syphilis in a Boston area insane asylum. In reality, however, Jennie died in 1957, at the age of ninety-one years, nine months and nine days, in McLean Hospital in Brookline, Massachusetts. The cause of death was possible abdominal cancer and jaundice. In answer to the question "Maiden Name of Mother" on her death certificate, "unknown" is written. Jennie was cremated in Cambridge, Massachusetts, although her name is incised on a stone in the Griffith plot, along with the names of Bill Riddle and their son, Griffith. Bessie Childs is also buried in the Griffith plot, along with the family she spent her life with.

The End of the Line

That was the end of the lot of them, but the town, of course, kept huffing and puffing on. Once automobiles had gotten popular, people traveled to Manchester or Rutland to do their shopping. So except for a barber and Abe's big store and Nichols, there wasn't much of any business being conducted on Danby's sagging Main Street. It looked much the same as ever except for the addition of a Catholic Church that had been built in the mid-forties on the big, old hotel lot on the corner.

By then, in Mount Tabor, Nature had reclaimed Silas's kingdom. And the Lake House, deserted and untended, had long since become a monument of times past. Vandalized, occupied only by hedgehogs (porcupines) and, on occasion, by town kids and hikers and fishermen who used it as a shelter for the night, it finally became one with the devouring forest.

It was probably in the 1950s that the beautiful, big iron horse-drinking fountain contributed by K.T. Griffith disappeared one evening from Main Street. The then-head of the Prudential Committee had gotten sick and tired of righting the fountain every time the town kids pushed it over; nor did he much care for the work involved in winterizing it and then starting it up again in the spring. So he solved his headache right efficiently by talking the Prudential Committee into contributing the Danby Fountain to the Shelburne Museum without so much as a by-your-leave from Danby's Select board. One morning the fountain just wasn't there anymore. The Museum turned it into a beautiful flowerpot where it can be seen as such today.

It was in 1962 that the State of Vermont re-routed Route 7 one long block east of Main Street, so that the village was no longer part of the main north-south artery. The once elegant House on the Hill had, by then, been transformed into a motel; and, as for the center of town, lacking its former traffic, the fine old structures along the block-long thoroughfare, largely vacant and dilapidated, fairly proclaimed, "Ghost Town in Progress."

The Revival of Danby

The buildings' crumbling condition enabled the late, famed author Pearl S. Buck to buy up most of Main Street for a song in 1970. Miss Buck's restoration effort consisted primarily of painting and cosmetic repairs. But the prestigious author's essential ownership of the village and its attendant press succeeded in drawing tourists in droves to see the white and Chinese red-trimmed buildings that ear-marked her holdings. Almost all were antique shops, but Miss Buck appropriated the old S.L. Griffith & Company store building for her own use. She installed offices on the top floor and a country store and a diner/soda fountain, The Maple Skillet, on the main floor, where she added a rear dining room.

But fame and achievement do not of themselves win friends among the Danby locals. They neither appreciated Miss Buck's coterie of followers nor, especially, some injudicious remarks the author made to the press concerning her adopted community. This undoubtedly is why, when asked to evaluate Buck's reign, one long-time native resident retorted succinctly, "We survived it."

Miss Buck's death in 1973 brought an immediate end to Danby's resurgence. Once again the buildings fell vacant. Soon, between lack of maintenance and repairs to structural damage brought on by the years, most of the buildings along Main Street sagged into appalling disrepair. In the mid-1980s, however, a group of concerned residents joined together to purchase, in block, just about all the buildings formerly owned by Miss Buck. And, over the following years, Main Street was restored to its 19th century grandeur.

The Name of Silas Griffith

In the many intervening years since Griffith's death, the name of Silas Griffith, for the most part, lay dormant. Though his name would be forever blazoned on the library, the most imposing building in town, Silas would have been lost to time along with the multitudes of other benefactors whose names garnish buildings across the nation. Yet every Christmas, in the Congregational Church, the children of Danby Borough and Mt. Tabor still receive gifts (and needed clothing, too) under a Christmas Tree given by the long-gone Silas Griffith.

But even at this well-loved and appreciated ceremony, on one occasion, when the Reverend said, "Let's clap for Silas!" one of the locals quietly muttered, "Clap, clap. That's what he died of." The blemish of his alleged syphilitic end has ever thus tarnished the benefactor's name.

So, what was the true cause of Griffith's death? Based on the facts surrounding his last weeks of life as we know it, infectious disease specialists have stated categorically that he did not die of syphilis of the brain, nor of the spinal cord, aorta, or bone, and that it is impossible to know if he had syphilis of the stomach or kidneys. Other physicians state very positively that he did not have syphilis. Nor can any medical expert explain the death certificate diagnosis of *Pityriasis Rubra,* even as a socially acceptable alternate to syphilis. This is especially true, they point out, since there is no rash whatsoever in the final syphilitic stage.

So, what *did* he die of?

Some years ago, a friend and fellow officer of the Mt. Tabor-Danby Historical Society visited this author's home with a client of his, a psychic who had heard little or nothing about Griffith's life. When she was told of a photograph of Silas in California that had turned amber, she asked to be permitted to "speak to it, in privacy." When she returned to us in the living room sometime later, she said to me, "You think he was murdered, don't you?"

"Yes," I replied.

"You think he was poisoned."

"Yes."

"Well, he wasn't poisoned," she announced to us, "but he *was* murdered. Although K.T. did not commit the act herself, she was behind it. Someone else did it," (presumably Ethel Cienfuegos) the psychic continued, "by inserting a long hat pin with a brown, tortoise shell ball at the end, in his navel, and he hemorrhaged internally."

While she was still in Danby, the psychic visited the grounds of the House on the Hill and, touching the big oak tree on the south side of the house near the present swimming pool, she "saw" two women dressed in white, telling secrets and dancing together, rejoicing for being alone to themselves.

A 19th century hat pin could be up to 8" in length. A former Medical Examiner of the state of Vermont has verified that death could indeed have resulted from internal bleeding from such a hat pin. Or, if the needle punctured his bowels, for example, there could have been *sepsis* or some other malady depending on what specific route and resulting damage the pin could have inflicted. In both the specific cases mentioned above, some interval of time would have elapsed before Silas would have fallen ill from the wound, eventually, falling into a coma and dying.

What is the true story? We will never know, but Silas's portrait, with those amber eyes peering forth, can be seen to this day on Main Street in Danby.

The End

Out for a ride, sitting in front: K.T.'s brother driving, sister Nellie in the front seat and K.T. and her father William Tiel in the back seat

ANN K. ROTHMAN

Interior of the Congregational Church with Silas Griffith's Easter Lilies

The Lake House

SILAS LAPHAM GRIFFITH

Lake Griffith

A country peddler's wagon, Woodstock, Vermont

At the Lake House

Emma J. Rising, K.T. Griffith's adopted daughter and heir

Ed and Florence Risdon picnic at the Griffith Lake House, 1920s

K.T. Griffith and friend at the lake

Lake Griffith House, left to right – Top Row: Ben Long, Anna Long, Nelson Nichols, William Nichols (baby), Florence Nichols. Middle Row: Charlie Raiche, Winona Raiche, Joe Raiche (baby), Alice (Otis) Davison, Sarah Otis, Anna Davison, Clare Bradford, Wendell Davison (little boy), Gene Davison, 1910

The Lake House

SILAS LAPHAM GRIFFITH

Train travel, First Class

ANN K. ROTHMAN

San Diego, California, early 1900s

Griffith family graves

SILAS LAPHAM GRIFFITH

K.T. Griffith

ANN K. ROTHMAN

Ackerts Cold Storage for ferns

Ferns

SILAS LAPHAM GRIFFITH

Inside Ackerts Cold Storage for ferns

ANN K. ROTHMAN

Johnny Ackert with fern packs

SILAS LAPHAM GRIFFITH

Mort Ackert grading ferns

FIRE IN DANBY DOES DAMAGE OF $70,000

Ackert Garage Is Destroyed and 8000 Cases of Ferns in Storage, Ruined

SUMMON OUTSIDE AID

(Special to The Herald.)

DANBY, Feb. 6—Fire of undetermined origin, which at one time threatened to wipe out the entire business district of this village, destroyed the P. I. Ackert garage and fern cold storage plant tonight, causing damage estimated at $70,000.

Firemen from Rutland, Wallingford and Manchester, aided by a bucket brigade made up of hundreds of volunteers working with 2000 pails, fought the blaze for three hours in the sub-zero weather before it was under control. It was the most disastrous fire in the history of the village.

In the cold storage plant, which is located in the basement of the garage, were 8000 cases of ferns, representing the summer's work of scores of fern pickers. It was believed tonight that the entire stock, worth $36,000, had been totally destroyed by the flames and heat.

Mrs. Risdon Discovers Fire.

Mrs. C. C. Risdon, whose home is located only a short distance from the garage, heard the crackling of flames about 7 o'clock. She looked out of the window of her home and saw flames bursting from the garage. The cry of "fire" was sent out and men and boys rushed from all parts of the village and formed a bucket brigade. Calls for help were sent to Wallingford, Manchester and Rutland. The Rutland department, with six men and a pump, made the 19-mile trip in 29 minutes. The Manchester and Wallingford departments also made quick trips through the freezing weather.

Business Section Threatened.

For a while it was thought that the flames were going to sweep through neighboring buildings, in which are located the majority of Danby's business houses. Hard work by the fire departments and volunteers averted that disaster.

The flame-swept garage was of stucco construction. Thousands of dollars worth of tools, machinery, a sleigh, and other articles were destroyed. Mr. Ackert tonight estimated the damage to the building, contents and ferns at about $70,000. He and his family reside in a large building, formerly the hotel here, which is located near the garage. When it looked as though the fire would spread neighbors helped move the furniture and other household goods from the house. The equipment and furniture in the restaurant, owned by Mrs. Maude Baker, was also moved out of doors.

Water was taken from Mill brook, which is a short distance from the scene of the fire. Thousands of persons from Manchester, Dorset, Wallingford and other nearby towns, attracted by the glare in the skies flocked to the fire.

Members of the Rutland Fire department who went to the aid of the village were: Capt. Ralph R. Beane, Firemen Frank Seward, James Rice, Frank Rice and William Mason.

News of the Ackert fire

SILAS LAPHAM GRIFFITH

Bond Hotel

After the fire

Bond Hotel

150th anniversary celebration, downtown Danby, 1911

Memorial Fountain donated by K.T. Griffith for the 150th celebration

ANN K. ROTHMAN

Old Home Week at Danby 150th celebration, 1911

Approaching Danby from the south

SILAS LAPHAM GRIFFITH

View from the East, Griffith Office center in front to RR station

Masonic Lodge, 1835

ANN K. ROTHMAN

Main Street Danby, looking south from Depot Street

Danby Village, Pen and Ink by I. J. Nichols

SILAS LAPHAM GRIFFITH

Abe Rosen, owned former Griffith Store 1919-1959

ANN K. ROTHMAN

The Corner Store

Safe from Silas Griffith store

Silas and the lily pond

ANN K. ROTHMAN

Pauline Rosen, wife of Abe Rosen

The Borough School before addition

The Borough School with high school addition

ANN K. ROTHMAN

Crane for the incline railroad, by the Marble Quarry

Tracks to bring marble out of The Marble Quarry

The Fish Hatchery

ANN K. ROTHMAN

The Fish Hatchery

Old job abandoned

SILAS LAPHAM GRIFFITH

Silas Griffith gathering maple sap

Danby Depot

Danby Depot and Mill

Griffith steam powered mill at Danby Depot
Plumb of black smoke in background is from charcoal kilns

Danby Depot, charcoal kilns and Big Barn

ANN K. ROTHMAN

Silas Griffith telephone

SILAS LAPHAM GRIFFITH

K.T. Griffith's ivory vanity set

ANN K. ROTHMAN

Sarah and Peter Ackert

Henry G. Lapham and Mrs. Lapham (Samantha Vail)

SILAS LAPHAM GRIFFITH

Silas Griffith Boys Club

The Greenhouse

Entry to Danby Green, 1990s

Annie's Kitchen, 1990s

Behind the Griffith Store, 2020

Green Mountains from behind Griffith Store

Griffith Store, 1990

Corner Store, 1990

Main Street, Danby, looking south, 1990s

Main Street, Danby, 2021

ANN K. ROTHMAN

Stone wall in front of Griffith Mansion, The top of the wall doubled as a sidewalk

Millbrook Professional Office, 1990s

Philips Mansion, 2014

ANN K. ROTHMAN

The Green Mountains from different views in Danby

SILAS LAPHAM GRIFFITH

The Green Mountains from different views in Danby

ANN K. ROTHMAN

Millbrook, 2000s

Taconic Range, 2020

SILAS LAPHAM GRIFFITH

South of Depot St. Extension to Railroad Tracks, 2000

ANN K. ROTHMAN

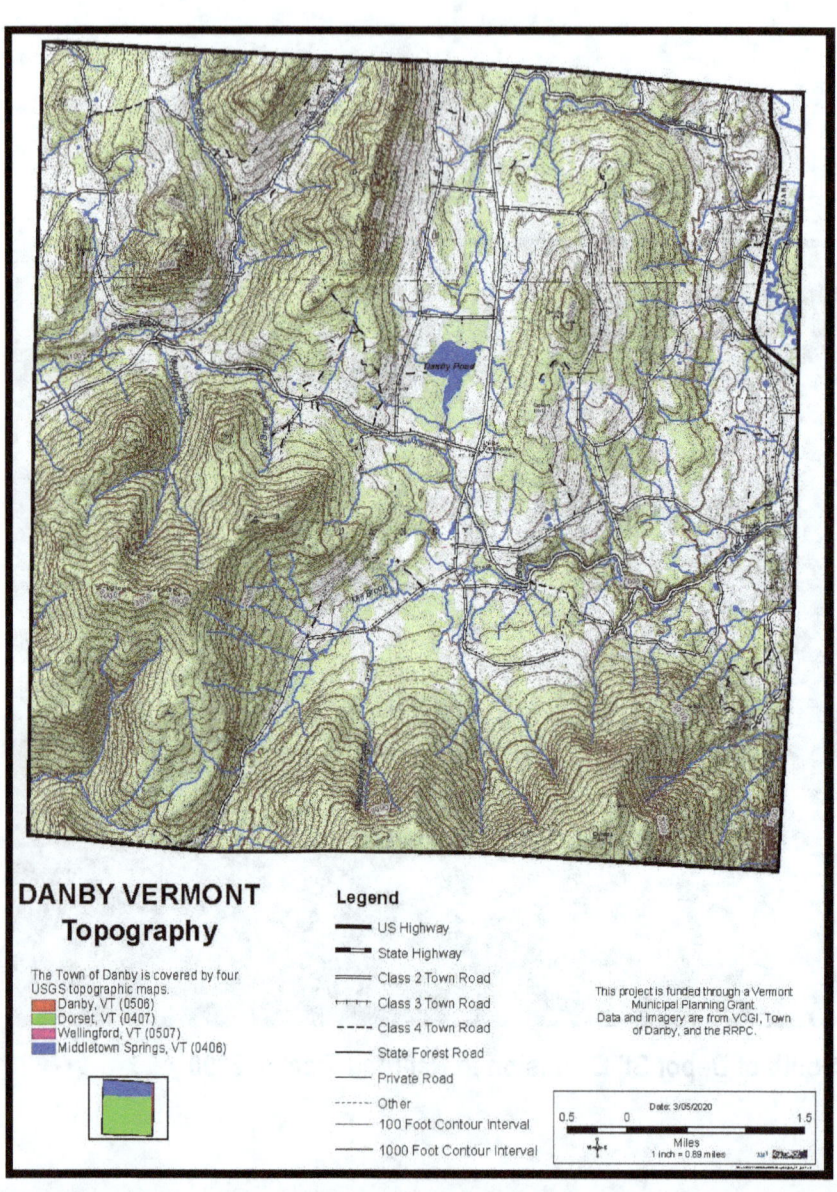

Danby, Vermont Topography Map

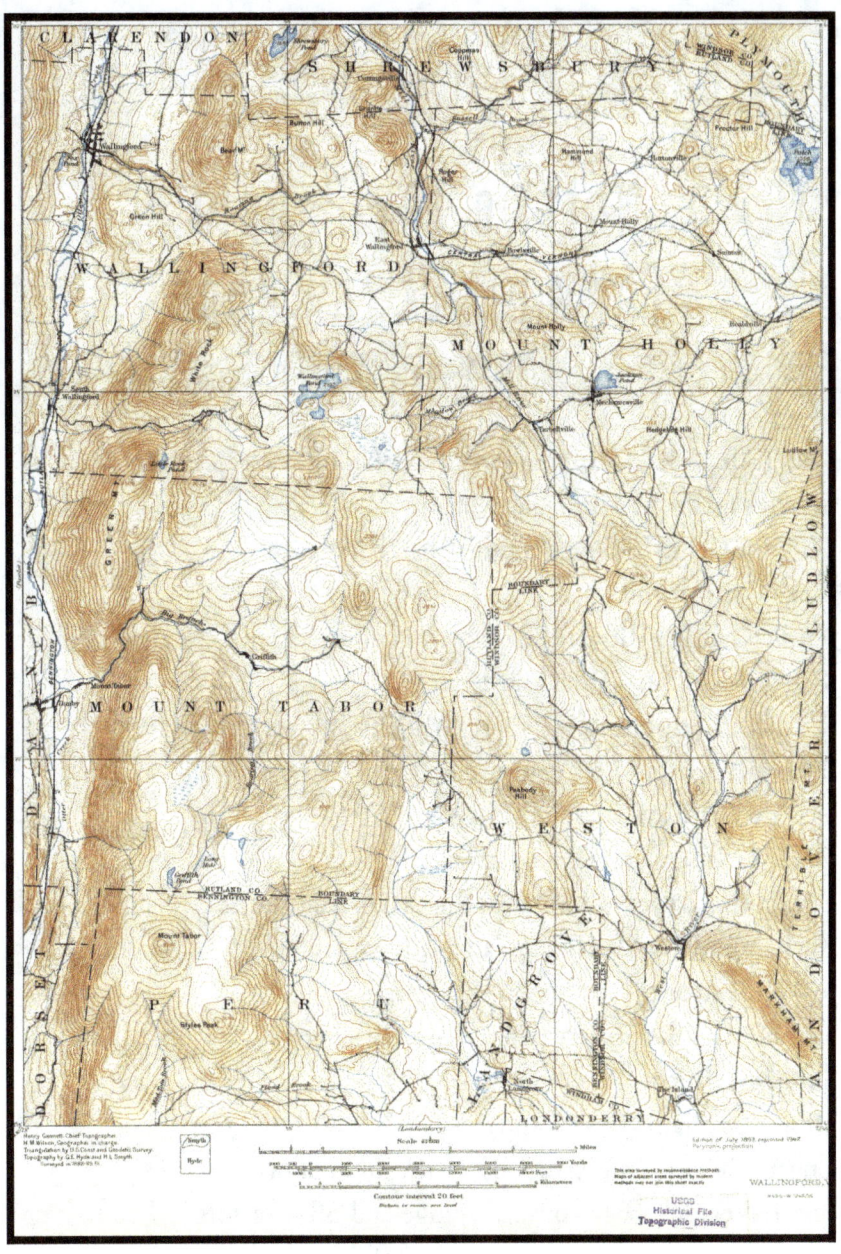

1893 U.S. Geological Survey Wallingford Quadrangle

ANN K. ROTHMAN

Noteworthy People Throughout the Book
In order of appearance

Silas (Sile, S.L.): Lapham Griffith: Vermont entrepreneur
Charles Griffith: Silas's older brother
William Griffith: Silas's younger brother
Mary Griffith: Silas's sister
Jennie Griffith Riddle: Silas's second child
William Riddle: Jennie's husband
K.T. (Katherine or Kate Tiel) Griffith: Silas's second wife
Barnum: Silas and K.T.'s chef
George Griffith: Silas's great uncle
David Griffith, Jr.: Silas's father
Elizabeth and Jesse Lapham: Silas's aunt and uncle
Nathan and Elizabeth Lapham: Jesse's parents
Joseph Button: Nathan's business partner
Lemuel Griffith: Silas's paternal grandfather
Sophia Griffith: Silas's mother
Henry Lapham: Jesse Lapham's son
Charlie Baker: Newspaper publisher and editor
Joel Baker: Charlie's cousin, a judge and Silas's attorney
Eugene McIntyre: Business partner of Silas, manager of the lumber and charcoal operations
W.H. Griffith: Silas's cousin and office manager
C.M. Bruce: Business partner of Silas, store owner

SILAS LAPHAM GRIFFITH

William Ames: Silas's cousin and childhood friend
Elizabeth Mary Staples (Libbie) Griffith: Silas's first wife
Lottie Griffith: Silas and Libbie's first child
Minnie Bushee: Silas's secretary and longtime mistress
Harry Ralph: Road builder and manager in Silas's lumber Works
Harry Griffith: Silas's fourth child
Eddie Staples: Superintendent in the lumber Works, Libbie Griffith's half brother and Silas's brother-in-law
William Pierce: Spiritualist, merchant, diary keeper
Austin Baker: Charles Baker's father
George Baker: Hotel proprietor
Peleg T. Griffith: Silas's second cousin
Senator William H. Barnum: Businessman and competitor
Agatha Griffith: Silas's third child
Bill Bond: Mason, hotel owner and merchant
Griffith Hatton Riddle and Marion Riddle: Children of Jennie and Bill Riddle, Silas's grandchildren
Odolphus (Dolph) Nichols: Yard boss and overseer at the lumber Works
Ellis Millard: Woods boss and merchant
Martin Foley: Legal adversary
Louie Griffith: Head bookkeeper, office manager
Wilbur Griffith: Silas's cousin, bookkeeper, financial manager
Jay Bromley: Eventually Minnie Bushee's husband
Emma Rising: Intimate friend of K.T. Griffith, later her adopted daughter
Julius Griffith: Silas's cousin, who accompanied him to California
Theron P. Griffith: Son of Peleg, nephew of Julius
James and Ethel Cienfuegos: Innkeepers in Tijuana
The Tiels: K.T. Griffith's family
Anivol Colvin: K.T. Griffith's driver
Nellie Tiel: K.T. Griffith's sister

ANN K. ROTHMAN

Griffith

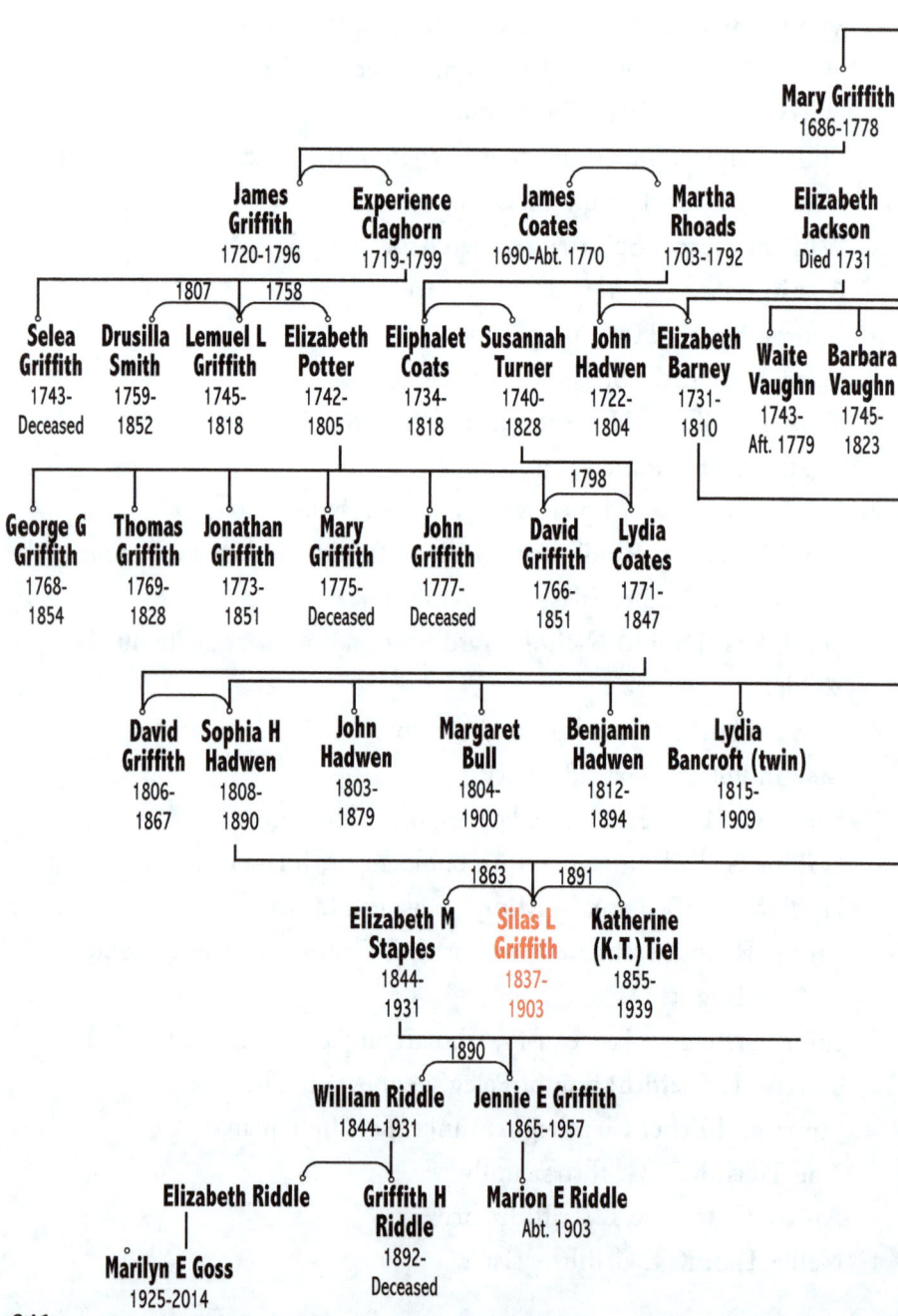

SILAS LAPHAM GRIFFITH

Family Tree

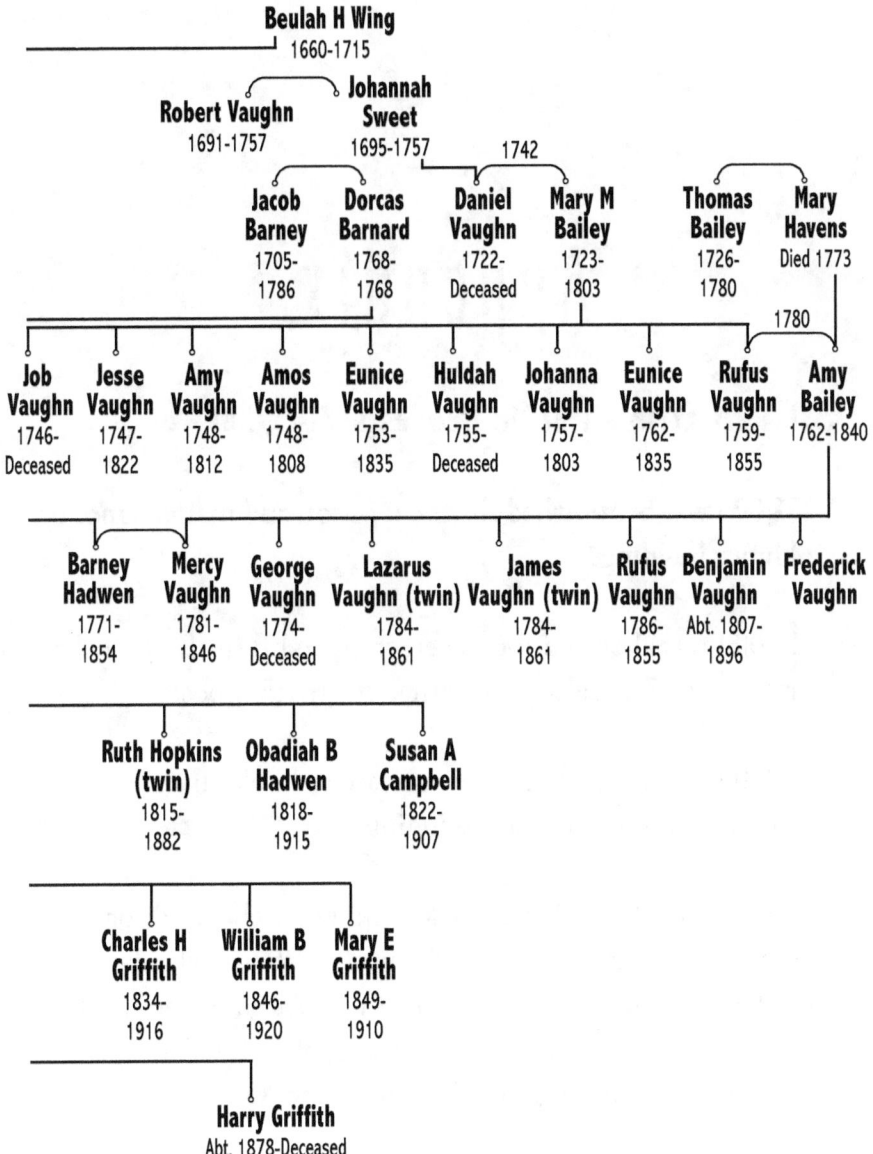

Every reasonable effort was made to verify the
Griffith Family Tree through history documents and www.ancestry.com.
Furthermore, we will not be held liable for any errors, inaccuracies or
omissions that may possibly occur, at any time.

ANN K. ROTHMAN

Appendix

Silas Griffith's Public Bequests: $105,000

$51,000 was bequeathed for the erection and maintenance of a library building.

$14,000 was allocated for the erection and furnishing of the structure on a lot also bequeathed for that purpose.

$5,000 was allocated for the purchase of books and periodicals...of high moral standing.

The income of a $32,000 Trust Fund was to be used for general maintenance and supplying the Library with books and periodicals. The yearly income was placed in the hands of a (compensated) committee consisting of K.T. Griffith, the pastor of the Congregational Church, and Wilbur Griffith.

Stipulations:
That the committee, empowered with general oversight of all matters, annually deposit with the Librarian for the

inspection of the public an itemized account of their receipts and expenditures.

That some suitable person have charge of the building and its contents and that the building be kept open at all proper hours for the free use of the public.

That the Library be enlarged from year to year by the addition of books and periodicals...of a high moral character

$11,000 was bequeathed to the Danby Cemetery Association plus ½ interest in a house.
The annual income and interest from a $5,000 Trust was allocated for keeping up, caring for, and beautifying the [Scottsville] cemetery.

Stipulations:
That no taxes or assessments be laid on Griffith's lot or lots.

That the Association provide a sum equal to ⅓ the bequest to be placed in trust with the income applied to the upkeep or that they raise each year a sum equal to at least ⅓ the income from Griffith's $5,000 trust.

Failure to comply with the foregoing conditions will result in the $5,000 reverting to the residuum of Griffith's estate.

The annual income and interest from a $6,000 Trust was allocated for keeping up, caring for and beautifying Griffith's circle of lots and on his land outside of driveway.

Griffith's ½ interest in a house co-owned by George Hadwen, to be used as a home for the custodian of the cemetery, provided Hadwen's interest be purchased promptly.

$23,500 to the Congregational Church
The annual income and interest of a $16,000 Trust to be given to the Pastor of the Church to be used in supporting Congregational preaching according to the usages of the Congregational Church.

Stipulations:
If Congregational Church preaching shall cease for a period exceeding six months, the $16,000 shall revert to the residuum of Griffith's estate.

The annual income and interest of a $3,000 Trust to be used for lighting and heating the church and paying the janitor.

The annual income and interest of a $3,000 Trust to be used for repairing, painting and keeping the church and grounds in good condition.

The annual income and interest of a $1,500 Trust for the purchase of books and periodicals for the church and Sunday School.

If the preaching of the gospel according to the Congregational Church and the meetings of the Sunday School shall cease for a period exceeding six consecutive months, the $7,500 bequeathed above shall revert to the residuum of Griffith's estate.

$2,500 Christmas Party Trust
The annual income and interest of a $2,500 Trust to be used for the yearly purchase of Christmas gifts for the children of Danby Borough and vicinity and Mt. Tabor, to be distributed from a Christmas tree in the Congregational Church.

Stipulations:
If Congregational Church no longer exists, the Christmas Tree may be located elsewhere in Danby Borough.

No distinction whatever is to be made among the children, whether or not they belong to any particular church or denomination.

$2,000 Christmas Clothing Trust
The annual income and interest of a $2,000 Trust to be used for providing the poor children of Danby Borough and vicinity and Mt. Tabor with shoes, clothing, and other needed items at Christmas time.

$15,000 Public School Trust
The annual income and interest of a $15,000 Trust to be used to support the public schools of Danby and Mount Tabor.

Stipulation:
That the amount each town is to receive shall be in proportion to the daily attendance of scholars in each town.

Silas Griffith's Private Bequests

In private bequests, ⅓ of the estate was to be held, in trust, for Jennie Riddle and her children (the same percentage K.T. would get), plus an additional bequest to his daughter, outright, the sum of $5,000.

To his grandchildren Griffith and Marion, $3,000 each.

To his brothers Charles and William, $2,000 each and to his sister Mary, $10,000.

As for K.T.'s share, for comparison, there were two different bequests, one from the original will and one from the codicil. The original will dated January 6th, 1903 read: "To my wife...such sum and such property and estate as she would by law be entitled to were this will not made.[i.e. ⅓] Should she desire the Danby homestead of about thirty acres, she could buy it completely furnished and equipped for $5,000, but reserving from it the Reservoir and one-half acre surrounding it to maintain pipes to the Grady spring."

The codicil executed on July 20th, 1903, read: " To my beloved wife...one-third of all the estate, but $10,000 shall be deducted from the one-third for the Danby homestead."

Stricken from the original will in the codicil was a bequest to destitute churches with the stipulation, "...I direct that the residue shall be placed in the general fund of my estate and divided equally, that is, share and share alike among the other devisees mentioned in my last will and testament."

Added to the codicil was a stipulation that the proceeds from the sale of "The Palms" be divided equally among the devisees and legatees. Which difference meant that K.T. would have to pay an additional $5,000 to the estate for the homestead and would share in the increased general fund.

The issue of the contest of the will was the Court's interpretation of the codicil's paragraph that read "...that the said residue shall be placed in the general fund of my estate and divided equally, that is, share and share alike among the other devisees mentioned in my last will and testament."

Possibly influenced by the wording "that the said residue shall be placed in the general fund of my estate and divided equally, that is, share and share alike among the other devisees mentioned in my last will and testament." compared to the wording of the disposition of "The Palms" in the same document, "...the proceeds thereof divided equally, that is, share and share alike, among the devisees and legatees mentioned in my last will and testament...," the infinite wisdom of the Probate Court, rendered on May 23rd, 1908, found K.T. and Jennie the only devisees, and, ignoring the ⅓ share specified for each, awarded them each ½ of the residue, (a ruling which likely had Silas turning around in his grave in Scottsville) and, for Charles, William and Mary, allocated a total amount of $46,600 including bequests and interest, plus their individual 1/7th share of "The Palms" which amounted to $741.14 per person. Between the three, they received $48,823.42.

It's no wonder Silas' siblings contested, claiming they were both legatees and devisees and, at a cost of $200.00, appealed the Decree of Distribution.

In dollars and cents, here's the difference:
Had the ⅓ provision for Jennie and K.T., as directed by Silas, been followed,

K.T. would have received the homestead, plus a total of $255,204.65.

Jennie (including the trust for herself and the children) would have received a total of $270,926.65.

Jennie's children, Griffith and Marion, would each have received a total of $38,394.08.

Charles and William would each have received a total of $37,150.08.

Mary would have received a total of $45,554.08.

By awarding 1/2 of the residue to Jennie and K.T., here's what everyone got:

K.T. ended up with the homestead, plus $325,028.

Jennie (including the trust for herself and her children) ended up with a total of $340,750.

Each of Jennie's children received $4,086.15.

Charles and William received $13,473.14 each, from which $37.06 was deducted from each for inheritance tax payable to the state of Vermont for the sale of "The Palms."

Mary received $21,877.14 less $37.06 deducted for inheritance tax payable to the state of Vermont for the sale of "The Palms."

On October 23rd, 1909, the County Court upheld the decision of the probate court.

K.T. Griffith's Estate

To her daughter, Emma Rising, K.T. left a total of $90,273.15 which included the house with all furnishings and stock, her jewelry, $15,000 in cash and $55,000.in trust, which amounted to $76,430, plus the $13,843.15 residue.

Stipulations:

Re: The $13,843.15 residue of the estate

To have and hold during her natural life, with the request that Emma dispose of the residue among needy relatives and friends, to the S.L. Griffith Memorial Library, to Rutland Hospital, The Women's Medical College of Pennsylvania or the Church of the Restoration, Universalist in Philadelphia and/or any other worthy cause or individual.

$3,000 was also awarded to Emma to be used in the education of certain children "whom I shall designate in a letter to her, and for such other purposes as I may direct."

$8,000 was bequeathed to her cousin Charles M. Griffith of Easton, Pennsylvania and $10,000 additional bequests went to other relatives.

The income and profit of a $10,000 trust, designated the Katherine T. Griffith Trust, was given to Vera H. Griffith for her lifetime, after which ¼ of that amount was allocated to Mt. Tabor schools and ¾ was allocated to Danby schools for improvements and equipment.

Stipulations:

"It is my desire that singing be taught in both Mt. Tabor and Danby schools," she directed.

After Vera's death, the funds were identified as the K.T. Griffith Trust Fund Music Account.

The income and profit of an $8,000 trust was given to one Edward Barrett of Danby" for faithful service."[unknown]. After his lifetime, $3,000 was to be paid to the Valley Forge Historical Society of Valley Forge, Pennsylvania (for reasons unknown by that institution), $1,000 was allocated to the American Bible Society, $1,000 for the Christmas Tree fund, and $3,000 to the Northfield School in East Northfield, Massachusetts.

The income and profits of a $10,000 Trust was earmarked for the S.L. Griffith Memorial Library, a $5,000 Trust was established for the Congregational Church and a Trust of $2,000 went to the Danby-Mt. Tabor Fire District #1 for streetlights, sidewalks, or a new water system.

Both Anivol Colvin and K.T.'s housekeeper each received $2,000.

The above bequests totaled $150,273.15, the remaining balance after paid expenses of the $261,463.17.

Emma Rising Brown's Estate

Emma left a gross estate of $237,968.52.

The House on the Hill, with furnishings, was valued at	$18,615.00
Notes, bonds, stocks and cash	$217,798.52
Car, truck, silverware, trinkets	$1,555.00
	$237,968.52

In addition, she left $4,862.00 in securities registered in two names (other than her husband's) and $34,669.05 in holdings registered in the names of Emma and her husband, as Joint Tenants.

Her husband, Jay Earle Brown received $25,000, the $18,615. House on the Hill and the $76,617.08 balance of K.T.'s $55,000 Trust Fund which Emma revoked, all of which amounted to $120,232.08, plus the additional $34,699.05 of security holdings registered in Emma's and his name as joint tenants.

In accordance with K.T.'s requests, Emma left $1,000. each to the Women's Medical College of Pennsylvania and to the Church of the Restoration, Universalist of Philadelphia. She gave $10,000 to Danby's Congregational Church plus $2,000 in Trust for floral remembrances to K.T.'s memory. She also bequeathed the followings sums, often in trust: $1,500. went to Danby's Public Schools, $1,000 went to Mt. Tabor's schools, $10,000 to the S.L. Griffith Memorial Library. $3,000 to the local Fire District and the balance to other charitable organizations and to friends and family.

Details of Questioning of Witnesses to Codicil by the Superior Court of San Diego

On September 2nd, 1903, the Superior Court of San Diego, California, pursuant to the commission issued out of the Probate Court of Rutland, Judge Norman H. Conklin called before him several gentlemen to testify concerning the codicil Silas executed the day before he died. After having been duly sworn, Eugene Daney, James Vernon, Theron P. Griffith and Linden Boone, testified as follows:

Linden Boone, the attorney who drew the codicil, testified concerning the legality of the document and to the fact that he was personally acquainted with Eugene Daney, Theron P. Griffith and

James Vernon, the witnesses produced to prove the execution of the codicil.

Eugene Daney [a prominent attorney] swore that on the 20th of July, Silas declared to him and James Scott, the other attesting witness, that this was a codicil to his will, and he signed it in their presence, acting without duress, menace, fraud or undue influence.

Q. Was anyone else present at the time he executed the codicil excepting yourself and Mr. Scott?
A. Yes, I think there was also present Mr. Theron P. Griffith, and possibly another gentleman was there whose name I do not recall; I think his name was also Griffith. WITNESS THERON P. GRIFFITH: My father. (Continuing) Yes. I do not know his initials, but there was an elderly gentleman there who was called Mr. Griffith; I think, if I remember correctly, there were four present besides the testator at the time he declared this to be a codicil (etc.)...

Q. What was his mental condition?
A. He was perfectly clear; his mind was just as bright and clear any one; he was a sick man, of course not vigorous physically, but his mind was as clear as any one's and he had a perfect conception of what he was doing and just what he had done. Theron P. Griffith testified that he was witness to the signing, but did not sign it, Eugene Daney, thinking it best for him not to sign. He also stipulated the document was signed without duress, fraud, menace or undue influence and that Silas' state of mind was "clear and bright as could be, so far as we could see it." James Vernon testified concerning witness James Scott, whom he had known for

thirteen years and who had been his companion nearly every day for the last five or six years when he was in town.
Q. What is his business?
A. He is a professional nurse.

Q. Do you know whether or not Mr. Scott nursed Mr. Griffith down at Paradise Valley?
A. I do, sir; yes, sir.

Q. Where is Mr. Scott at the present time?
A. On his way to London; that is what he left for, and I presume that is where he is going; that is he left, and I saw him buy a ticket for New York to go to London.

Q. When was that?
A. Last Sunday week — two weeks ago Sunday.

Q. What did he say to you at the time he bought the ticket, if anything?
A. He said he was going to London and from that down to his home, and that he would write me from England.

Q. Is he an Englishman by birth?
A. By birth, yes.

Q. Well, did you see him off — see him on the train?
A. Yes, sir, I was on the cars with him until the cars started.

SILAS LAPHAM GRIFFITH

Acknowledgments
from the author

In the course of writing this book, I made some wonderful new friends from the list below, and lost too many good ones.

I am indebted to every one of the people named here, all of whom were kind enough to contribute the significant bits and pieces on which this volume is largely based.

Without the community's lore, legends and stories, there would have been no book. Without the forthrightness and humor, it would have been dull. Without the family legends and skeletons from the closets of the families Griffith, Lapham, Staples, Tiel and Rising, supplied by brave family members, it would have been a text instead of a tale.

I can only offer my sincerest thanks and pray this effort is worthy of their time and help.

Richard Ackert
William Ackert, Sr.
Mary Tone Atkins
Leonel Audy
Arthur Beauregard

William Beauregard
Hugh Bromley
Mott Bromley
Virginia Colvin
Robert Cressy
Anne and Goodwin Crosby
William Crosby
Wendall Davison
Kathleen Despres
Joseph Felsoe
Thomas Fuller, Sr.
Anthony Gaiotti
Margaret Staples Gaiotti and Charles Gaiotti
Marilyn Riddle Goss
Marion and Chauncey Griffith
Edward Griffith
John B. Griffith, Sr.
John B. Griffith, Jr
Mildred Griffith
Robert Fiske Griffith
Cecile Hawes
James McLellan
Hazel and Edward Merrow
Donald Nelson Nichols
Isaac J Nichols
John Nichols
Mary and William D. Nichols
Edward Raiche
Edward Risdon
Susan Rising Sowersby
Blanche Spangler

SILAS LAPHAM GRIFFITH

Edward Staples
George Stone
Marion Stone
Dorothy Wilson Strong
Vivien Brown Wetmore
Mrs. Vernon Young

Locally, I wish to express my deepest thanks to the S.L. Griffith Memorial Library, for entrusting me with the historic photographs found throughout this volume. My thanks also to Cheryl Colby who bravely entered the lion's den and attempted further Mt. Tabor research after I had become *persona non grata* and to Ida Beauregard, Mt. Tabor's present town clerk, for her substantial help. My thanks also to Helen Macheski for researching the *Rutland Herald*, to Sam Lloyd for the Lapham charts and to Bradley Bender for his help in providing snippets of fine information and frequent doses of help, when needed.

For their endless time and patience, interest and help, and for fetching and carrying endless weighty town record books back and forth,-back and-forth and helping me locate data, I can't thank Danby's town clerks Janice Arnold and Elizabeth McLellan enough. Quantities of thanks also to Gay Johnson, Clerk of the Rutland County Court for her substantial time, help and input and especially for ferreting out Foley v. Griffith from the archives.

I am indebted to the San Diego Historical Society and to Barbara Palmer in particular, for the remarkably thorough research concerning "The Palms," Griffith's Palm Hill fruit ranch. My thanks, also to the Western Washington University for their astounding research through the Whatcom County land records that detailed his extensive real estate dealings in the state of Washington.

I also wish to thank Mrs. Wallace, formerly with the Valley Forge

[Pennsylvania] Historical Society, for her input concerning K.T. Griffith's bequest to that organization and Mr. Richard Tyler, the Philadelphia Historian, who provided the information about 19th century Wood Street. Also, thank you Susan Schulman for the Tia Juana research you were kind enough to provide.

My appreciation to the Daughters of the American Revolution and the Vermont Society of the Colonial Dames, for kindly providing me with Katherine Griffith's applications to their organizations. Thanks also to Donna Connors for entrusting me with the Pierce Diaries. I am especially grateful to the Reverend Lester Tufts, former minister of Danby's Congregational Church, who devoted days of his time with me as I pored over the Union Meeting House records he provided for my study, while intermittently providing invaluable help by tutoring me in 19th century philosophical thought and Christian beliefs.

For their professional input and opinions on various subjects, my thanks to Nina Rubin, Charles Richardson, Patrick A. Naughton, Henry Greenwald, M.D. and Eleanor E. McQuillen, M.D., former Medical Examiner of the State of Vermont.

To my friend, Flo Larson, my gratitude and appreciation for endlessly reading and critiquing and, most of all, for putting up with me. To my daughters, my apologies for what my writing cost them and my unlimited thanks for their enduring love and affection. I am truly blessed for having them. Last of all, my thanks to Ferris Mack, whose enjoyment of my work gave me the confidence to keep on writing.

Ann Karfiol Rothman May 16th, 1931—June 5th, 2010
Courtesy of Donna Rothman, Annie's daughter

About the Author

Ann Karfiol Rothman, known affectionately as Annie, was a talented writer and decorator in Manhattan before moving to her second home in Danby, Vermont, at the age of 55. She was an iconoclastic thinker who lived on her own terms. Behind the happy-go-lucky exterior was a serious and successful business woman. She was loved and admired by those with whom she interacted. Annie passed away in June of 2010 at Rutland Regional Medical Center after a period of declining health.

While living in Danby, she became a passionate champion for the town and its preservation and revitalization. She owned many historic buildings along Main Street in Danby, collectively known as Danby Green. She operated the Gallery at Danby Green and Annie's Kitchen, a shop selling decorative house and kitchen ware. She also founded and served as Secretary of the Mt. Tabor-Danby Historical Society, and was recognized by the State of Vermont for her efforts to restore the Town. Through her efforts, the Society got its first home in the Pearl S. Buck house on Brook Road in Danby in 2002.

She spent more than 20 years conducting exhaustive research into the life of the Town's benefactor, Silas Lapham Griffith, sometimes called "the Santa Claus Bandit." Her Silas research became an obsession, and she wrote several manuscripts about him, including the one upon which this book is based. Consistent with her enthusiasm for "all things Silas," she had a "SILAS" license plate on her car and eventually bought his bedroom furniture from Paolo Zancanaro. This is the last and best of her Silas books, and was the opus she believed would put Silas and her beloved town on the map of history.

www.ingramcontent.com/pod-product-compliance
Lightning Source LLC
Chambersburg PA
CBHW071226230426
43668CB00011B/1323